ECONOMIC AND SOCIAL CONDITIONS OF ĀNDHRA DEŚA

ECONOMIC AND SOCIAL CONDITIONS OF ĀNDHRA DEŚA

(A.D. 1000 to 1323 A.D.)

K. PRAMILA

BHARATIYA KALA PRAKASHAN
DELHI (INDIA)

First Edition : 2002

Published by **C.P. Gautam**
BHARATIYA KALA PRAKASHAN
3421-A, IInd Floor Narang Colony, Tri Nagar,
Delhi-110035. Phone : 7153083

ISBN : 81-86050-92-2

Laser Type Setting by
A-ONE GRAPHICS
X-4, Gali-2, Brahmapuri, Delhi-110053
Phone : 218 3470

Printed at Santosh Offset Press
40, Anand Nagar, Inderlok, Delhi
Phones : 511 6763, 511 7390

DEDICATED

TO MY FRIEND,

PHILOSOPHER & GUIDE

MY HUSBAND

PREFACE

This work is substantially the same of my thesis submitted to the Nagarjuna University, Nagarjuna Nagar (A.P.) for the award of Ph.D. Degree in 1989.It took a long period of time to make the press copy ready and get published. During serious personal setbacks occurred and circumstances due to services transfers could not make it possible for me to work further on this aspect. However studies on this period have appeared and they are given there under.

Cynthia Talbot (1991)	Temples, Donors and Gifts : Patterns of Patronage in Thirteenth century South India, Journal of Asian Studies, 50, pp. 308-40.
(1992)	A Revised view of Traditional India : Caste, Status and Social mobility in medieval Andhra, South Asia,15, pp. 17-52.
(1993)	Rudrama Devi, The Female King : Gender and Political Authority in Medieval India. In, David Shulman, Syllables Of The Sky, Studies in South Indian Civilisation, Delhi, pp. 391-430.
C.V. Ramachandra Rao	The Kākatīya Polity, Society. And Economy : Presidential Address, Medieval Section, A.I., History Congress, Warangal, pp. 59-75.
K.M. Srimali	Reflections on Recent Perceptions of Early Medieval India : Presidential Address, Historiography Section, A.P. History Congress,Tenali, pp. 124-130.

ACKNOWLEDGEMENTS

In the course of my Research several scholars have guided me. It is my moral duty to convey my gratitude to them.

I express my deep sense of gratitude to Prof. Dr. B. Rajendra Prasad, Dept. of Ancient Indian History, Culture and Archaeology, Sri Venkateswara University (Formerly Reader, Department of Ancient History & Archaeology, Nagarjuna University) for his scholarly guidance and supervision at every stage in the preparation of this work. I am very much beholden to him.

I take this opportunity to express my gratitude to late Prof. R. Subrahmanyam who was responsible for initiating me in historical research.

I thank late Dr. B.S.L. Hanumantha Rao, former Professor of Buddhist Studies, Nagarjuna University for his scholarly suggestions and Mrs. B. Priyamvada for her co-operation in the course of my study.

I am thankful to my husband late Dr. B. Kameswara Rao Former Reader in Physics, D.K. Govt. College for Women Nellore, and my children for their encouragement and co-operation in the course of the work.

I express my thanks to Dr. V.V. Krishna Sastry and late Dr. Mukunda Rao of the State Government Department of Archaeology and Museums for having permitted me to copy down some unpublished epigraphs from the collection.

I am thankful to Sri O. Sambaiah former Lecturer in History, J.K.C. College and to Sri M. Somasekhar, lecturer Hindu College Guntur for their encouragement in the course of my work.

I must thank profusely to Sri C.P. Gautam of Bharatiya Kala Prakashan, Delhi for bringing out my work neatly and in an efficient manner.

K. PRAMILA

ABBREVIATIONS

A.B.O.R.I.	:	Annals of Bhandarkar Oriental Research Institute
A.P.A.R.E.	:	Andhra Pradesh Annual Report on Epigraphy
A.P.A.S.	:	Andhra Pradesh Archaeological Series
A.P.G.A.S.	:	Andhra Pradesh Government Archaeological Series
A.R.	:	Annual Reports
A.R.S.I.E.	:	Annual Reports on South Indian Epigraphy
C.I.T.D.	:	Corpus Inscriptions of Telangāṇa Districts
Cp.	:	Cuḍḍapah District.
E.A.	:	Epigraphic Āndhrica
E.C.	:	Epigraphic Carnaṭica
E.I.	:	Epigraphic Indica
I.A.	:	Indian Antiquary
I.A.P.	:	Inscriptions of Āndhra Pradesh
J.A.H.R.S.	:	Journal of Andhra Historical Research Society
K.C.S.C.S.	:	Kandūri Coḍula Śāsanamulu (Inscriptions) Caritra-Samskṛti
km.	:	Khammam District
kn.	:	Karimnagar District
M.A.R.	:	Mysore Archaeological Reports
Mn.	:	Mahaboobnagar District
L.R.	:	Local Records
ma.	:	Marturu
N.D.I.	:	Nellore District Inscriptions
Nlg.	:	Nalgoṇḍa District

P.I.	:	Perūr Inscriptions
Proc. A.P.H.C.	:	Proceedings of Andhra Pradesh History Congress.
Proc. I.H.C.	:	Proceedings of Indian History Congress
S.I.I.	:	South Indian Inscriptions
Tel. Ins.	:	Telangāṇa Inscriptions
Wl.	:	Warangal District

CONTENTS

MAP - I
TELANGANA—POLITICAL

POLITICAL CONDITION : [A.D. 1100]

SAMANTA STATES : -------------- I. SABBI NAD II. POLAVASA III. ANMAKONDA. IV. MUDIGONDA. V. KANDURUNADU VI. KOLLIPAKA.

POLITICAL CONDITION : [A.D. 1250]

KAKATIYA KINGDOM :————————————

MAP - II
TELANGANA IN ANDHRA PRADESH

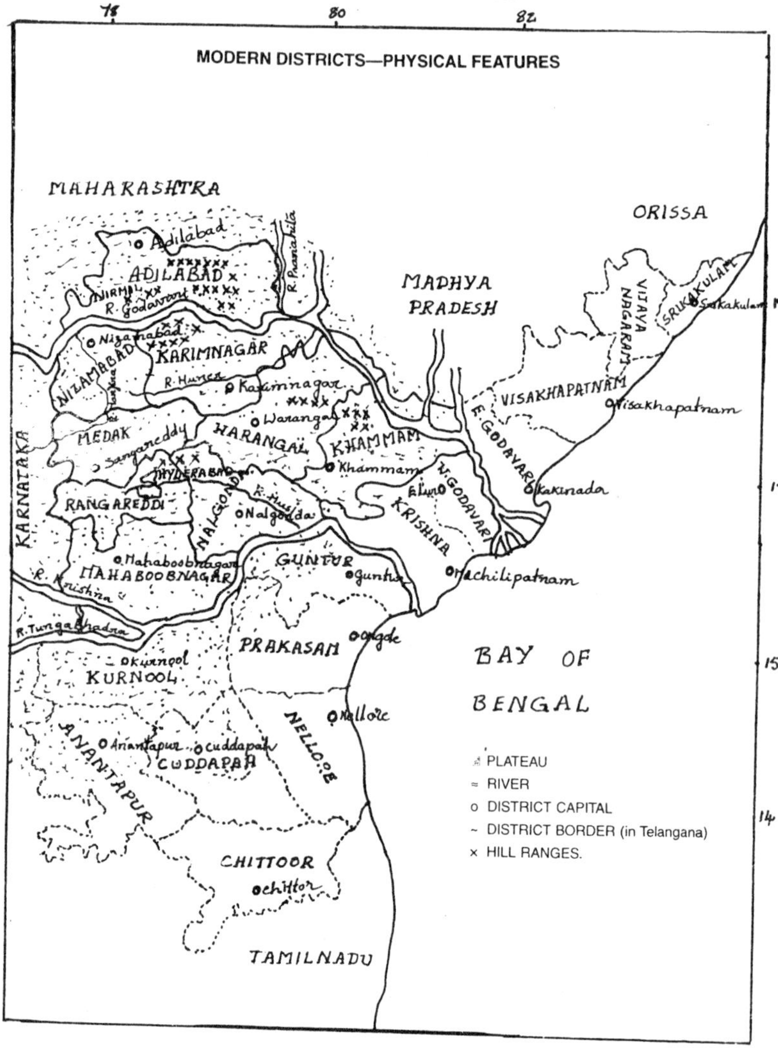

MAP - III
TRADE CENTRES—TRADE ROUTES

INTRODUCTION

Scope of the subject

Telangāṇa* is one of the three natural regions of Āndhra Pradesh. It comprises the ten North-Western districts of the state extending between 77° 5' and 82° E. Longitude and about 16° and 20° N. Longitude. The region is bounded on the north by the states of Mahārāṣṭra and Madhya Pradesh and by Karṇāṭaka and Mahārāṣṭra on the west. On the east it touches the coastal districts of Guntur, Krishna and East Godavari. On the south it is separated from Rāyalasīma by the river Krishna. Within these boundaries Telangāṇa has an area of 1, 14, 864 sq. kms. and an approximate population of 20 millions.

Inspite of certain points of similarity with Rāyalasīma comprising the districts of Anatapur, Chittor, Cuddapah and Kurnool and with parts of Guntur and Krishna districts, Telangāṇa has physical idetity and individuality of its own, with a fairly good rainfall, dense forest and a variety of mineral wealth. The region invites the attention of scholars with ample scope for study.

* Telangāṇa is also called Telingāṇa. The word Telingāṇa is explained with reference to the three śaiva *kṣctras* (three *liṅgas*) of Śriśailam (Kurnol District), Dākṣarāmam (East Godavari District) and Kāleśvaram (Karimnagar District). with the exception of the last place, rest are located out side the region. Therefore, Teligāṇa is not an appropriate name to the region. The word Telangāṇa is explained as the land of Telugu speaking people, (Telugu + *Ānemu*). But Telugu is not only the language of the region but of the entire Āndhra people. During the period covered by the present study, Āndhradeśa and Triliṅgadeśa were used as synonyms. Early Muslim writers used the word Teling or some of its variants to denote the Kingdom of Prataparudra which embraced almost entire Āndhradeśa. After the formation of Hyderabad *subah* by the Asaf Jhahis, which included Telugu, Kannaḍa, and Maratwāḍa regions, it is likely that the Telugu-speaking parts were called Telingāṇa or Telangāṇa. As the latter word is being widely employed in recent times, it is adopted to denote the region in this study.

Politically till the rise of Kākatīyas to sovereign authority (A.D. 1163), Telangāṇa formed a part of the Cālukya and Rāṣṭrakūṭa imperial systems and absorbed many social elements and cultural traits flowing from the western Deccan. Even after the fall of the Qutb Shahis (A.D. 1687) and till the formation of Āndhra Pradesh in 1956, Telangāṇa remained separate from the rest of Āndhradeśa.

Telangāṇa, fo: the above reasons, merits a special study. But so far, no attempt has been made at it. The importance of regional and local history in understanding the complexity of national culture is being recoginsed and regional imbalances in Indian historiography are held responsible for the emergence of extreme type of regionalism, plagueing India.[1] Further, as the Japanese scholar Karashima[2] points out that for historical investigation, a small area and short period are best suited. Such a selection gives good scope for a detailed study of the forces at work in the area and during the period and their impact on the people and enables one to arrive at more accurate results.

The author, therefore, has chosen the econimic and social forces at work in Telangāṇa during the period A.D. 1000-1323 for her study.

Review of earlier work

Till recently the interest of the authors of Deccan history has been centred round dynasties such as the Early Cālukyas, Rāṣṭrakūṭas and Later Cālukyas and in their scheme the socio-economic aspects occupied an insignificant place and much less regarding the regions like Telangāṇa as they formed parts of mighty imperial systems. Morover, as the above dynasties had their seats in Karṇāṭaka, their kingdoms are generally known as Karṇāṭaka empires and engrossed the attention mostly of Kannaḍa historians. It is natural that the regions like Telangāṇa, though extensive in area, received scant attention from such historians. In The Early History of The Deccan edited by G. Yazdani,[3] dynastic approach has been adopted. The major dynasties like the Sātavāhanas, Vākāṭakas, Early Cālukyas, Rāṣṭrakūṭas, Later Cālukyas and Kākatīyas only attracted the attention of the historians and therefore the work suffers from two serious shortcomings: (1) the lack of continuity and (2) omission of an acount of the feudetory or sāmanta ruling families which played a conspicuous role in the economy and culture of their respective regions. However, N. Venkateramanaiah has made a special study of the history of Cālukyas of Vemulavāḍa[4] because of their significant role in the conflicts between the Rāṣṭrakūṭas and Eastern Cālukyas.

Though Telangāṇa was the core-region of the Kākatīya kingdom, historians of Āndhra laid emphasis on the Kākatīya efforts at the unification of all the Telugu-speaking areas of Deccan under their rule. M. Rama Rao may be said to have been the first to make an attempt at a comprehesive account mainly on the political history in his book 'The Kākatīyas of Warangal'[5] However, his entire work on the dynasty has not seen the light of the day. The Kākatīya Sañcika edited by him in Telugu contains articles on different aspects of the period but it is limited by the extremely meagre source material available during the thirties.[6]

In the Early History of the Deccan there is a lengthy chapter on the Kākatīyas, contributed by N. Venkataramanayya and M. Somasekhara Sarma.[7] This is no doubt a comprehensive account but written from the point of Āndhradeśa. Further, the scholars could not describe in detail the social and economic developments during the period because of the limited scope of the project.

The 'Kākatīyas' of P.V. Parabrahma Sastry[8] is the latest and very valuable work on the history of the period. Sastry has made remarkable contribution to the early history of the Kākatīyas including their relations with other Cālukyan feudatories in the region. His work which has fully utilised the epigraphical evidance so far available gives an insight into the administration and society in Āndhra during the Kākatīya period. Pratibha and Kanaka Durga worked on the individual reigns of Rudramadevi[9] and Gaṇapatideva[10] and their times respectively.

On the socio-economic history of the period 'The Corporate Life in Medieval Āndhra' of R. Narasimha Rao[11] may be called a pioneer study. It throws welcome light on various artisan and merchant guilds and their role in the social and economic activities. The Studies in Economic and Social conditions of Medieval Āndhra (A. D. 1000-1600) by K. Sundaram[12] is too sweeping an account over a long period and the author's main interest was in the conditions of the coastal districts. A. Vaidehi also has made a study of the Social and Economic Conditions in Eastern Deccan (A. D. 1000-1250) but she limited her study to the eastern Deccan i.e. coastal districts of Āndhradeśa.[13] Her account contains a description more of social and religious condition and less of economy. Suravaram Pratapa Reddy has written the Social History of Āndhras in Telugu (Āndhrula Sānghika Caritra) but it is based mainly on literary sources.[14]

Several articles by different scholars on various aspects of life during the period appeared from time to time in journals like J.A.H.R.S. , Itihās and Bhārati.

Present Approach

The present work is an attempt at a study of the economic and social conditions in some detail and their mutual interaction in the limited area of Telangāṇa during a period of 300 years (A.D. 1000-1323) in the light of the latest trends in Indian Historiography. Since the British conquest of India, several European writers have taken keen interest in understanding her past. With the limited sources and administrative reports prepared by the officers of the East India Company, they developed interesting ideas. One of such is the Marxian concept of Asiatic mode of Production.[15] The essence of the concept is that for ages the Indian economy and, as a consequence, the Indian society have been stagnant being based upon self-sufficient village economy till the British rulers gave it a push during the 18th and 19th centuries.

The concept of Asiatic mode of Production has been a subject of much debate. Very early S.A. Dange[16] applying Marxian dialectics has tried to prove that the Indian society was not totally immobile and stagnant and that a careful study would reveal different stages of social evolution. Romila Thapar[17] emphasised the inadequacies of the concept. Karashima has rightly pointed out that self-sufficient and isolated village communities are almost a myth. Recently, Katheleen Gough,[18] limiting her study to the district of Tanjavur, tried to vindicate the concept in a modified form. But her conclusions are open to question. D.D. Kosambi has rightly warned that mechanical application of Marxian theories to the Indian situations would not yield satisfactory results.[19]

More complicated is the problem of feudalism.[20] The political and socio-economic order of medieval Europe is generally referred to as feudalism characterised by the following features:

1. Heirarchy of rulers resembling a pyramid with the king at the top and with extreme decentralisation of political power.

2. Agriculture being the main scource of national income, the nature of landholding determined the relations between the different strata of society.

3. Landlords or local magnates appropriating the surplus produce which is not channelised into productive avenues but wasted away on luxuriant life.

4. Self-sufficient village production, with minimum trade in which money rarely played any role. The economy was thus mainly rural and little helpful to social mobility.

Scholars admit that the features of European feudalism are not aplicable to the Indian conditions. Horbans Mukhia[21] even denies the very existence of feudalism in India. D.D. Kosambi[22] held that Indian feudalism was mostly 'from above' implying thereby that it was more political. D.N. Jha[23] is of the opinion that from the later period of Gupta rule to about A.D. 1000, a mode of production similar to European feudalism was prevalent at least in north India. R.S. Sarma[24] observes that the history of Indian feudalism is uneven because of vastness of size and perplexing diversity in regional situation. Even in a particular age, no uniform pattern can be applied throughout India.

Recent studies by Champakalakshmi,[25] Subbarayalu[26] (Tamilnad) M.G.S. Narayanan[27] (Kerala) and N.R. Nandi[28] (Karnataka) reveal a fresh approach to the history of South India from the above points of view with encouraging results. Particlularly the studies in Cola history by Burton Stein, [29] Kenneth Hall[30] and Noboru Karashima[31] and others are significant in the application of the concepts of feudalism and the segmentary state.

This work is a modest attempt to study the socio-economic development in the Telangāṇa region from the above point of view. It begins with a survey of the political background keeping in view of the concepts of oriental despotism which became one of the articles of faith with the English historians Sir Henry Maine and James Mill and the concept of 'segmentary state'which Burtan Stein applied to the Cola empire. How far the polity developed feudal characteristics has been examined.

In chapter II different types of landholding such as Crown lands, Agrahāras, Devabhogas and the nature of landholding in peasant villages are examined. The keen interest evinced by the kings, sāmantas, officials, guilds and private individuals in the development of irrigational facilities is discussed. Agricultural production pattern is described. Land and agricultural taxes are discussed at the end of the chapter. Taxation was no doubt heavy but did not break the backbone of the peasant.

The channelisation of surpluses in the agricultural production into industrial activity is discussed in chapter III. Among the indsutrial activities, the growth of textile manufacture and oil production and the artisan communities involved in these industries are explained. Non-agricultural industries such as the metal industry and other miscellaneous types of production are outlined in this chapter. Taxes on industrial communities are briefly outlined.

Chapter IV deals with trade. The various organisations of trade such as the Nakaram and Pekkaṇḍru are discussed. The growth, expansion and diversification of Nakaram network and its integration with itinerent merchant guilds such as Ayyāvali-500 and artisan guilds like Telivevuru into larger corporations such as Ubhayanādesi pekkanḍru are discussed. Various trade centres and trade routes are outlined. Taxes on trade and the mechinery of tax collection are also discussed. The Kākatīyas attempted to standardise land measure, coinage and units of measurement as necessitated by economic development. This aspect is briefly outlined in the Appendix.

The next three chapters are devoted to the study of contemporary society with a view to examine social changes that occured during the period under the impact of the above economic developments.

A discussion on the social sturcture forms the content of the chapter V. The inadequacy of the Cāturvarṇa system and the concept of Aṣṭādaśamahāpraja to explain the contemtporary social structure is examined. The major factors that were responsible for the structural changes in the society such as the absorption of aboriginals, economic developments, religious movements and political fortunes are outlined.

The classification of society on the basis of occupations appears to be more appropriate than the traditional methods of looking at the society as a conglomoration of castes. As such, the society of the period is analysed into four major social grops viz., priestly class, ruling class, agricultural communities and merchant and artisan communities. The role of these groups in the contemporary social, political and economic formations and the changes that took place as a result of the factors are explained in chapter VI.

The developments in the economic, religious and political fields resulted in mobility of social groups on the status scale. This is known as social mobility. Two types of social mobility, horizonatal and vertical are witnessed. These factors are outlined in chapter VII. The migration of brāhmaṇas from various parts of India to Telangāṇa, decline of Kṣatriya community and the rise of peasant-warrior community are considered. The mobility of non-elite groups is briefly outlined.

The expansion in wetland agriculture, growth of industry and trade, large scale temple building and establishment of *sāmanta* and *māṇḍalka* principalities led to the development of several urban centres all over the region. The process of urbanisation is discussed and the growth of some prominent towns and cities is outlined in chapter VIII.

The results of this study are presented in Conclusion.

Sources

The study is naturally based upon (1) literature (2) epigraphy and (3) monuments. A serious student of history generally prefers archaeological i.e., epigraphical evidence to literary account because literary works are prone to subjective elements such as imagination and fancy and author's preferences. They are further prone to alterations and interpolations. The archaeological evidence epigraphy, numismatics and monuments are free from such defects.

The historical research in Telangāṇa received stimullus with the establishment of Lakṣmaṇarāya Pariśodhaka Maṇḍali. Under the auspices of the Maṇḍali, Dūpāti Seshāchāryulu and Dūpāti Ramaṇāchāryulu known as Seshādri Ramaṇakavulu, Ādirāju Veerabhadra Rao and Gaḍiyāram Rāmakrishna Sarma collected a large number of inscriptions and published them in two volumes entitled -Telangāṇa Śāsanamulu. In the Hyderabad Archaeological Series, P. Srinivasachar edited 'The Corpus of Telangāṇa Inscriptions ' in three volumes. The fourth volume of the corpus was prerared by Mallampalli Somasekhara Sarma, and edited by R. Subrahmanyam and published by the Government of Āndhra Pradesh. P.B. Desai and P. Srinivasachar compiled the Kannaḍa Inscriptions of Āndhra Pradesh. The inscriptions in the Alampūr Museum and the Inscriptions of Perūr have been edited in two different volumes by Abdul Waheed Khan and Nelaturu Venkata Ramanaiah respectively. B. N. Sastry has published Śāsana Samputi in two volumes, containing the inscriptions from Telangāṇa Districts and another volume of the Inscriptions of Kandūru Coḍas. The Āndhra Pradesh State Department of Archaeology and Museums has planned to bring out a district-wise inscriptions in separate volumes and so far the inscriptions of Warangal and Karimnagar districts have come out.

The inscriptions especially from temple towns and trade centres such as Perūr, Alampūr, Bekkallu, Māṭeḍu and Warangal contain a good account of the religious conditions, trade guilds and taxes. But the districts of Adilabad and Nizamabad yielded practically no inscriptions. Even from other districts most of the inscriptions are donative records, generally short in size. Rarely do we come across historical *praśastis,* royal edict and administrative records as in Tamilnāḍ and Karṇātaka. The inscriptions, therefore,do not give a comprehensive picture of the socio-economic condition of the region and the period. This is one of the serious disadvantages under which the student of Āndhra history in general and Telangāṇa history in particular has to work.

Geographically and ecologically several parts of coastal Āndhra and Rāyalaseema, Krishna, Guntur, Prakasam and Kurnool districts are contiguous with Telangāṇa though seperated by river Krishna. As such a number of epigraphs from these regions are also consulted. These inscriptions are published by the Archaeological Survey of India as *South Indian inscriptions* in volumes IV, V, VI and X.

Literary Sources

The history of Sanskrit literature in this period may be said to begin with *Mānasollāsa* a Manual on Polity author by the royal poet Someśvara III. Many poets are known to have received patrcnage at the court of the Kākatīyas. Most of them composed their works in sanskrit, but none of them are very useful as source of historical information. Rudradeva is believed to have composed the Nītisāra, but it is not available. A few verses of Nītisāra translated into Telugu are included in Nītisāra Muktavali of Singana. Vidyānātha was the court poet of Pratāpa Rudra and his Pratāparudra Yaśobhūṣaṇam tries to derive the name Kākatīya and referes to the caste of the Kākatīyas. The Nṛttaratnāvali of Jāyapa, the Gajasāhini of Gaṇapatideva throws light on the condition of arts during the period. Nṛsimhakavi, son of Viśveśvara composed Siddhodvāha inscribed on Ursuguṭṭa contains beautiful descriptions of Āndhradeśa and the city of warangal. Rāvipāṭi Tripurāntaka is believed to have composed a Vīdhināṭaka named Premābhiramam on the life in the city of Warangal but it is not available in original.

Much literature was produced in Telugu. Its history in the period begins almost with the Āndhramahābhāratam of poet Nannaya (A.D. 1056) followed by the Gaṇitasārasaṃgraha of Mallana (A.D. 1060) and the Kumārasambhavam of Nannecoḍa (C. A.D. 1150). During the period under study much literture was produced. Under the patronage of Telugu Coḍa rulers of Nellore, Tikkana translated the Mahābhārata. He had friendly relations with the Kākatīya king Gaṇapatideva and tradition recounts his visit to Warangal. His junior contemporary, Ketana translated the Mitākṣara under the title Vijñāneśvaram, a commentary on the Yajñavalkyasmṛti prepared at the court of Vikramāditya VI. Baddena (C.A.D. 1100) wrote the Nītisāra Muktāvali besides Sumatīsatakam. These works throw light on several aspects of polity and society. Mārana dedicated his Mārkaṇḍeya Purāṇam to Gannaya, an officer at the court of Prataparudra, whom the work describes as the Mayor of the city of Warangal. During the same period Gona Buddhā Reḍḍi composed the Ranganātha-rāmāyaṇam. The translation of Bhāskara Rāmāyaṇam was completed under the patronage of Sāhiṇi Māraya. The most outstanding Telugu poet of Telangāṇa of the age was Pālkuriki Somanātha. The Paṇḍitārādhya caritra and the Basava Purāṇam contain useful information on the socio-economic conditions

The Telugu works that came after the fall of the Kākatīyas but are useful for the history of their age are the Palnāṭivīracaritra, the Krīḍābhirāmam and the Nītisāramuktavali. The first work is generally attributed to Śrīnātha and is a mine of information on social conditions of the period. The Krīḍābhirāmam of Vallabhāmātya is a translation of Premābhirāmam of Tippana, who was contemporary of Prataparudra. It contains a graphic description of the city of Warangal, its dirrerent Vāḍas (wards), market places, temples and temple festivals. Mamidipudi Venkatarangaih says that Kriāḍābhirāmam "throws a flood of light on social conditions on the great kingdom of Telangāṇa under Pratapa Rudra, and as such its value to students of research and historians is immense". It is a mirror of life in Warangal. The Siddheśvara Caritra of Kāse Sarvappa is a very late work of the 17th century and give the traditional account of the Kākatīya dynasty. It is based upon an earlier work Pratāpacaritra of Ekāmranātha. These works contain information more legendary in nature than historical. To this class belongs also the Somadevarājīyam of Kūcimanci Jaggakavi of about the 17th-18th centuries.

Monuments

The large number of temples and tanks that are spread all over Telangāṇa are the mirrors of the social, religious, economic and cultural conditions of the people in the medieval period. The temples built by the Cālukyas of Kalyān, the Coḍas of Kandūr and Kākatīyas and several other subordinate rulers have been studied by a number of scholars, G. Yazdani, M. Rama Rao, M. Radhakrishna Sarma, B. Rajendra Prasad and S. Gopalakrishna Murthy. The temples at Ālampūr, Pānagal, Pillalamarṛi, Anmakoṇḍa, Warangal and Pālampet are some of the best examples of art and architecture reflecting the culture-contacts of the Deccan. The Rāmappa lake, the Pākhal lake, Kesarisamudram, Udaya Samudram are some of the living examples of the large tanks that were built during the period under study. They reflect the high technical skills as well as the aesthetic sense of the people.

REFERENCES

1. Romila Thaper, 'The scope and singnificance of Regional History', 'Ancient Indian social History', (New Delhi, 1978).
2. N. Karashima, South Indian History and Society (A.D. 800-1800) Introduction, P. XX (Delhi, 1984).
3. G. Yazdani, (ed) The Early History of the Deccan., (London, 1960).
4. N. Venkataramanayya, The Cālukyas of L(V) emulavāḍa, (Hyderabad,

1953).

5. M. Rama Rao, The Kākatīyas of Warangal, (Hyderabad, 1952).
6. M. Rama Rao, (ed) Kākatīya Sañchika (Telugu) Rajahmundry, 1935.
7. N. Venkataramanayya and M. Somasekhara Sarma in The Early History of the Deccan, (London, 1960).
8. P. V. Parabrahma Sastry, The Kākatīyas. (Hyderabad, 1975).
9. Pratibha, Rudramadevi and her Times (unpublished) Ph. D. Thesis, 1972. Andhra University,Vishakhapatnam.
10. Kanakadurga, Gaṇapatideva and his times. unpublished Ph.D. Thesis, 1984 (Nagarjuna University), Nagarjuna Nagar.
11. R Narasimha Rao, Corporate life in Medieval Āndhra, Secunderabad, 1967.
12. K. Sundaram, The Studies in Economic and Social conditions in Medieval Āndhra (A. D. 1000-1600), (Machilipatnam, 1968).
13. A. Vaidehi, Social and Economic Conditions in Eastern Deccan (A.D. 1000-1250) Secudarabed 1970.
14. S. Pratapa reddy, Āndhrula Śānghika caritra. (Hyderabad, 1982).
15. Karl Marx, The Capital, vol. I, quoted in Precapitalist economic Formations (ed) e. J. Hobsbawm, (London, 1964).
16. Dange S.A., India from Primitive Communism to Slavery, (Bombay, 1947).
17. Romila Thapar, Ancient Indian Social History - Some Interpratations. (Delhi, 1984).

    R.A.L.H. Gunavardana, The Analysis of Precolonial Social Formations in Asia, in the writings of Karl Marx, I.H.R. II, W. 1976.
18. Katheleen Gough, Modes of Production in Southern India, Economic and Political Weekly, annual Number, Ferbruary, 1980, pp. 337-364.
19. D.D. Kosambi, An Introduction to the Study of Indian History, (Bombay, 1956) Introduction.
20. N. Karashima, op. cit., Introduction, p. XXX.
21. Harbans Mukhia, Was there Feudalism in Indian History?

    The Journal of Peasant Studies, vol. VIII, No. 3, (New Delhi, 1981).
22. D.D. Kosambi, op. cit., p. 295 ff.
23. D.N. Jha, The Early Indian Feudalism—a Historiographical Critique, Presidential Adress, Section I, Proc. I. H. C., 1979.
24. R.S. Sharma, Indian Feudalism, (Delhi, 1980).
25. R. Champakalakshmi, Growth of Uraban Centress in South India, Kudamukku - Palaiyarai, The Twin-City of the Colas, Studies in History vol. I, No. 1 1979.

26. Y. Subbarayalu, The Cola State, Studies In History, vol. IV. No. 2, 1982.
27. R. N. Nandi, Feudalism of the State in Medieval south India-Social science Probing, vol. I, No.1, March, 1984, pp. 33-57.
28. M.G.S. Narayanan, Reinterpretations, in South Indian History, Trivandrum, 1977.
29. Buton Stein, Peasant State and Society in Medieval South India, (Delhi, 1980).
30. Kenneth R. Hall, Trade and Statecraft in the Age of the Colas, (Delhi, 1980).
31. N. Karashima, *op. cit.*

CHAPTER—I

POLITICAL BACKGROUND

Telangāṇa played a subordinate role in the political history of Deccan till the rise of the Kākatīyas as an independant power. For long time the region was ruled by imperial powers such as the Rāṣṭrakūṭas and later Cālukyas from their capitals outside Āndhra. The efforts of these powers to bring the fertile and rich coastal Āndhra, which was ruled by the weak Vēṅgi Cālukyas further complicated the poilitical situation of the region. The imperial armies moved frequently across Telangāṇa retarding her economic growth. The imperial powers stationed subordinate ruling families at positions of strategic importance and appointed mostly generals as their agents over the other important parts of the region. If the Cālukyas of Vemulavāḍa[1] were subordinates of Rāṣṭrakūṭas, the Cālukyas of Mudigoṇḍa[2] were feudatories of the eastern Cālukyas and their principalities served as the buffere between Mānyakheṭa and Vēṅgi. The Kākatīyas were posted at Anmakoṇḍa[3] (Koṛavi) by the Rāṣṭrakūṭas to check the aggressive activities of the Mudigoṇḍa Cālukyas and assist their own subordinates. These chiefs and generals owed nominal allegience to the imperial powers and ruled their region quite independently. The Rāṣṭrakūṭas were overthrown in A.D. 973 and with them disappeared the Cālukyas of Vemulavāḍa.

There are three distinct phases in the political history of Telangāṇa from the time of the overthrow of the Rāṣṭrakūṭas (A.D. 973) to the fall of the Kākatīyas (A.D. 1323). This is the period of the present sutdy. The first phase is characterised by the rule of the Cālukyas of Kalyan through their sāmantas, especially the Kākatīyas and the Kandūr Coḍas. The second phase witnessed the emergence of the Kākatīyas as a political force, consolidation of their authority and their rise as sovereign, rulers. The third phase which may also be called the imperial phase is marked by territorial expansion of the Kākatīyas, administrative reorganisation characterised by centralisation and the growth of the nāyankaras.

FIRST PHASE

Rule of Cālukya Sāmantas

With the overthrow of the Rāṣṭrakūṭas in A.D. 973, Telangāṇa passed under the rule of the later Cālukyas.[4] The Cālukyan monarachs appear to have paid special attention on Telangāṇa having realised its geo-political significance, particularly in their conflict with the Colas of Tanjāvūr. Taila II, who overthrew the Rāṣṭrakūṭas, had made Telangāṇa his base of political and military operations and took the title, Lord of Trilingadeśa.[5] Though he started his independent rule from Mānyakheṭa,[6] his sucessors shifted their capital to Poṭlaceṛuvu (poṭlakeṛe). According to the Kannaḍa Basavapurāṇa,[7] Jayasimha rule from Poṭlakeṛe which is identified with modern Paṭāncheṛuvu near Hyderabed and it remained the capital of the Cālukyas till Someśvara made the city of Kalyān his permanent capital. Even afterwards, the emperors and princes frequently visited the region.

Someśvara (A.D. 1042-1068), the successor of Jayasimha, was a powerful ruler. During his time the Cola-Cālukya conflict over Vēṅgi assumed fearful proportions[9] and both Telangāṇa and coastal Āndhra became a big battle field. Someśvara had reorganised the administration of Telangāṇa in view of the political and military reuquirements.

Someśvara granted various regions of Telangāṇa among subordinate or sāmanta ruling families. The Anmakoṇḍa viṣaya was conferred on Prola I of the Kākatīya family as a military fief.[10] The Kākatīyas entered Telangāṇa as generals of the Rāṣṭrakūṭas and consolidated their position under Beta II. After the Rāṣṭrakūṭas were overthrown, they shifted their loyalty to the Cālukyas and, by their meritorious service, won the confidence of their overlords. The family rose to the position of sāmantas under Beta I.

The Coḍas of Kandūr, who had hailed from Eṛuvanāḍu (Kurnool dt.)[11] as generals attained the sāmanta status by about A.D. 1050.[12] They first appear as rulers of Kollipāka, but gradually settled down in Kandūrunāḍu, a region on the northern bank of the river Krishna comprising several parts of Nalgoṇḍa and Mahaboobnagar districts,[14] with Koḍūr as their early headquarters. As it became an extensive principality, it came to be divided into two rājyas, the Pānagallu rājya and Kandūru rājya.[15]

Polavāsa in the Jagityāl taluq of Karīmnagar District was another seat of a feudatory family.[16] Govindāpuram was their subsidiary headquarters.[17] They too rose to power under the Rāṣṭrakūṭas and continued as the subordinates of the later Cālukyas. They became a powerful family under Vikramāditya VI.[18] The sāmanta states are shown in Map I. Their growth is noted in Table - I.

There is not much evidence for clearly defining the relationship between these sāmantas and their soverigns. However, they took the title sāmanta[19] and mahāsamnta.[20] The sāmantas of the Cālukyas that functioned in Telangāṇa are noted in Table - I. The sāmantas developed their own bureaucratic set-up.There were māṇḍalikas under powerful mahā-sāmantas such as the Kandūr Coḍas, whose principalities were considerably large in size.[21] It is not known whether these sāmantas paid regular tribute.There are instances where the sāmantas attended the coronation ceremonies of their overlords and most probably on such occasions paid gifts and presents to the overlord. It is learnt from the Koravi epigraph that Kusumāyudha of Raṇamarda family installed Cālukya Bhīma on the throne of Vēṅgi and ornamented his neck with raṇama rdakanṭhika.[22]

As the sāmantas paid only nominal allegience to the overlord, they enjoyed much freedom.[23] Their principalities were called kingdoms and their courts were smaller replicas of the imperial courts. The sāmantas tried to augment the economic resources of the principalities. They also built temples, of course, for the health and victory of their overlords. Several inscriptions of the period note the construction of temples and tanks by the Kandūr Coḍas and early Kākatīyas. This is a proof of expansion of resource base of these kingdoms. The famous tanks of Udayasamudram, Coḍa-samudram and Bhīmasamudram were created by theCoḍas of

Kandūr.[24] Among the early Kākatīyas, Prola I built Periyakeṛia[25] and Prola II was responsible for Kesarisamudram.[26] The combination of tank and temple led to the growth of agriculture and the emergence of rural townships providing favouraable conditions for urbanisation. With these developments, Telangāṇa could find a place in the economic map of Deccan attracting trade guilds even from outside. Inscriptions from Gangāpuram[27]and Perūr[28] reveal that both the places become busy trade centres with merchant guilds being active and diverting some of their rich profits into tank and temple building.

The sāmantas participated in the campaigns and wars of their overlords. One of the early Kākatīyas, Garuḍa Beta had the title colacamūvārdhi pramathana[29] which makes it evident that he took part in the Cālukyan expeditions against the Cola kingdom. Prola II helped, Vikramāditya VI in suppressing Paramāra Jagaddeva of Kollipāka and Meḍarāja of Polavāsa who rose against the cālukyan authority.[30] Prola II helped Someśvara III in putting down the rebellion of his own brother Tailapa, the governor of Gangāpuram.[31] But, whenever the emperor showed signs of weakness or whenever the imperial dynasty was disturbed by disputed successions, the sāmantas grew stronger, mutually aggressive and tried to assert independence. The wars between the Kākatīyas and the Cālukyas of Mudigoṇḍa[32] and those between the former and the Kandūru Coḍas[33] could not have been at the instance of the imperial Cālukyas. Even as a subordinate of the Cālukyas of Kalyān, Prolla II made efforts to expand his own principality at the expense of the Coḍas of Kandūr and the Durjayas of Velanāḍu. It is said that after his victory over Kandūr Coḍas, Prola visited Śrīśailam and erected a pillar of victory.[34]

The Cālukyan empire fell on evil days after Vikramāditya VI. The civil wars during the reigns of Vikramāditya VI (A.D. 1076-1126)[36] and Someśvara III (A.D. 1126-1138)[36] and the innumerable expeditions of the former had weakened the economy of the kingdom. Tailapa III (A.D. 1141-1162) could not arrest the process of disintegration and the Cālukya subordinates such as the Kālachūris, the Hoyasālas, the Yādavas and the Kākatīyas asserted independence.[37]

TABLE I

Sāmantas and Māṇḍalikas under The Cālukyas and The Kākatīyas

Sl. No.	*Place district*	*Sovereign King/date*	*Feudatory with title*	*Subordinate*	*Reference*
(1)	(2)	(3)	(4)	(5)	(6)
1.	Sanigaram (Karimnagar)	Someśvara-I A.D. 1051	Mahāsāmanta Betarasa	-	I.A.P. Kn. 14
2.	Sanigaram (Karimnagar)	-do- A.D. 1053	Mahāsāmanta Prolarasa	-	I.A.P. Kn. 15
3.	Poṭapalli (Karimnagar)	-do- A.D. 1066	Mahāsāmanta Chaṇḍayyarasa	-	I.A.P. Kn. 16
4.	Bānājipet (Warangal)	Vikramāditya-VI A.D. 1082	Mahāmaṇḍaleśvara Medarasa	-	I.A.P. Wl. 14
5.	Vemulavāḍa (Karimnagar)	-do- A.D. 1083	Mahāmaṇḍaleśvara Rājāditya	-	I.A.P. Kn. 18
6.	Kollipāka (Nalgoṇḍa)	-do- A.D. 1088	Mahāmaṇḍaleśvara Toṇḍarasa	-	Tel. Ins. I, P. 123
7.	Ujjili (Mahaboobnagar)	-do- A.D. 1097	Mahāmaṇḍaleśvara Vallabhacola	-	Tel. Ins. II, p. 66
8.	Kāzipet (Warangal)	-do- A.D. 1098	Mahāmaṇḍaleśvara Durgarasa	-	I.A.P. Wl. 15
9.	Niḍigoṇḍa	-do-	Mahāmaṇḍaleśvara Natavāḍi Buddharājulu	-	I.A.P. Wl. 16

(1)	(2)	(3)	(4)	(5)	(6)
10.	Niḍigoṇḍa (Warangal)	-do- A.D. 1104	Māṇḍalika Duggarasa of Natåvādi	-	I.A.P. Wl. 17.
11.	Kollipāka (Nalgoṇḍa)	-do- A.D. 1105	Mahāmaṇḍaleśvara Jagaddeva Nārāyaṇå	-	Tel. Ins. I, p. 147
12.	Pudūr (Mahaboobnagar)	-do- A.D. 1105	Pundur Hallikarasa	-	Tel. Ins. I, p. 128-129.
13.	Sanigaram (Karimnagar)	Vikramāditya-VI	Mahāmaṇḍaleśvara Betarasa	-	I.A.P. Kn. 19
14.	-do-	-do-	Mahāmandaleśvara Jagaddevarasa	-	-do-
15.	Bhuvanagiri (Nalgoṇḍa)	-do- A.D. 1115	Daṇḍanāyaka Lakshmīdevayya	-	Tel. Ins. II, p. 59
16.	Peddakaḍumur (Mahabubnagar)	-do- A.D. 1116	Saudhare Bollenāyaka	-	Tel. INs. II,
17.	Māṭeḍu (Warangal)	-do- A.D. 1120	Mahāmaṇḍaleśvara Prolerāju	Mahāsāmanta Mallenāyaka.	I.A.P. Wl. 24
18.	Paṭāncheruvu	-do-	Mahāmaṇḍaleśvara Amalamayya Daṇḍanātha		C.I.T.D. IV, (Medak) p. 18
19.	Govindāpuram (Warangal)	-do- A.D. 1122	Mahāmaṇḍaleśvara Meḍarāja		I.A.P. Wl. 26 not
20.	Sanigaram	Someśwara III A.D. 1128	Mahāmaṇḍaleśvara Prolarasa	Savadore Kuṛavaraju	I.A.P. Kn. 21

(1)	(2)	(3)	(4)	(5)	(6)
21.	Gangāpuram (Karimnagar)	-do- (A.D. undated)	Sāmantha Guṇḍeraju	-	I.A.P. Kn. 23
22.	Sirikoṇḍa (Khammam)	Jagadekamalla A.D. 114	Udayacoḍa	Mahāmāṇḍa-lika Ketaya	K.C.S.C.S., 193
23.	Sanigaram (Karimnagar)	-do- A.D. 1149	Mahāmaṇḍaleśvara Prolarasa	Mahasamanta Kurvaraju	I.A.P. Kn. 24
24.	Perūru (Nalgoṇḍa)	Bhimanacoḍa A.D. undated	Mahāmāṇḍalika Mallenāyaka	-	P.I. 6
25.	Peruru (Nalgoṇḍa)	Udayanacoḍa A.D. 1136	Māṇḍalika guṇḍaya	-	P.I. 8
26.	Perūru (Nalgonda)	-do- A.D. 1147	Māṇḍalika Mallenāyaka	-	P.I. 9
27.	Rāchūr (Mahabubnagar)	-do- A.D. 1159	Savadara Rāvitorti Prolenāyaka	-	K.C.H.C.S., P. 199
28.	Lingala (Nalgoṇḍa)	-do- A.D. 1168	Māṇḍalika Toṇḍ	-	-do- p, 220
29.	Nelakoṇḍapalli (Khammam)	A.D. 1176	Udayanacoḍa Mallināyaka	-	C.I.T.D., III, P. 31
30.	Nagurūr (Karimnagar)	Rudradeva A.D. 1171	Māṇḍalika gangarāju	-	I.A.P. Kn. 25
31.	Yellampeṭa (Warangal)	-do- A.D. 1178	Māṇḍalika Prole nāyaka	Preggaḍa Perama Reḍḍi	I.A.P. Wl. 39
32.	Pillalamaṛṛi (Nalgoṇḍa)	-do- A.D. 1195	Māṇḍalika Recherla Nāmireḍḍi	-	Tel. Ins. I, p. 17

(1)	(2)	(3)	(4)	(5)	(6)
33.	Manthena (Karimnagar)	Ganapatideva A.D. 1999	Allum-prolarāja	-	I.A.P. Kn. 28
34.	Jalālpuram (Nalgonda)	-do- A.D. 1202	Māṇḍalika Ceṛaku Bollayya	-	Tel. Ins., II, p. 103
35.	Koṇḍaparti (Warangal)	-do- A.D. 1203	Malyāla Chauṇḍ senāni	-	I.A.P. Wl. 48
36.	Pillalamarri (Nalgonda)	Gaṇapati A.D. 1200	Māṇḍalika Recherla Bati Reḍḍi	-	Tel. Ins. I, p. 31
37.	Vāḍapalli (Nalgoṇḍa)	-do- A. D. 1222	Three Nāyakas (1) Komara Nāyaka (2) Beta Nāyaka (3) Rudra nāyaka	-	Tel. Ins. I., p. 38
38.	Pālampeṭa (Warangal)	-do- A.D. 1213	Māṇḍalika Recherla Rudra Senāni	-	C.I.T.D. II, p. 138
39.	Rāmannapet (Warangal)	-do- A.D. 1213	Mahāsāmantha Malreḍḍi	-	I.A.P. Wl. 50
40.	Chapur (Warangal)	-do- A. D. 1217	Māṇḍalika Kāṭaya Reḍḍi	-	I.A.P. Wl. 54
41.	Vardhamāna puram (Mahabubnagar)	-do-	Māṇḍalika Gonaganapayya A.D. 1224	-	C.I.T.D. III 46 PP. pp. 94-97
42.	Pammi (Khammam)	-do- A.D. 1236	Mahāsāmantha Viriyāla Nāgasānamma	Mairāju and Mummaḍirāju Devarapre-ggaḍa	C.I.T.D. III, p.31

(1)	(2)	(3)	(4)	(5)	(6)
43.	Koṇḍaparti (Warangal)	-do- A.D. 1245	Malyāla Kāṭaya Chamūpati	-	C.I.T.D., III, P. 46
44.	Vardhamāna puram (Maha-bubnagar)	-do A.D. 1245	Māṇḍalika Malyala Guṇḍaya	-	Te,. Ins. II, P. 107-114
45.	Budāpūr (Maha-bubnagar)	-do- A.D. 1249	-do-	-	Tel. Ins. I, pp. 55-61
46.	Jalālpuram (Nalgonda)	-do- A.D. 1253	Māṇḍalika Ceṛaku Immaḍi Viśvanātha	-	Tel. Ins. I, p. 115
47.	Kūcimañci (Khammam)	-do- A.D. 1260	Piṇḍipolu Pina Maldevarājulu	-	C.I.T.D., III, pp. 19-21
48.	Myḍāram (Krimnager)	Gaṇapatidēva undated	Mahāsāmanta Mydeśvara Pallava Mahārāja	-	I.A.P. Kn. 33.
49.	Rāmakrishnapuram (Khammam)	-do undated	Māṇḍalika Vīrapasāyata	-	C.I.T.D. III, pp. 35-36
50.	Pānugallu (Nalgonda)	Rudramadēvi A.D. 1265	Yādava Sārañga Permāḍi	-	Tel. Ins. I, p. 75
51.	Būrugugaḍda (Nalgonda)	-do- A.D. 1268	Pradhāni Bollamarāju	-	Tel. Ins. p. 71
52.	Umāmaheśwaram (Mahabubnagar)	A.D. 1280	(1) Viśvanatha nāyaka of Goukāpuram (2) Bhaṇḍaru Mahādeva Nāyaṅkara of Umāmaheśwaram (3) Bramhanāyaṅkara of Vāvilāla	-	C.I.T.D., III p. 86

(1)	(2)	(3)	(4)	(5)	(6)
53.	Āgāmotkur (Nalgoṇḍa)	-do- A.D. 1282	Mahāmaṇḍaleśvara Rāmanāthadeva Coḍa	-	K.C.S.C.S. 32
54.	Kollipāka (Nalgoṇḍa)	-do- undated	Potināyaka	-	Tel. Ins. I. p. 80
55.	Perūr (Nalgonda)	-do- undated	Māṇḍalika Maṭṭuri Nāyaka	-	P.I. No. 15
56.	Kandikoṇḍa (Khammam)	Pratāparudra A.D 1285	Recherla Veṅna p. 5-7	-	C.I.T.D., III
57.	Gārla (Khammam)	Pratāparudra A.D. 1287	Recherla Boppaya pp. 5-8	-	C.I.T.D. II,
58.	Amarābad (Mahabubnagar)	-do- A.D.1290	Mahāsāmanta Cheraku Immaḍi Bollaya Reḍḍi	-	C.I.T.D. III, Mn. 5, pp. 38-39
59.	Gaṇapavaram (Nalgoṇḍa)	-do- A.D. 1292	Mahāpradhāni Nāyankara, Gangidevamayya	-	C.I.T.D. III
60.	Rāmpūr (Warangal)	-do- A.D. 1293	Uttamagaṇḍa Eṛva Paṇḍri	-	I.A.P. Wl. 85
61.	Magatala (Mahabubnagar)	-do- A.D. 1297	Gajasāhiṇi Guṇḍayanāyaka	-	Tel Ins. II, p. 120
62.	Magatala (Mahabubnagar)	-do- A.d. 1298	Gajasāhiṇi Mādaya Reḍḍi	-	Tel. Ins. II, p. 123
63.	Mellacheruvu (Nalgonda)	-do- A.D. 1311	Nāyankara Bāmirāju Eṛṛaya preggaḍa	Bollamarreḍḍi, Pradhāni of Nāyankara	Tel. Ins. p. 92

(1)	(2)	(3)	(4)	(5)	(6)
64.	Ṭekumāla (Medak)	-do- A.D. 1311	Mahāpradhāni Puravari Mahādevanāyaka	-	Tel. Ins. p. 91
65.	Maṇūr (Medak)	-do- A.D. 1314	Vilem Rudradeva Nāyankara	Adhikāri Anumakoṇḍa Annuvenka	C.I.T.D. II, p. 162
66.	Chittāpūr (Karimnagar)	-do- undated	Mahāmaṇḍaleśvara chinni Rudradevamahārājulu (Nāyamkara of Pariyāla)	-	I.A.P. Kn. 38

SECOND PHASE

Expansion and consolidation of Kākatīya rule

The Kākatīyas occupy a significant place in the history of Āndhradeśa. Scholars have pointed out that the Kākatīyas, starting from their core region (Telangāṇa), succeeded in bringing almost all the Telugu-speaking parts of the Deccan under their rule.

They entered Āndhra as the generals and frontier gaurds of the Rāṣṭrakūṭas about the beginning of 10th century A.D. From the Bayyāram Tank Inscription of Mailama[38] it is learnt that one of the early members of the family, Guṇḍa Rāṣṭrakūṭa took part and probably lost his life in the wars of Krişṇa II in Vēṅgi. In recognition of his faithful services, Krişṇa appointed Guṇḍa's son Eṛiya Rāṣṭrakūṭa as the governor of Kuṛṛavaḍi, which was situated between the Rāṣṭrakūṭa and Eastern Cālukyan kingdoms, comprising parts of the present Khammam and Warangal districts.[40] The early Kākatīyas came into conflict with the Cālukyas of Mudigoṇḍa who were their neighbours and subordinates of Vēṅgi.[41] However, they succeeded in winning the sympathy and support of some of the local ruling families.

After the fall of the Rāṣṭrakūṭas, Piṇḍi Guṇḍa or Kākartya Guṇḍyana became Independent.[42] He is the first known Kākatīya. In his aggressive wars against the Mudigoṇḍa Cālukyas, Guṇḍa lost his life.[43] But the local chieftains, Viriyāla Kāmasāni and a certain Pallavarāya, supported Guṇḍa's son Garuḍa Beta.[44] They secured the help, probably of Vikramāditya V, and installed Beta on the throne at Kākatipura, probably the traditional seat of the Kākatīyas.

There is no unanimity on the identification of Kākatipura. P.V.P. sastry, following the family account in *Sidheśvara Charitra* identified it with Kandārapura near Nandeḍ in Mahārāṣtra.[45] M. Ramarao suggests that Kākatipura must have been situated in Koṛavideśa (The Kākatīyas of *Warangal* p. 10.) But the Gūḍūr inscription of the Viryāla family states that Kāmasāni installed Beta at Kākati which therefore should have been in Telangāṇa itself. B.S.L. Hanumantha Rao identifies it with Warangal on the basis of the presence of the temple of Kākitamma, the family goddess of the Kākatīyas in the city.[46] There is no clear evidence to associate the early Kākatīyas with Anmakoṇḍa or Warangal. The inscriptions of Beta and his son Prola I are found at Sanigaram in the Karīmngar district.[47] It is possible that the Cālukyan overlords shifted Beta to Sanigarm, a subdivision of Sabbi-1000 from Koṛavi. An inscription from Sanigaram (A. D. 1053) records the gift of lands to god Madhupīśvara of Khaṇḍisanigara by Prola I.[48] The Khājīpet inscription of Tribhuvanamalla Durgā (A.D. 1090) says that Prola I obtained Anmakoṇḍa *visaya* from Trailokyamalla[49] as a permament fief.

Beta II (A. D. 1075-1108) who took the title *Vikramacakri*[50] tried to expand his principality while being loyal to his Cālukyan overlord. The title *Tribhuvanamalla* taken by his son Durgā[51] indicates that he too acknowledged the overlordship of the western Cālukyas. But his loylty was shortlived. Duraga appears to have joined Meḍa of Polavāsa and Paramāra Jagadddeva and rebelled.[52] But he was defeated and was overthrown by his own bother Prola II.[53]

Prola II (A. D. 1117-1158) was an energetic and ambitious prince. He mapped out the lines of future expansion of the Kākatīya principality and prepared the gound for their independence, while continuing as a trusted subordinate of the Cālukyan emperor Vikramāditya VI. The most striking feature in the geo-political history of Deccan is the constant efforts of the western powers to expand eastwards and gain control of the east coast with its busy ports. Prola realised it as the natural direction of Kākatīya expansion. He helped Vikramāditya in suppressing the revolts of Meḍarāja of Polavāsa and Govinda Daṇḍanāyaka and Coḍa Bhīma of Kandūr.[54] The death of Vikramaditya (A.D. 1126) was followed by a conflict between his sons Someswara and Tailapa. Prola supported the former and helped him in securing the throne.[55] The Rudreśvaram (Thousand pillar-temple) inscription of Rudradeva mentions that Prola took Tailapa captive but released him out of consideration.[56] It seems that Prola considered his suppression of Coḍa Bhīma as a personal victory as he planted as noted above, a pillar of victory at Śrīśailam.[57] It foretold the expansion of his successor upto that famous śaiva *ksetra*.

Having thus strengthened his position in Telangāṇa, Prola made an attempt to expand into coastal Āndhra. he invaded Vēṅgi sometime about A.D. 1156 but was defeated and killed by the rulers of Velanāḍu as indicated by the title '*Kākati Prola nirdahana*'[58] taken by Gonka II and his ally, Koṭa Bhīma. Prola II thus left Kākatīya authority consolidated in Telangāṇa and his kingdom was much enlarged with future palns of further expansion.

Rudradeva (A. D. 1158-1195) succeeded his father Prola II at a time when the conditions in Deccan and Āndhra were favourable for proclaiming Kākatīya soverignity and expanding their kingdom in all directions. The time of Rudra's accession appears to have synchronised with the proclamation of independence by the Kālachūris, another subordinate family of the Cālukyas[59] (A.D. 1156-57). In his Rudreśvaram inscription dated in the year A.D. 1163 Rudra does not owe allegience to any overlord and therefore that year is generally taken to mark the proclamation of independence by Rudra.[60] The same record of Rudra describes his victory over a number of rulers in Telangāṇa including Meḍa prince, Coḍa Bhīma of Vardhmānapura and Udaya Coḍa of Pānagal. Rudra made secure the Kākatīya authority in the newly conquered regions by appointing loyal offifcers.[61] These are noted in Table I.

With his victories, Rudra's kinngdom embraced almost the entire Telangāṇa where his authority became unrivalled. Having thus become confident of his power and probably after the death of Tailapa, Rudra proclaimed independence. At this time, the Kākatīya kingdom was bounded by the sea on the east, Śrīśailam on the south, Kalyān on the west and Mālyavanta hills (most probably the Nirmal hill ranges on the banks of Godāvari) in the north.[62]

Rudradeva, in order to avenge the death of his father turned his attention towards the east coast. The war of Palnāḍ (A. D. 1180-82)[63] waged between the vassals of the Durjayas of Velanāḍu destroyed the military might of their kingdom. Taking advatage of the situation, Rudra extended his authority over Vēṅgi[64] and reduced the Koṭas and Koṇḍapaḍumaṭis of Velanāḍu to subjection.[65]

The imperialism of Rudra and the expansion of the Kākatīya kingdom roused the jealousy of the Kālachūris and Yādavas. Rudra appears to have been successful against the Kālachūris,[66] but he lost his life at the hands of Yādava Jaitugi.[67] His brother and successor Mahādeva was also killed in a war of vengence against the Yādavas and Gaṇapatī deva was taken captive.[68] The Kākatīya power thus suffered a temporary eclipse in Telangāṇa.

THIRD PHASE

Territorial expansion-Imperial Organisation

The three kingdoms that ultimately sprang up on the ruins of the Cālukyan empire, the Yādava, the Kākatīya and the Hoyasāla were engaged in expansionist warfare against each other. About the closing years of the 12th century, the Yādava-Hoyasāla conflict became very fearful. Moreover, the Yādavas were already experiencing attacks from the Delhi Sultans.[69] In these circumstances, Jaitugi released Gaṇapatideva who ascended the Kākatīya throne in A. D. 1199.[70] In a short time Gaṇapatideva could consolidate his authority at Anmakoṇḍa-Warangal with the loyal support of the generals and *māṇḍalikas* of the Recerla, Ceṛaku, Malyala, and Gona families.[71] It was during the reign of Gaṇapati (A.D. 1199-1262) that Āndhradeśa was brought under one rule and the Kākatīya dynasty reached the zenith of its power and glory.

Gaṇapati was an ambitious conqueror and a wise statesman. He realised that the Kākatīya kingdom should expand eastwards and southwards to which the chief opponents would be the Durjayas of Velanāḍu. He had secured the northern frontiers of his kingdom by friendly relations with the Yādavas[72] and forged an alliance with the Tikka Coḍa of Nellore[73] who was also fighting with the Durjayas.[74] He then launched an attack on Velanāḍu. Prithvīśvara, the king of Velanāḍu[75] was killed and Divi and Velanāḍu were occupied. The feduatory chiefs of the region, the Ayyas, the Koṭas and the Telgu Coḍas became the subordinates of the Kākatīyas. The Cālukyas of Vēṅgi were subdued and the Kākatīya empire extended upto the confines of Kalinga.[76] The expeditions that Gaṇapatideva sent against Kalinga did not yield any permanent results.[77] Meanwhile, Manumasiddhi, the Telugu Coḍa king of Nellore, sought the help of Gaṇapatideva to recover his throne from his enemies.[78] Gaṇapati led the southern expedition and reinstated Manumasiddhi. The Southern expedition resulted in the extention of his authority upto Kānchi and incorporated Mārjavāḍi into the Kākatīya empire.[79] The political reorganisation of Pānugal *rājya* was made by Gaṇapatideva by including the territory of Mārjavāḍi and making Pānugal as the capital. The reorganised Pānugal Mārjavāḍi *rājya* was conferred on kāyastha Gangaya Sāhiṇi who was earlier ruling from Vallūripaṭṭaṇa in Mārjavāḍi. With these conquests, the Kākatīya empire embraced all the Telugu-speaking parts of Deccan, justifying the titles *Āndhrādhīśvara*[80] and *Triliṅgadeśa parameśvara*[81] taken by Gaṇapati. The Telangāṇa districts as the core region of the Kākatīya kingdom are shown in Map I.

The expansion of the empire necessitated the reorganisation of its administration, in which Gaṇapati displayed deep political insight. His policy may be characterised as a compromise between local autonomy and centralised control and an attempt at harmonising feudalism with absolutism. In the conquered regions of Velanāḍu and Vēṅgī, he had retained the erstwhile rulers as his subordinates. They include the Koṭās of Dharaṇikoṭa, Telugu Coḍas of Koṇidena and Nellore, Yādavās of Addanki, Kāyasthās of Vallūr-Gaṇḍikoṭa and the Cālukyās of Vēṅgi. Gaṇapati treated them as his equals as they were allowed to take such high-sounding titles like *Mahāmaṇḍaleśvara* which he himself had. He entered into matrimonial alliances with the Kotās,[82] the Natvāḍis,[83] the Cālukyas[84] and the Ayyās,[85] He reorgnised Telangāṇa and appointed faithful members of the Recherla, Ceṛaku and Malyāla families over several principalities. These chiefs caled themselves *māṇḍalikas* and enjoyed great autonomy. Table II notes the estates rewarded to civil and military officers some of which developed into *māṇḍalika* principalities. As suggested by the Chiṭyāla inscription (A.D. 1213)[86] the *māṇḍalikas* were not always hereditary. Kāṭaya of the reocrd claims that by pleasing the king with his valour and fighting skill he received from him the title māṇḍalika and a throne and two fly-whisks. During the rule of Gaṇnapatideva the *māṇḍalika* heirarchy served as a bulwark of the Kākatīya authority. The *māṇḍalikas* and *maṇḍaleśvaras*—the chiefs of Natavāḍi, Manumasiddhi of Nellore, the Recerlās and the Ayyās helped Gaṇapati in extending and consolidating the Kākatīya authority.

Gaṇapatideva, at the sametime, developed an elaborate bureaucracy, consisting 72 *niyogās*[87] such as *mahāpradhāni, sandhivigraha, sarvādhikāri, srīkaraṇādhipati, katakarakṣhapāla.* This bureaucratic machinery is a sign of the centralilsation of administration. But as it appears the *māṇḍalika* system and the bureaucratic machinery were overlapping. The *maṇḍaleśvara* of Ganḍikoṭa, Kāyastha Jannigadeva was appointed as *Bāhattara niyogādhipati*[88] whereas the *gajasāhiṇi* Jāyapa, received Chebrol as a military fief.[89] But shortly he was replaced by Malleboya.[90] Thus the members of bureaucracy received military fiefs and *māṇḍalikās* held positions in the bureaucratic machinery.

The system of local administration with its village, *sthala* and *nāḍu* divisions which was in force during the Cālukyan period was retained but reinforced. The popular assembiles such as the *mahājanas* in *agraharas,* the *aṣṭādaśamahāpraja* in peasant villages and the merchant and trade guilds in towns and cities functioned more effectively. In villages, the assembly worked in collabroation with the twelve *Āyagārs,*[91] including *pedakāpu, karaṇam,* and *talāri* which was a quasi-government machinery. The village assemblies, trade and marchant guilds managed water resources in rural areas and supervised the market palces in urban centres promoting social harmony and there by palying a vital role in the economic development of the land.

The early Kākatīyas were Jains.[92] Since the time of Beta II they had changed the the Kālāmukha Śaivism and became the desciples of Rameśvara Paṇḍita, the pontiff of Śillāmaṭha at Śrīśailam.[93] Rudradeva showed preference to the brahmanical system[94] with its emphasis on the brāhmṇas and temples. Inspite of this, creation of *agrahāras* that declined in Phase I was revived and continued to be a striking feature. The building and endowing

TABLE II

Estates of Government Officials and Military Officers and Soldiers (A.D. 1100 to 1325)

Sl. No.	Place Dist.	King & Date	Name of the Recipient	Status of the recipient	Nature and Extent of the estate	Remarks	Reference
(1)	(2)	(3)	(4)	(5)	(6)	(7)	(8)
1.	Koṇḍaparti (Warangal)	Gaṇapati	Chauṇḍa Senāpati	Senāpati (army commander)	Sankīśadeśa	Chauṇḍa was made a chief of a military fief known as Sankīśa (deśa) whose chief town was Koṇḍaparti	I.A.P. Wl. 48
2.	Pālampeṭ	Gaṇapati A.D. 1213	Recherla Rudra	Senāpati and Māṇḍalika (Governor)	Large No. of villages are mentioned in his fief	Nekkoṇḍa Upparȧpalli, Borlapalli, Naḍakuḍi. Ākunuru appears to be a new town which must have been the head-quarters. Recherla Rudra liberally donated two villages Podanapalli and Boḍupāḍu.	I.A.P. Wl. 50

(1)	(2)	(3)	(4)	(5)	(6)	(7)	(8)
3.	Māṭeḍu	Prola II A.D.1120	Vemrabola Boḍama Mallenāyaka	Mahāsāmanta	Military fief and a province Māraṭeḍu as chief village	-	I.A.P. Wl. 24, 25
4.	Chiṭyāla-Pāḍu	Gaṇapati A.D. 1213	Recherla Kāṭaya	Māṇḍalika	Military fief in Mulug Taluk	Kāṭaya was also made a māṇḍalika along with Recherla Rudra. Kāṭaya was Mandaḍi of the king.	I.A.P. Wl. 52
5.	Ramannapeṭ A.D. 1213	Gaṇapati	Malli Reḍḍi	Mahāsāmanta	--	--	I.A.P. Wl. 53
6.	Garla (Khammam)	Rudrama A.D. 1287	Recherla Boppa-Yaraya	Padmanāyaka Chief	Military fief	--	C.I.T.D. II, p. 6-8
7.	Sirikoṇḍa	Udayana-Choḍa A.D. 1148	Ketaya	Mahāmāṇḍalika	Military fief	--	K.C.S.C.S. pp.193-195

(1)	(2)	(3)	(4)	(5)	(6)	(7)	(8)
8.	Manthena (Karim-nagar)	Gaṇapati	Allumprolarāju	Chennurideśa-Palaka (Māṇḍalika)		-- Kn. 28	-- I.A.P.
9.	Goḍiśāla (Karim-nagar)	Gaṇapati A.D. 1236	Kāṭayanayaka	--	Military and official fief	--	I.A.P. Kn. 30
10.	Myḍāram (Warangal)	Gaṇapati	Myḍeśvara Kn. 34	Mahāsāmanta	--	--	I.A.P.
11.	Chittāpūr (Karim-nagar)	Pratāpa-rudra	Chinnirudradeva	Nāyankara	--	--	I.A.P. Kn. 38
12.	Vekkallu (Bekkallu (Warangal)	Tribhuva-namalla, Rudra	Vrekkanṭi Mallireḍdy, Māṇḍalika	--	--	--	I.A.P. Wl. 20 Wl, 42
13.	Vardhamā-napuram	Gaṇapati	Malayāla Guṇḍaya		Military fief	--	C.I.T.D. III, Mn.47
14.	Magtala	Pratāparu-dra A.D. 1297	Guṇḍayanayaka	Gajasāhini & Mandalika	Military fief Magatala Sthalam (8Vgs. including an agrahara are mentioned	Guṇḍaya was succeeded by the Mādaya-reḍḍi. The later was succeeded by Annaya Venka Reḍḍy	Tel. Ins. II. pp. 122-127

(1)	(2)	(3)	(4)	(5)	(6)	(7)	(8)
15.	Amarābad (Mahabubnagar)	Gaṇapati A.D. 1264	Cheṛaku Immaḍi Viśvanātha	Sāmantha	Military fief	Military fief of the Cheṛaku chiefs succession of chiefs Immaḍi Viśvanātha (1264) Bollaya Reḍḍi (1286). Immaḍi Jeṭṭi Bollaya (1290)	C.I.T.D. III, Mn, 4
16.	Vardhamānapuram (Mahabubnagar)	Gaṇapati A.D. 1224	Gona Gaṇapayya	Māṇḍalika	Mililtary fief	Gaṇapaiah became the Māṇḍalika of kandūru-1100	C.I.T.D. Mn. 46
17.	Pānugallu (Mahabubnagar)	-- A.D. 117	Kandūri Muṭṭaya	Savadora (dist. head)	Bhīmapura-12	--	C.I.T.D. IV. 11
18.	Pillalamarri (Nalgonda)	Rudra A.D. 1195	Recherla Nāmireḍḍy	Senāni and Māṇḍalika	Military fief	The Recheruvula Reḍḍy family split into two branches 1. Pālampet Branch 2. Pillalamaṛṛi Branch.	Tel. Ins. I pp.17-38

(1)	(2)	(3)	(4)	(5)	(6)	(7)	(8)
19.	Nāgulapāḍu (Nalgoṇḍa)	Gaṇapati A.D. 1234	Recherla Kāṭ Reḍḍy, S/o. Nāmi Reḍḍt	Daṇḍanāyaka	Subordinate fief	The Pillala-maṛṛi region appears to be subdivided into two small areas	Tel. Ins. I, p. 40-68
20.	Bairāni-palli (Nalgoṇḍa)	Tribhuva-namalla A.D. 1108	Reva	Daṇḍanāyaka	Military fief	Nanganur-190 Part of Kollipāka-1000	Tel. Ins. II, pp. 73-74, 75
21.	Jalālpuram (Nalgoṇḍa)	Gnṇapati A.D. 1202	Cheṛaku Bollaya	Senāni	Military + Personnel fief	Cheṛaku-12	Tel. Ins. II, pp. 103-107
22.	Anumula (Nalgoṇḍa)	Toṇḍa A.D. 1096	Amātya Prolama Raju	Amātya	Civil Estate	Chagamaṛṛi -12 Toṇḍijparti-12. Proprietary + hereditary rights are given	K.C.S.C.S. pp. 105-107
23.	Rāmalingāla gūdem (Nalgoṇḍa)	-Bhīma A.D. 1105	Kāvaliya-Brahma Devaiah	Kāvaliya	Military fief	Tipparti	K.C.S.C.S. pp. 129-134

(1)	(2)	(3)	(4)	(5)	(6)	(7)	(8)
24.	Paraḍa (Nalgoṇḍa)	Udayana A.D. 1143	Karaṇam Brahma Devaiah	Karaṇam	Civil Estate	Nemmāni is a village in Podileru-70 a district in Kandūrunadu-1100	K.C.S.C.S. pp. 181-184
25.	Pānugallu (Nalgoṇḍa)	Gokarṇa A.D. 1121	Bhīmana Preggada	Govt., officer	Civil estate	Māḍuvula (village in Kukkaḍam-30)	K.C.S.C.S. pp. 156-160
26.	-do-	-do-	Doḍḍaya Bhaṭṭu	-do-	-do-	Addaluru (village in Āmanakallu-70)	K.C.S.C.S. pp. 156-160

temples and making land gifts to learned brāhmaṇas became widespread and it reached climax during the time of Gaṇapatideva. Gaṇapatideva patronised Śaivism of pro-vedic Goḷaki *maṭha* with its numerous branches headed by Viśveśvara Śiva, was the principal channel through which royal benefactions were distributed to the religious and educational institutions. The members of the royal family, state officers, *māṇḍalikas*, and rich merchants and landlords built large number of temples and tanks. The freedom from interrecine warfare and political unity which Gaṇapatideva achieved and guaranteed by his efficient administrative system stimulated diverse economic enterprise in the kingdom. Gaṇapatieva, more than any other Kākatīya king, encouraged trade and commerce as indicated by his *abhaya śāsana* at Moṭupalli[96] through which he gave assurance of favourable conditions to foreign merchants trading with his empire. The temple of Pālampeṭ built by māṇḍalika Recerla Rudrireḍḍi[97] stands as a symbol of the imperial glory and prosperity of Gaṇapati's reign.

Rudramadevi (A.D. 1262-1292) succeeded her father Gaṇapati in about A.D. 1268. During A.D. 1262-1268, she seems to have functioned as co-regent. She tried her best to keep the kingdom intact. It seems that soon after the death of Gaṇapati, the Yādavas of Devagiri became agressive and Rudrama had successfully repulsed Yādava attack in the north.[98] But during her time, the weakness of *māṇḍalika* system became manifest and it began to show signs of break-up. Powerful *māṇḍalikas* tried to assert independence, thereby weakening the central authority. Especially Ambayadeva, the Kāyastha chief of Gaṇḍikoṭa, soon after his accession (A. D. 1272),[99] proclaimed independence over a vast area extending upto Tripurāntakam. Rudramadevi, realising the defects of the system attempted at reorganising the state on the *Nāyankaras system.* It may be inferred from Table I that *Nāyankaras* made their appearance during the later part of Rudrama's reign as evidenced by her records dated in the year A. D. 1280. [100]

Pratāpa Rudra (A. D. 1292-1323) the grandson and successor of Rudrama was the last of the Kākatīyas. Pratāpa Rudra's reign was full of disturbances. He ascended the throne when Ambadeva was still in revolt. Rudra put down the revolt and brought Mārjavāḍi and Nellore under his control.[101] But the region was exposed to Hoyasāla agression under Ballala III. Kampilarāya of Ānegondi assumed a hostile attitude and Pratāpa Rudra had to send an expedition against him.[102] As Pratāpa Rudra was busy in the south, the Yādava Kingdom was attacked by the Turks under Ala-ud-din Khilji and Rāmachandra became a vassel of the Delhi sultan.[103] This should have been a serious warning to Pratāpa Rudra.

Pratāpa Rudra should have therefore felt the need of strengthening his state by thoroughly organising it on the basis of *Nāyankara* system inaugurated by Rudramadevi. Already most of the *maṇḍaleśvaras* even in coastal Āndhra became weak and their principalities were on the decline. The powerful *manḍaleśvaras* proved rebellious. Therefore Pratāpa rudra, according to the local records and the *Siddheśvara Caritra*[104] divided the kingdom into 77 or 75 small *nāyankaras* and distributed them among those whom he considered faithful. Each *Nāyankara* was therefore small in size and no single *nāyankara* because of the limited resources at his command, could think of revolting against the emeperor. There was only a remote chance of severl *nāyankaras* joining together against the emperor. The system therefore, was expected to be a guarantee against internal revolt, especially in the event of an external attack. No clear information is available on the powers and obligations of the nāyankaras. But it may be said that the nāyankara maintened peace and order in his domain, supervised the local officers in the collection of revenue and other levies and maintened a small force to be supplied to the emperor whenever required. The Nāyankaras thus appear to have combined in themselves the revenue, judicial and military powers and the system worked for thorough decentralisation. A close examination of the list of nāyankaras in the Pratāpa carita would make it clear that the nāyankaras were recruited from the powerful section of the śūdras namely the Reḍḍis and Velamas. But already there developed caste rivalrics among the śūdras. As most of the Nāyankaras were bestowed on the Velamas, the Reḍḍis grew jealous of them and were displeased with the emperor.[105] Such of the nāyankaras took advantage of the frequent Muslim attacks on Warangal from A.D. 1303 and tried to strenghten their own position. With the meagre information available, it is difficult to assess whether the system ultimately proved a source of strength to the king or weakened his position.

Meanwhile, the Muslims started attacking Warangal. Pratāpa Rudra successfully repulsed the first Muslim attack in A.D. 1303[106] but was defeated in 1310 by Mālik Kāfur and agreed to become a vāssal of the Delhi Sutlan, Allaudin Khilji. He paid an enormous quantity of wealth as indemnity and tribute.[107] In order to replenish his treaty he appears to have reclaimed forests in Guntūr, Kurnool and Cuḍḍapah districts. He undertook a southern expedition in A.D. 1313 in the course of which he defeated the Hoyasālas and Pāṇḍyas and proceeded as far as Jambukeśwaram.[108] This proved a drain on his military and financial resources.

Later, the Muslim attacks became more determined and Prince Juna invaded Warangal in A.D. 1322. Pratāpa Rudra scored initial success. But ultimately, deserted by the Reḍḍi section of the army, according to the Pratāpa Carita,[109] Pratāpa Rudra was defeated and taken captive in A.D. 1323. On his way to Delhi, Pratāpa Rudra lost his life on the banks of Narmada.[110] The Kākatīya dynasty came to an end and the Kākatīya kingdom was incorporated into Delhi Sultanate.

REFERENCES

1. N. Venkataramanaiah, The Cālukyas of L(V)emulavada (Hyderabad, 1953) p.15 ff.
2. I.A. XXXII, p. 231 ff; E.A. II, p. 39 ff.
3. I.A.P. W1. 15.
4. K.A.N. Sastri in the Early History of the Deccan. Ed. G.Yazdani (London, 1960), pp. 317-323.
5. E.A. IV, p. 143.
6. K.A.N. Sastri , op.cit., p. 322.
7. P.B. Desai, Jainism in South India, p. 102.
8. K.A.N. Sastri, op.cit., p. 330.
9. N.Venkataramanaiah, The Cālukyas of Vēṅgi (Madras, 1950) p.218 ff.
10. I.A.P. W1. 15.
11. B.N.Sastry, K.C.S.C.S. Introduction, pp. 1-2.

12. Tel.Ins., I p.123.
13. Ibid.
14. K.Isvara Dutt, Pracīnāndhrabhūgolam, (Hyderabad,1979) pp. 56-57.
15. P.V.P. Sastry, The Kākatīyas (Hyderabad, 1978),p. 66.
16. Ibid, pp. 58-64.
17. I.A.P. Wl. 26.
18. P.V.P. Sastry, op. cit.
19. I.A.P. Kn. 23.
20. I.A.P. Kn. 14.
21. P.I. No. 7, K.C.S.C.S., p. 193-195.
22. I.A.P. Wl. 6.
23. The *mahāmaṇḍaleśvara* titles taken by feudatories such as Kākati Beta II (I.A.P. Kn. 19) and Kandūri Toṇḍaya (Tel. Ins. I, p. 123) indicate the freedom enjoyed by them.
24. Tel. Ins. I, pp. 169-172. Ibid, pp. 73-74.
25. I.A.P. Kn. 15.
26. I.A.P. Wl. 29.
27. Tel. Ins. I, pp. 105-106, 108, 118, 119.
28. P.I. No. 4 and 6.
29. I.A.P. Wl. 15.
30. I.A.P. Wl. 36.
31. Ibid.
32. P.V.P. Sastry, op. cit., pp. 51-57.
33. I.A.P. Wl. 36.
34. J.A.H.A.R.S., XXXVI-1, Ap. 4.
35. K.A.N. Sastry, op. cit, p. 355.
36. Ibid, p. 370-372.
37. P.B. Desai (Ed) *A History of Karnataka* (Dharwar, 1970) pp. 183-185.
38. E.A. I, p. 71 ff.
39. Ibid, p. 57 ff.
40. P.V.P. Sastry, Op. cit., pp. 39, E.A. I, pp. 71 ff.
41. Ibid, pp. 51-57.
42. Ibid, pp. 39-42.
43. Ibid.
44. I.A.P. Wl. 27.
45. P.V.P. Sastry, Op. cit., pp. 22-23.
46. B.S.L. Hanumantha Rao, *Āndhrula Caritra* (Telugu) (Guntur, 1983) pp. 293-353.
47. I.A.P. Kn. 14, 15, 19, 22, 24.
48. Ibid, 15.
49. I.A.P. Wl. 15.
50 Ibid.
51. Ibid.
52. P.V.P. Sastry, Op. cit., pp. 49-50.
53. Ibid.

54. I.A.P. Wl. 36.
55. Ibid.
56. Ibid.
57. J.A.H.R.S. XXXVI-1, Ap. 4.
58. S.I.I. IV, 1242.
59. P.B. Desai, op. cit.
60. I.A.P. Wl. 36.
61. I.A.P. Kn. 25, Tel. Ins., 1, pp. 17, 19.
62. Ibid.
63. P. Lakshmikantham, Introduction to Śrīnātha's *Palnāti-Vīracharitra* (Vijayawada, 1961). p. 15.
64. Ibid, p. 13.
65. P.V.P. Sastry, op. cit., p. 98.
66. Ibid, p. 94.
67. Ibid, p. 100.
68. Ibid, pp. 103-104.
69. P.B. Desai, op. cit., p. 228.
70. Ibid.
71. P.V.P. Sastry Op. cit., pp. 116-117.
72. Ibid, p. 114.
73. Ibid., pp. 108-109.
74. Ibid.
75. P.V.P. Sastry, *Select Epigraphs of Andhra Pradesh*, p. 64., S.I.I.V., 1254.
76. P.V.P. Sastry, *The Kākatīyas,* pp. 109-112.
77, Ibid.
78. Ibid, pp. 112-114.
79. Ibid.
80. Vallabhāmātya, op. cit., v. 155.
81. Vidyānātha, *Pratāarudrayaśobhūṣhaṇam, Nāṭakaprakaraṇam* quoted by K. Isvara Dutt, *Prācīnāndhra chāritraka bhūgoḷam,* p. 72.
82. E.I. VI., p. 147.
83. I.A.P. Wl. 57, 58, 59.
84. S.I.I. X 360.
85. P.V.P. Sastry, op. cit., p. 108.
86. I.A.P. Wl. 52.
87. K. Isvara Dutt, *Śāsana Śabdakośam* (Hyderabad, 1967) p. xliv., S.I.I. X 332.
88. I.A.P. Cp. I, 142, S.I.I.X. 332, Ibid. 464.
89. Venkataramanayya N., Somasekhara Sarma, M. In *the Early History of Deccan,* (ed) G. Yazdani, p. 602, E .I.V. pp. 142-150.
90. S.I.I. X, 211.
91. T. Venkatesvara rao, Local Self-Government in Medieval Āndhra, J.A.H.R.S. XXXI Parts 1-4, pp. 113-123.
92. N. Venkataramanaiah and M. Somasekhara Sarma in *The Early History of the Deccan,* Ed. G. Yazdani, Vol. II, p. 712. I.A.P. Kn. 14.

93. I.A.P. Wl. 15.
94. The *trikūṭa* temple built by Rudra in A.D. 1163 (I.A.P. Wl. 36), and the encouragement to his ministers and governors like Gangādhara (I.A.P. Kn. 25) to build temples and create *agrahāras* indicates his shift to brahmanical religion.
95. S.I.I. X, 395.
96. E.I. XII, p. 183ff.
97. I.A.P. Wl. 50.
98. S.E.A.P. No. 21.
99. I.A.P. Cp. I, 146.
100. C.I.T.D. III, p. 86, P.V.P. Sastry, The *Kākatīyas*, pp. 129-131.
101. P.V.P. Sastry, op. cit., 134-135.
102. Ibid.
103. Elliot, H. M. and Dowson, J.—*The History of India as told by its own Historians* (Allahabad, 1970), Vol., III, Tarikh - I' alai p. 77.
104. Kāse Sarvappa - *Sidheśvara Caritra* (ed. K. Lakshmiranjanam) p. 146.
105. N. Venkataramanaiah (ed.) *Velugotivāri Vamśāvaḷi* (Madras, 1939) v. 25.
106. Elliot, H. M. and Dowson, J., op. cit. Tarikh-i-Fferoz shahi (Allahabad, 1970) pp. 202-203.
107. Ibid.
108. E.A. IV, p. 121.
109. Ekāmranātha, *Pratāpa Caritra*, pp. 168-169.
110. A.R. 1938-39, Copper plate 5.

CHAPTER—II

AGRICULTURE

GEOGRAPHICAL AND ECOLOGICAL ASPECTS

Telangāṇa, comprising the ten districts of the north-western part of Āndhra Pradesh, forms a part of the penisular plateau. It extends between 77°5' and 82° E Longitudes and about 16° and 20° N Latitudes. It occupies the central and eastern parts of the plateau, flanked on the east by the eastern-most fringes of western ghats.[2]

Hills

The land mass is generally made of pre-Cambrian grantie and gniess.[3] The hills of this region are mostly of granite and sandstone. They are weathered down by sun and rain and at many places they have become domic, facilitating the building of formidable forts. Bhuvanagiri, Hanmakoṇḍa, Nalgoṇḍa and Khammam are some of them which played an important role in the politics of Medieval Āndhra. Denudation and weathering over long milleniums resulted in sandy peniplanes all over the region. The granite and sandstone available in Telangāṇa gave ample scope for the stone worker and this resulted in a variety of architectural feats and sculptural wealth. In Table III are given the district-wise physiographical data of the region. These data are explained below. Prominent physical features of the region are shown in Map-II.

Minerals

The Telangāṇa plateau abounds in several kinds of minerals. Large deposits of iron and coal have been discovered in the Godavari valley in Adilābād, Warangal, Karīmnagar and Khammam districts. The districts of Nalgoṇḍa, Mahaboobnagar and Adilābād have large deposits of limestone. Glass-grade sand is found in Medak and Mahaboobnagar districts.

River systems

The Godāvari and Krishnā are the two major river systems, in Telangāṇa. The Godāvari enters the region at Bāsar in the Nizāmābād district and runs almost east forming the boundary between the Adilābād district in the north and Nizāmābād and Karīmnagar districts in the south. Then it turns almost south to meet the sea. The river Mañjira joins Godāvari immediately after it enters Telangāṇa. The Prāṇahitā and Pengangā are the two other major tributaries of Godāvari that flow in Telangāṇa.

The river Krishna enters Āndhra Pradesh in the Mahaboobnagar district and the Tungabhadra joins it near Alampūr. Afterwards, the Krishna runs as an interdistrict border between the Mahaboobnagar and Nalgoṇḍa districts in the north and Kurnool and Guntur Districts in the south. The Krishna enters the plain near Amarāvati and takes a south-eastern course to reach the Bay of Bengal.

Mūsi, a tributary of Krishna is another river of the Telangāṇa region. it meets Krishna at Vāḍapalli between Nāgārjunakoṇḍa and Amarāvati.

There are minor rivers and streams in the Telangāṇa region. These are given in the Table III.

Forests

The total area under forests in Telangāṇa today is about 27 lakh hectares.[4] It must have been more five or six centuries ago i.e., in 12th and 13th centuries A.D. Most of the forest area lies on both sides of the Godāvari river, spread in Adilābād (6.2. L.H.) Karīmnagar (2.5 L.H.) Warangal (3.7 L.H.) and Khammam (7.5 L.H.) districts. The forests are thick in vegetation and rich in timber. Good Quality teak wood and a variety of forest products are available in these forests. Here live a large number of tribes like the Goṇḍs, Bhills Śabaras and Chenchus. The north-eastern part of the peninsular plateau received its name Goṇḍwana from these aboriginals.

Rainfall

The average rainfall in the Telangāṇa districts is in the range

TABLE III

Physiographical Information.

District	*Annual Rainfall (Normal)*	*Soils*	*Minerals*	*Forests*	*Major Rivers*	*Any other information*
Warangal	978mm	B-21% C-64% D-14%	Iron, Coal	3.71 L.H Good timber	Godāvari, Maner Pāler, Ākeru, Pākeru.	
Karīmnagar	977mm	B-8% C-27% D-65%	Iron, Coal	2.52 L. H. Good timber.	Godāvary, Maner. Kudaleru	
Medak	886mm	B-45% C-40% D-7%	Quartz. Ochre, clay.	0. 88 L. H.	Manjīra, Kudaleru.	
Mahaboob-nagar	705mm	B-20% C-67% D-13%	Limestone	3.04. L.H. Thick forest	Krishna, Mūsi, Ḍimḍi, Tungabhadra	
Nalgoṇḍa	702mm	B-9% C-44% D-47%	Limestone	0.83 L. H.	Kṛṣṇa, Mūsi, Āleru. Ḍinḍi, Pāleru.	
Khammam	1018mm	B-29% C-40% D-28%	Coal, Corundum, limestone, graphite.	7.55 L. H. Rich timber	Godāvari, Śabari, Wyra, Munneru, Pāleru, Ākeru.	

(1)	(2)	(3)	(4)	(5)	(6)	(7)
Nizāmābād	1025mm	B-55% C-45%	--	1.68 L. H.	Godāvari, Manjīra.	
Adilābād	1051 mm	B-72% C-9%	Limestone, Iron	6.20 L.H. Rich timber	Godāvari, Kaḍem, Prāṇahita, Peṅgangā	
Rangāreḍḍi						Information not available

Note :—Soils B-Black, C- Chalka, D-Dubba (Sandyloam). L.H.=Lakh Hectares of 800-1000 mm. The area receives most of its rainfall (80%) from the south-west monsoon during June to September. The north-east monsoon (October-November) brings 20% of the annual rainfall. From December to May, It is a continuously dry season.

The general climate of Telangāṇa is typically tropical and continental. The summers are very hot the temperatures going to a maximum of 44°C in May-June and winters are cold, the temperatures going down to 15°C - 12°C in December-January. The climate is generally dry and the humidity low.

Soils

The soils in Telangāṇa are generally of three types :

(1) black soil (2) red soil and 3) sandyloam. Other types of soils are found in small areas.

Black soil

The back soil is generally known as black cotton soil. Its colur is balck because of it contains a good quantity of iron oxide. It is made up of fine grain and retains wetness. This is a very fertile soil. The soil is spread on either side of the Godāvari river in the districts of Medak, Adilābād, Nizāmābād, Karīmnagar, Warangal, and Khammam. A narrow tract along the Krishna river also contains this soil. Nearly 30% of the total area in Telangāṇa is black cotton soil. Cotton, oil-seeds, sugarcane and fine quality of rice are grown in these soils.

Red soil

This is red sandy soil formed from the weathering of the granite and gniess. This is soft and light but as it contain sand it does not retain water. In fertility it is next to black cotton soil and is useful for agricluture where good irrigation facilities are available. Nearly 45% of the soil in Telangāṇa is of this type. It is largely found in the interior areas of the districts. These areas are known for the cultivation of rice and jowar.

Sandyloam soil

The third type of soil in Telangāṇa is the *Dubba* or sandyloam. This is whitish in shade and has the least water retentivity and poor in fertility. Nearly 20% of the land in Telangāṇa is of this type. This is not particularly useful for any major crop variety.

Alluvial soil

The most fertile type of soil, the aluvial, is present in Telangāṇa only in small patches formed by the overflow of the rivers. These are limited to the banks of the major rivers. These patches are used for the cultivation of good varieties of rice and sugarcane.

LAND TYPES IN INSCRIPTIONS

In the records of 11th to 14th centuries A.D. we find that land was classified according to content and fertility and various crops were grown depending on the nature of the soil. Five major types of soil were frequently mentioned. They are : (1) *śāli*[5] (2) *Kriṣṇa*[6] (3) *eṛṛanjenu*[7] (4) *pāṇḍura*[8] and (5) *Karamba.*[9]

Śāli kṣetra

This is the best soil which may be called aluvial in nature and is caled as *śāli kṣetram*. This land is fit for producing rice and sugarcane. This is limited to river banks and some lands constantly watered by tanks.

Kriṣṇa kṣetra (Regaḍa)

This is black soil which is also mentioned as *regaḍu nallanjenu* and *kriṣṇa kṣetram* This come next to *śāli kṣetram* in fertility and was used for the growing of cotton, oil-seeds like gingelly and turmeric.

***Eṛṛanjenu* (Red soil)**

This is red soil and comes next to black soil in fertility. This is used for the cultivation of a variety of crops including rice, oil-seeds and pulses.

Pāṇḍura

This is pale yellowish white soil and was used for growing millets, oils seeds, fruits, vagetables and flower gardens.

Karamba

This is a mixed type of land inferior in fertility. In inscriptions, this land was differently mentioned as *karamba, jadālu* and *gaḍḍanala*.

These are the five main types of soils which are mentioned in inscriptions. Other types referred to are: *gaḍḍanela*[10] (rocky soil), *aṇḍanālu*[11] (high field) and *Ootapolamu*[12] (marshy land).

Besides these, we come across various names of fields. The name indicate the various characteristic features of a particular field such as its level *(nerapuguṇṭa)*,[13] content *(chauṭa cenu*[14]*)* ownership *(sattapunāyanidūba*[15]) and *poḍubhūm* (land brought recently under cultivation after clearing the forest).

The land names having the suffixes such as kuṇṭa,[17] *dūba,*[18] *tippa,*[19] *maḍi,*[20] *Chenu,*[21] *kayya*[22] and *polamu*[23] are found in inscriptions. This indicates the thorough knowledge of land of the medieval people.

Burton Stein defines in *The Cambridge Economic History of India*[24] three eco-types of land on the basis of the irrigation facility in south India. The three eco-types are: 91) land with assured irrigation facility such as a tank, called wet land, (2) land without any assured irrigation facility and solely depending upon rainfall and (3) land of mixed type having a small source of irrigation such as a well or pond and also supported by rainfall. This is called semi-arid or semi-dry land. This classification applies to the Telangāṇa as well.

These three eco-types of lands were mentioned in the contemporay inscriptions of the period. They are (1) *nīrunela*[25], (2) *karamba* or *Jadālu*[26]and (3) *velipolamu or bāhyakṣetramu.*[27]

LANDHOLDING

One of the important problems of medieval Indian economy is that of land ownership. Some European historians expressed the view that in India, the king was the owner of all land and that there was no private property in land.[28] The *Dharmaśāstras* do not definitely say this. *Manusmriti* fixed the share of the king in land and its produce.[29] The *Gautama Dharmaśāstra*[30] lays down that the land belonged to the people who cultivated it and paid a part of the produce for the maintenance of the king. However, it was an assumption that land theoreticaly belonged to the state, whose seven components include the king. Thus, land belongs to the state, but as monarchy became absolute, kings appear to have appropriated the authority over the land.

The question is to be examined on the basis of inscriptional information corroborated by works on polity like the *Vijñāeśvaram*. The ownership of land was generaly referred to as *Aṣṭabhoga-svāmyam* meaning eight right of possession. These are : *nidhi* (natural hoard), *nikṣepa* (treasure hidden by some one), *akṣīṇa* (permanent benefits), *āgāmi* (future benefits), *sañchita* (benefits already available), *jala* (water sources) *taru* (trees), and *pāṣāṇa* (stone). The inscriptions of the period help uis to classify the land in the following way on the basis of ownership:

1. State lands and crown lands
2. *Agrahāra* lands
3. *Devabhoga* lands
4. Lands in peasant villages

State lands

In the period under study, the state lands are referred to in inscriptions as *Prabhutvamu polamu,*[31] *Racapolamu*[32] and *Rācādīnamu*[33] *(Rājādhīnam)*. These lands were allotted to various persons as *vrittis* either in reward of their service to the state or in lieu of wages for officials. This allotment was done either by the sovereign king himself or a *sāmanta* chief. *Agrahāras* and *devabhogas* are established by them. Moreover, the kings and feudatory chiefs retained parts of cultivable and uncultivable lands as their personal property in many villages.

Agrahāras

The practice of donating an entire village or a part therein or a group of villages to brāhmaṇas or temples was widespread during the medieval period. A village donated by a king or chief to one or many brāhmaṇas is called an *agrahāra*.As such, *agrahāras* may be considered as a class of landowners. Scholars like Stein[34] and Karashima[35] have pointed out that there was at least one *brahmādeya* or *agrahāra* village among a group of villages konwn as *'nāḍu'* during the Cola period. In the coastal Āndhra, Cālukyas of Vēṅgi established several *agrahāras*. This practice was also

TABLE IV
Agrahāra Villages

Sl. No.	District	King/Donor and date	Name of the New Name	Agrahāra village Old Name	Type of Agrahāra	Other information	Reference
(1)	(2)	(3)	(4)	(5)	(6)	(7)	(8)
1.	Warangal	Natavāḍi Buddharaja- A. D. 1101	Indrapuram	Bidramkunṭa	Sarvam- ānya	A large number of Brāhmins belonging to various gotras are settled	I.A.P. Wl. 16
2.	Warangal A. D. 1090	Kākati Durgā	Śivapuram	--	Sarva mānya Ekabhoga	Rāmeśvara Paṇ- ditas of Malli kārjuna Śilā- maṭha	Ibid., Wl. 15
3.	Warangal	Kākati Prola II undated	Śivapura	Vaijanapalli	Ekabhoga Agrahāra	Rameśvara Panḍita of Lakuleśvara School	Ibid., Wl. 35
4.	Warangal	Chaunḍa Senāni A. D. 1203	Chaunḍapura	--	Tax free grant to brāhmaṇas	Number of Brāhmins received lands.	Ibid., Wl. 48
5.	Warangal	Kundamāmba A.D. 1210	Kundavaram	Vemulatomṭa	--	No. of Brāhmins are settled	Ibid., Wl. 58

(1)	(2)	(3)	(4)	(5)	(6)	(7)	(8)
6.	Khammam	Pratāparudra A. D. 1303	Kaṭukūr	--	--	--	C.I.T.D. III pp. 16-17
7.	Medak	Tribhuvanamalla Vikramāditya (undated)	Kuchenūru	Kuchenūru	Ekabhoga	Donee is Suryā bharaṇa paṇḍita	C.I.T.D. IV. pp. 32-35
8.	Nizāmabad	Rudramadevi A.D. 1273	Vaināyakapuri	--	--	A number of brāhmins	C.I.T.D. III pp. 114-118
9.	Karīmnagar	(Gaṇapatideva) Manchibhaṭṭo-Padhyaya Allum Prolarāju	Mallikārjuna-puram, new agrahara (name not known)	Koṭapalli	No. of Brāhmins	Allum Prolarāa made a gift of land to the priest to build a village and a tank.	I.A.P. Kn. 28
10.	Karīmnagar A. D. 1171	Gangādhara mantri	-- --	Dinḍomṭa	No. of Brāhmins	--	I.A.P. Kn. 25.
11.	-do- A. D. 1236	Kāṭayanāyaka	--	Pinchara-Palli	Brāhmins & Temple.	The village is both an agrahāra and Devabhoga	I.A.P. Kn. 30
12.	Mahaboob-nagar undated	Gokarṇa Coḍa	--	Vellaṁkoṭi	Ekabhoga Agrahāra	One Nārāyaṇa Paṇḍita received the village	C.I.T.D. III, pp. 68-69

(1)	(2)	(3)	(4)	(5)	(6)	(7)	(8)
13.	Nagoṇḍa A. D. 1208	Beti Reḍḍi	Eṛakapuram	--	--	No. of Brāhamaṇas	Tel. Ins. I, pp. 31-38
14.	-do- undated	Mailamāmbika	Bhīmanārayaṇa puram	Piṭṭam-palli	Brāhmins & Temples	Agrahāra-Devabhoga	C.I.T.D. IV, p. 114.
15.	Nalgoṇḍa A.D. 1213	Devapālanāyaka	Gaṇapāpuram	--	--	Agrahāra-Devabhoga (A new settlement)	C.I.T.D. II, pp. 73-78.
16.	-do- A. D. 1119	Kumāra Tailapa	--	Tāḍimatta	Brāhmaṇas & Temples	Agrahāra Devabhoga.	P.I. No. 3
17.	-do- undated	Mallināyaka	--	--	--	An agrahāra name not mentioned	P.I. No. 14
18.	Nalgoṇḍa undated	Maṭṭūrināyaka		--	--	An agrahāra whose name is not mentioned	P. I. No. 15
19.	-do-	Gokarṇa	--	Chiṭṭākoḍūru	--	Agrahāra	K.CS.CS. p. 21.
20.	-do- A. D. 1124	Mailama	Kāśyapalli	kaśyapalli	Śutradhāri Brahmoju	Ekabhoga Agrahāra	Tel. Ins. I, pp. 169-172
21.	-do- A. D. 1253	Cheṛaku Viśva-nātha Daṇḍanā-yaka	Rempuṇḍi Verjinta Sūrepali	--	Sūtradhari Kāsu Malloju	devabhoga Agrahāra	

prevalent under the Cālukyas of Kalyān, their subordinates and successors.

The establishment of an *agrahāra* was, no doubt, considered as an act of piety[36] and an encouragement to brāhmaṇa schoars and brāhmanical religion. However, it was also a method of bringing new lands under cultivation. The inscription of Manthena[37] dated in the year A.D. 1199 (incidentally the first date of Gaṇapatideva's reign) refers to the establishment of two *agrahāras*. An old village Koṭapalli was converted into an *agrahāra* (Table IV) by Machibhaṭṭopādhyāya. Again this priest received some land from Allumprolarāju, a *māṇḍalika* ruling in the Chennūrideśa at the instance of the king Gaṇapatideva. The inscription clearly refers to the four boundaries of the land thus received. Manchinārya built a tank and a village in that land and invited brāhamaṇas from Mantrakūṭa, to live in the new village. Formation of an *agrahāra* is mostly individual. Each brāhmaṇa was alloted a piece of land and endowed with hereditory rights. In the Kundavaram *agrahāram* established by Kundamāmbika, the land received by each brāhmaṇa is clearly indicated. The land belonging to an *agrahāra* and its resources were administered by the assembly of the brāhmaṇas known as *brahmasabha* or *mahājanulu*. Two Perūr[39] inscriptions call the brāhmaṇas as *grāmasvāmulu* and *mahājanulu*.

The *agrahāras* may be classified into several kinds. If an *agrahāra* was shared between a temple and a group of brāhmins it is known as a *devabhoga agrahāra*[40] Some of the *agrahāras* were free from payment of taxes. These were mentioned as *sakara agrahāra* grants. These were also referred to as *'sarvānamasya' 'sarvamāya'* and *'sarvabādhāparihāra'* grants.[41]

The brāhmaṇas in an *agrahāra* rarely cultivated the land. The tilling was done by others such as share-croppers belonging to peasant communities.

Devabhogas

During the period under study, building of temples coupled with tank excavation became widespread and as a result *devabhoga* grants outnumbered *agrahāra* establishments. This development may be attributed to the influence of the Bhakti movement which

TABLE V

Devabhoga Villages

S. No.	District	Date	Donor	Names of villages granted	Names of the temple or god	Other recipients of land	Remarks	Reference
(1)	(2)	(3)	(4)	(5)	(6)	(7)	(8)	(9)
1.	Warangal	A.D. 1185	Rudradeva	(su) Maḍapalli	Śiva Temple	--		IAP. Wl. 41.
2.	,,	A. D. 1206	Natavāḍi Rudra	Chintapalli	Buddheśvara Muppeśvara	--	--	,, 49
3.	,,	A. D. 1213	Recherla Rudra	1) Nekkoṇḍa	Rudreśvara	--	--	
				2) Upparapalli	Gaureśvara	--	--	
				3) Borlapalli				
				4) Naḍakuḍi	Kāṭeśvara	--	--	50
				5) Aṭuku	Kāmeśvara			
4.	,,	undated	Recherla Kāṭaya	1) Boḍapāḍu 2) Peḍanapalli	Mallikārjuna of Śrīśailam	--	--	51
5.	,,	A. D. 1213	Mahāsāmantha Malli-Reḍḍi	Koṭyaboyani-meṭṭa	Lord Muppi-ḍeśvara	--	--	52
6.	,,	A. D. 1217	Venna Peḍḍi	Vennayapalli	Rameśvara Keśavadeva	--	--	' 54
				Boḍukoḍūru	Ekkeśvara Pāṭidevara			
7.	,,	A. D. 1217	Recherla Kāṭaya	Gollakuṇṭa	Yeleśvara	--	--	" 55

(1)	(2)	(3)	(4)	(5)	(6)	(7)	(8)	(9)
8.	,,	A. D. 1219	Queen Kundamāmbika	Part of Kundavaram	Rudreśvara Mahādeva Sūrya Ganapeśvara	--	--	' 57
9.	Warangal	A. D. 1236	Kāṭaya	Pinchara-palli	--	--	--	CITD III p. 166-170
10.	Khammam	A. D. 1235	Devana-preggaḍa	--	--	--	--	CITD III p. 31-35
11.	Nizāmābād	A. D. 1273	Viriyāla Sūra	Vaināyakapuri	Purushottama	--	--	C.I.T.D. III pp. 114-118
12.	Karīmnagar	A. D. 1108	Tribhuvana-mala Vikra-māditya VI.	Illindikunṭa	Harikeśvaradeva	-- --		I.A.P. Kn. No. 21
13.	Karīmnagar	A. D. 1199	Allum Prla-rāju and Manchi Bha-ṭṭopādhyāya	Koṭpalli	Keśavadeva Mahādeva	--	--	I.A.P. Kn. No. 28
14.	Karīmnagar	A.D. 1236	Kāṭaya	Pincharapalli Pañchalingala	Śiva	--	--	I.A.P. Kn. No. 30
15.	Mahaboob-nagar	A. D. 1294	Stānu-Chamūpati	Kannenāyaka-palli	Malinātha of Magatala	--	--	Tel. Ins. II pp. 153-157
16.	"	A. D. 1178	Bhīma & Gokarṇa	Māmiḷḷapalli Mañchikunṭa	Nṛisimha	--	--	C.I.T.D. III Mn. 26
17.	"	A. D. 1280	Bhanḍāru Pochāya	Trakkavrolu	Rudreśvara Rāmanātha Mallinātha Somanātha Pocheśvara	--	--	C.I.T.D. III Mn. 41

(1)	(2)	(3)	(4)	(5)	(6)	(7)	(8)	(9)
18.	"	A. D. 1224	Śrīkaraṇam Bhīmadevara Preggaḍa	Peddapali	Buddeśvara Sahasraliñga-Gaṇapatiśvara Lakṣhminarasimha Nārāyaṇa Prasanna Bhairava	--	--	Ibid., Mn. No.46
19.	Mahaboob-nagar	A. D. 1168	Māṇḍalika Taṇḍa	Kārapamūla	Bhīmanrāyaṇa Kanneṇvara Gokarṇa Mārkaṇḍa	--	--	Kandurico-dula Sasana mulu Caritra Samskriti pp. 220-222
20.	Nalgoṇḍa	A. D. 1258	Pradhāni Bollamaraju	Prochāpuram	Gopīnātha	--	--	Tel. Ins. I, pp. 71-72
21.	"	A. D. 1132	Mailāmbika (queen)	Part of Piṭṭampalli	Coḍa Bhima-narayana	--	--	Tel.Ins. I, p. 157
22.	"	A. D. 1253	Cheṛeku Immaḍi Viśvanātha Daṇḍanāyaka	Rempuṇḍi	Bolleśvara Malleśvara Gaṇapeśvara Vishṇu Mallikārjuna Keteśvara.	--	--	Tel Ins. II pp. 115-121.
23.	"	undated	Rudramadevi	Ambalapalli	Yeleśvara	--	--	CI.T.D. IV No. 26
24.	"	A. D. 1250	Mangaya Gaṇapayya (Gajasāhiṇi)	Tāḍimaḍa	Yeleśvara Mahādeva	--	--	Ibid., No. 30

(1)	(2)	(3)	(4)	(5)	(6)	(7)	(8)	
25.	"	undated	Gokarṇadeva	Beṭākoḍuru	Yeleśvaradeva	--	--	Ibid., No. 40 p. 87
26.	"	undated	Tribhuvana Vallabha Mallidevaṇḍu	Gummalamu Krttalūru Epuru Agaḍu	Yeleśvara	--	--	Ibid., No. 43
27.	"	undated	Anegumgana-rāju (Palnāḍ) Pendoṭa Nārapapalli	Rachchamalla-nipalli	Yeleśvara	--	--	C.I.T.D. IV No. 45
28.	Nalgoṇḍa	undated	Rāmadeva mahārāju	Tekulapalli	Yeleśvara	--	--	Ibid., No. 48
29.	"	undated	Podakanuri Siddhirāju	Vepunūr	-do-	--	--	" 56
30.	"	undated	Guḍivāḍa Malreḍḍy	Kambālapalli	-do-	--	--	" 57
31.	"	A. D. 1119	Kumāra Tailapa	Half of Tadimatta	Svaymbhu Someśvara of Perūr	—	--	Pl. No. 3
32.	"	A. D. 1290	Nāyakas	Kompalli	Swayambhu Someśvara of Perūr	--	--	Pl. No. 13
33.	"	A. D. 1100	Kumara Koṇḍaya	Kollūru	Vishṇu	--	—	K.CS.CS. pp. 15.

became predominent in the Telugu country during the 11th, 12th and 13th centuries.[42] More-over, greater distribution of land among various sections of the society was achieved as the temple servants received land as *vrittis*. In many cases, tank-digging went hand in hand with temple-building which contributed to the development of agriculture.,

The villages granted for the maintenance of temples are called *devabhoga* villages. A list of Devabhoga villages is given in Table V. Thus temples became big landlords.In addition to *devabhoga* villages large areas of cultivable and uncultivable land were granted to the temples. The Korapolu inscription[43] of Āhavamalladeva's time mentions a grant of 403 *marturs* of land irrigated by six tanks to god Bileśvara by Somapermāḍilakshmī-barasiyar. An undated inscription at Maktala[44] refers to the grant of 168 *nivartanas* of four types of land to god Svayambhu Mallinādha. Such land grants are known as *Devamānyas*. Thus, we see the temple emerging as a big landlord. However, the temple lands were distributed among the temple servants. When *karaṇam* Brahmadevayya built a temple at Paraḍa in the name of his father, he gave lands to the gardener (one *Martur* and two *khaṇḍugas*) and stone masons, Betoju and Āryanoju (one *martur* and two *khaṇḍugas* each).[45]

Landholding in peasant villages

The village was the basic unit of land and revenue administration. The lands belonging to each village were clearly defined. We find in inscriptions[46] several villages mentioned with boundaries or limits on all four sides known as *polimera* of that village. The lands belonging to each village were administered by the village assembly, the *aṣṭādaśapraja*. When a village land was donated to a brāhmaṇa or to an *agrahāra* or to a temple, the consent of the *aṣṭādaśamahāpraja* was generally taken.[47] In exceptional cases, the approval of the leading community such as the *ekkaṭivīraparivāramu* of the village was obtained for making land gifts.[48]

The village assembly had to supervise the various types of land holdings in a village. The functions of the village assembly have been discussed in Chapter I. The lands of the village may be classified as follows :

1. Crown lands and government lands
2. Brāhmaṇa lands
3. Temple lands
4. *Vritti* lands
   a) Civil tenures
   b) Military tenures
5. Private landholdings

CROWN LANDS AND GOVERNMENT LANDS

The crown or the state had lands in every village. As already noted, these are known as *rāchapolamu* or *rāchādinamu* or *prabhutvamu polamu.* In A.D. 1236 Kāṭayanāyaka, the son of Rājānāyaka, built temples, tanks and gardens and granted the village Pincharapalli to Pañchaliṅga Śiva[49] at Upparapalli in Karīmnagar district. At the end of the inscription, a gift of 10 marturs of land by Gaṇapatideva mahārāja is recorded. Evidently, this gift by Gaṇapatideva should have been from the *rācapolamu* of the village.

When land was brought under cultivation through new irrigational facilities by private enterprise, the State claimed a share in the land. But its share differed from one instance to the other. The Annavaram inscription[50] states that Nāmireḍḍi built a tank called Nāmasamudram to the east of Nāgulapāḍu. The newly reclaimed land brought under cultivation was shared by the builder of the tank and the state equally. But the Chiṭāpūr inscription records that the state claimed 2/3 of the land under Sakala-samudram built by the guild of *Ayyāvaḷi* 500 headed by Bairi-seṭṭi,[51] Thus, in these instances the local assembly had no share and the land became part of the Crown land or *rāchapolamu*. The government created new service tenures out of this land.[52] The *Vijñāneśvaram* of Ketana mentions that around each village, between the living houses and cultivated fields a space of 100 bows width should be left vacant. It should be 200 bows wide around a *kharvaṭa* (a small market palce) and 400 around a town. It is government land for common use.

The crown lands were cultivated by the local people by an arrangement known as *ardhāya*.[52a] Half of the produce was claimed by the government as rent. The cultivators engaged in this arrangement were known as *ardhasīri*[52b] cultivators, (*ardha* - half, *sīri* - plough) i.e. share-croppers.

Brāhmaṇa lands and devamānya lands

In addition to *agrahāras* and *devabhoga* villages, brāhmaṇa scholars and temples were given lands in villages. Such lands were either purchased from others or were granted with the consent of the village assembly.[53]

Vritti lands

Vritti lands are small or large estates granted by the state or the village assembly to a person or a group of persons for the service rendered by the latter. The *vrittis* can further be classified into a) civil tenures and b) military tenures.

a) *Civil tenures*

In the medieval period each village had twelve *āyagārs* who rendered service in conducting the village affairs.[54] This aspect of vilage administration has been already discussed in the chapter- I. The *āyagārs* are 1) *pedakāpu* (Village headman), (2) *Karaṇam* (village accountant), (3) *talāri* (village gurad), (4) *purohita* (priest), (5) *kamsāli* (goldsmith) (6) *kanchari* (coppersmith), (7) *kammari* (blacksmith) (8) *kummari* (potter), (9) *cākali* (washerman), (10) *mangali* (barbar), (11) *veṭṭi* (village servant) and (12) *carmakāra* (leather worker). These *āyagārs* received lands for the services they rendered in lieu of salary. In course of time the offices as well as *vrittis* became hereditary. Another type of *vritti* is the *Daśavatha mānyam* .

b) *Military tenures*

In several villages military personnel were settled and they were given lands in reward of their services and in lieu of their salary. The Ākunūru inscription[55] (A. D. 1172) of Rudradeva's time refers to the building of a temple and a tank by soidires. In A.D. 1224 Gaṇapati mantri, son of Ādityāmātya, the *Śrikaraṇā-dhikāri* built three temples and a tank at Koṇḍapāka, Medak district and donated 3 *marturus* of wetland with the permission of the king and also of the *ekkaṭivīraparivāramu* (corporation of soldiers).[56] Thus, it appears that the military personnel had acquired rights in lands.

Private landholding

The criteria for deciding whether there was private land ownership are as follows:

1. Sale and purchase of land by individuals
2. Mortgage of land
3. Hereditory rights and
4. Land disputes

Table VI gives a list of sales and purchases of land in the period under study. Most of the purchases are made by merchants and were meant for granting them to temples. Most of the persons that sold the lands were brāhmaṇas.[57] In one case, a lady sold away the land.[58] Another inscription records land assignments to various individuals by the *Asankhyāta māheśvarulu.*[60] In both the cases, the donors prohibited sale or purchase or mortgage of the land thus granted. A verse from *Vijñāneśvaram*[61] suggests the existence of hereditary rights in land and other types of property.

No evidence is available regarding the land disputes between individuals. But there are two instances of dispute over land and water sources between villages. The Pālem inscription[62] refers to dispute between two *agrahāra* villages, Vellamkoṭi and Vasanthapuram, the former being newly formed. A dispute arose between the two *agrahāras* about their boundaries. The dispute was settled by the *mahājanulu* of the two *agrahāras*. In the settlement some lands were transferred and money was paid in lieu of certain other lands. The settlement also included an equitable division of *rāṭnams* or water wheels. Another instance of land dispute come from the Karīmnager district. A copper plate record (A. D. 1246)[63] refers to a dispute regarding the canal named *gonugukāluva* of Chāmanapalli, which was claimed by the neighbouring villages. The dispute was referred to the King. After taking the evidence from the elders and brāhmaṇas of the villages concerned, the canal was restored to Chāmanapalli.

TABLE VI

Sale and Purchase of Land

Sl. No.	*Place& Date*	*By whom the purchase was made*	*From whom it was made*	*Area of the land*	*Amount of money paid*	*purpose*	*Other delails*	*Refe- rence*
(1)	(2)	(3)	(4)	(5)	(6)	(7)	(8)	(9)
1.	Kūcimañci (Khammam dt.) undated Ganapati's time.	Ponkala Bolseṭṭi	Not mentioned	4 marturs of Nirunela	Not menti oned	For grants to gods Gopīnatha and Dhar- manātha.	--	C.I.T.D. III, p. 21-23.
2.	Pedapariyāla (Karimnagar dt.)	Bairiseṭṭi (Head of the Virbalañja community)	1) Brāhmins 2) Mandanḍa kannaya (a private indi- vidual) 3) Devaya 4) Vāsappayya 5) Pochamakka Mallaya.	1 ma, of wet land 1 ma " ½ma " ¼ma " ½ma "	Total 3 ma paid 100 māḍas.	For grant to the new temples for Gods Baireśvara, sakaleśvara and Nāgeśv- ara.	--	I.A.P. Kn. 38

(1)	(2)	(3)	(4)	(5)	(6)	(7)	(8)	(9)
3.	Alampūr (Mahaboob-nagar dt.) A. D. 1299 Prataparu-dra's time.	some settis	not mentioned	5 marturs	Not menti-oned	For grant to God Gaureśvara	1. The land is measur-red with a pole of 32 spans. 2. The tra-nsaction was atte-sted by a witness 'Vireśe Beri' perhaps another merchant.	Tel. Ins. II, pp. 135-136.
4.	Amarābad, (Mahaboob-nagar dist.) undated.	Mallisetti	Not mentioned	Not mention oned (may be I ma of land).	30 māḍas	For grant to Svayam-bhu Saman-thas	For the irriga-tion fa-cility, perhaps a tank. Mallisetti paid 25 madas and 10 visas.	C.I.T.D. III, Mn. 741 pp. 40-41

(1)	(2)	(3)	(4)	(5)	(6)	(7)	(8)	(9)
5.	Māmiḷḷa-palli (Maha-boobnagar dist) A. D. 1115 Gokarnadeva of Kandur	Bgūpāla Nāviseṭṭi	Pinnaguṇḍya Peddana (perhaps a gāvuṇḍa) and some Māñgalulu as the land is referred to Mangaṇḍla Kāmechenu	40 vrittis of land	Not men-tioned	For grant of god Nrisimha	Mangaṇḍla Kāmechenu is men-tioned (may be belon-ging to Mangalis, barbers).	C.I.T.D. III, Mn. 27 pp. 63-64
6	Ramakrish-ṇāpurm (Khammam dist.)	Not mentioned	Komarusāni	Not men-tioned	Not men-tioned	Grant to an agrahara	Woman's private property.	C.I.T.D. III, pp. 35-36
7.	Umāmaheśva-ram (Maha-boobnagar Dist.) undated	Not mentioned	Not mentioned	1 ma of land ½ ma of land	80 tanks 40 tanks	For grant to God Basavana Maheśvara	--	C.I.T.D. III, Mn. 43 pp. 91-92
8.	Āgamotukūr Nālogṇḍa dist. A. D. 1282 (Rudrama)	Mahāmandale-śvara Rāma-nātha deva coda	A Brāhmin belonging to another village (Epur)	Not men-tioned	Not men-tioned	For grant to god Viramalnā-tha deva	--	K.C.S.C.S. pp. 242-248

Note :— The Paraḍa inscription (A. D . 1143) and the Umāmaheśvaram inscription (A. D. 1320) contain grants by Karaṇam Brahmadevayya and land assignments by Asankhyāta Māheśvarulu. In both the inscriptions borrowing and mortgaging of the lands granted were prohibited. Moreover, the donors prohibited the sale and purchase of the lands granted.

These instances make it clear that the land belonging to a village was clearly marked out with well-defined boundaries on four sides. Great care was taken to fix the boundaries. But inside a village, the land was distributed among the individuals. If any dispute arose regarding the ownership or succession, the village assembly settled it.

A verse from *Vijñāneśvaram*[64] says that if a person wanted to dig tank or a well for common good and if some-body else's land came in the way, he must obtain the permission of the land owners. This indicates the existence of individual ownership in land.

THE FARMING CLASS

The agricultural community of the medieval period may be divided into three classes.[65]

Land lords

Those who owned large areas of cultivable and unclutivable land, large numbers of cattle, agricultural implements and who employed share-croppers and wage earners for cultivation are generally called landlords. In the medieval period, temples are an example of such a land lord. Others include large estate holders like high civil and military officers and *agrahāra* brāhmaṇas. These land owners never personally cultivated the land. They engaged share-croppers (*Ardhasīri*).

Small farmers

Small farmers are those who have small plots of cultivable and uncultivable land. These small farmers themselves tilled the soil and engaged daily wage-earners. Also it can be said that these small farmers were engaged as share-croppers by the big land lords, temple and *agrahāra brāhmaṇas*. Irfan Habib opines that a person having a cultivable land and possessing two bullocks and a plough might be called a small farmer.[66] It may be said that, most of the agricultural population of this period, generally known as '*Kāmpulu*' belonged to this class.

The *Vijñāneśvaram* refers to the conditions imposed on a

share-cropper. If a share cropper failed to cultivate the land he had taken, the village assembly or any other authorised agency had the authority to re-allocate it to someone else who was prepared to cultivate it.[67] This condition ensured continuous cultivation of land.

Landles labour

These were wage earners who had no land of their own and worked only in agricultural seasons. The Ākunūru epigraph[68] (A.D. 1172) records the grant of some amounts to god Rudreśvara by several communities including *Anāmikkulu* which means nameless persons. These people might be landless labourers. During other times they engaged themselves in other activities. It may be said that they constituted the poorest section of the population. Generally they preferred to live in villages with a large number of tanks where there were plenty of agricultural opportunities.

Some of the landless people were engaged as shepherds and cow-herds. These husbandmen were generally drawn from tribal communities. The *Vijñāneśvaram* mentions[69] the wages to be paid to a cowherd. The daily wage was the 1/8 of the milk produced and the husbandman was given one animal from time to time as the flock increased.

IRRIGATION FACILITIES

Telangāṇa is a region of moderate rainfall. The avarage rainfall in the region is around 75 cm (Table III). The agriculture in this region is mainly rain-dependent. Though there are two major rivers, the Godāvari and Krishṇā with many tributaries, they are not of much use for irrigation purposes because they flow in rocky terrain. These could be harnessed only by modern engineering methods. Moreover, other rivers and streams in Telangāṇa region are most of the time dry. They have water running along them only occassionally during the seasons of heavy rains. So, they are not dependable for agriculture. Prior to the 12th century A.D., wells and small tanks were the only irrigational facilities. Water from the wells was lifted into the fields by means of water wheels referred to in a number of inscriptions in Medak and Karīmnagar districts.[70] Slowly tanks substituted for the wells, though well

TABLE VII

Tanks mentioned in Inscriptions

Sl. No.	*District*	*No. of Samudras (Big tanks)*	*No. of ceruvus (Medium) tanks)*	*No of Kuntas (Small tanks)*	*Total No. of tanks*
1.	WARANGAL	17	30	13	60
2.	KARIMNAGAR	7	23	6	36
3.	MEDAK	3	3	2	8
4.	MAHABOOBNAGAR	15	49	10	74
5.	NALGONDA	27	64	16	107
6.	KHAMMAM	8	30	10	48
	TOTAL	77	199	57	333

irrigation continued side by side. It is of interest to note that even now a large number of wells are used. The expansion of irrigation network, in the form of tanks in the Telangāṇa region from the 11th century, was mainly due to the new thrust given by the *sāmantas* who sought to optimise resource mobilisation in their respective regions through the construction of tanks. The temple institutions became the nuclei of such agricultural enterprise, which gradually expanded in several ecological zones of Telangāṇa. As a result, even the drier eco-zones of Nalgoṇḍa and Mahaboobnagar districts received intensive agricultural expansion.

In the medieval period the construction of a tank was considered as a meritorious deed. Several inscriptions of the time, such as the Karimnagar inscription (A.D. 1171) of Gangādhara,[71] a minister of Kākati Rudradeva and Gaṇapavaram inscription[72] refer to *Saptasantānas*. Further the ecology of Telangāṇa necessitated tank-digging to augment economic resources of the state by providing greater irrigational facilities for the development of agriculture. Under the Cālukyas of Kalyān many tanks were dug in the region to satisfy irrigational requirements. The undated Korapolu inscription of Āhavamalladeva's[73] time mentions six tanks which were already existing. The Ollāla inscription[74] (A.D. 1098) mentions two tanks, one of them being referred to as *kottaceruvu* a newly built tank.

The Kākatīyas, whose core region was Telangāṇa, had to continue the policy with greater vigour and intensity. They paid much attention to agricluture not only for it was the prime source of revenue and augmented the resources of the state but also because it was the main occupation of the people.

In many inscriptions of the period it is interesting to find frequent invocations of Varuṇa, the god of rain and of *Jaladhara*, the god of water.[75] This is a clear indication that most of the crops in the region depended more on rain (*varṣādhāra*).

On the basis of the suffix applied to the tanks they may generally be classified into three main kinds. Some are called *samudras* and others as *ceruvus* or *taṭākams* and other *kunṭas*. The samudra or sāgara, which literally means sea, is a big tank and *taṭākam* or *ceruvu* come next in size. They are medium-sized tanks. The *kuṇṭa* is a small pond. The Table VII shows the medium size tanks outnumbered the other two types. Canals were dug from the tanks to carry water to the fields. Almost from the beginning of their rule, the Kākatīya kings, the members of the royal family, their subordinates, generals and ministers built a large number of tanks all over Telangāṇa. Generally, tank-digging was not an isolated act. With the growth of the *Bhakti* movement, temple-building received great stimulus. Each temple was accompanied by a tank and raising up of a new village in its vicinity. As a result, the land around was brought under cultivation. When Kundamāmba converted the village Vemulatomṭa into Kundavar *agrahāra,* built the temples of Rudresa, Mahadeva, Sūrya and Gaṇapeśvara and caused the digging of several tanks.[76] Much land was brought under cultivation. It is interesting to note that the fields around the *agrahāra* were known by different names such as *Vemulatomṭa* which means a grove of neem trees (margosa), *jammipaḍiya, bādamkuṇta, niluvurāyi* (standing stone) and *cauṭa* (fallow land) revealing their chief characteristics.[77] These inscriptions reveal how different aspects in the socio-economic life proved complimentary to one another. The grant of *agrahāras,* temple-building and digging of a tank led to growth of new settlements, increased agricultural activity and helped movement of people to the developing villages.

Tanks built by kings and members of royal families

The kings and members of the royal families were directly involved in the tank-building activity. Though, there is no direct evidence to say that the Cālukyan monarchs built any tanks in the Telangāṇa region, the Coḍa and the Kākatīya chiefs built many tanks.

Toṇḍarasa (A. D. 1093) of the Coḍa family is credited with the construction of big tank at Koppolu.[78] His successor, Mallikārjuna Coḍa (A. D. 1098) built a tank at Ollāla.[79] Many tanks are mentioned at Pānugallu (Nalgoṇḍa dt.) with names Toṇḍayakeṛiya,[80] Bhīmasamudram,[81] Coḍasamudram[82] and

Udyasamudram,[83] and Udayāditya samudram[84] is a huge tank built by Udayāditya Coḍa (A. D. 1235-1260).

The Moṭupalli epigraph of Gaṇapatideva (A. D. 1244) mentions the building of a large tank by Prola I (A. D. 1053-1075) known as Kesarisamudram.[85] His son and succesor, Beta II (A. D. 1076-1108) is credited with building of two tanks.[86] Prola II (A. D. 1117-1158) founded a tank near Anmakoṇḍa called Sarisamudram.[87] The Siddhesvaracharitra records that Prola II built another tank called Kamasamudram.[88] The Anmakoṇḍa inscription of Rudra (A. D. 1163) states that the king, after destroying the fort of king Coḍodaya, built a big tank.[89] *Pratāpa charitra* mentions that Gaṇapatideva founded many tanks at Gangāpuram, Gaṇapāpuram, Ekaśilāpuri and other places.[90] The same work mentions that Rudramadevi and Pratāparudra also built many tanks.[91]

Members of the royal family, especially the queens, took keen interest in building tanks. Mailamadevi, sister of Gaṇapatideva and wife of Natavāḍi Rudra built a tank called Mailasamudram.[92] The Bayyāram tank near Mahaboobabad (Warangal dt.) was built by the same queen.[93] Kundamāmbika, her sister and co-wife, built a tank known as kundasamudram at Niḍigoṇḍa (Warangal dt.) and established an *agrahāra* called Kundavaram.[94]

One of the inscriptions refers to another Kundasamudram tank and Kundavara *agrahāra* built by the same queen on the northern bank of Godāvari in the present Adilabad district.[95]

Tanks built by subordinates and officials

The māṇḍalikas, ministers, generals and chieftains valid with one another in building tanks and augmenting irrigation facilities in their respective jurisdiction. Mahāsāmantha Vemabola Boḍḍama Mallenāyaka,[96] a puḷinda general and chieftain under Mahāmanda-leśwara Kākatīya Prolarāja built a large tank, Mallasamudram at Māṭeḍe in A. D. 1120. He built three temples for Īśvara, Nārāyaṇa and Āditya and endowed them with dry and wet lands, irrigated by the new tank. He also established a Brāhmaṇa settlement, Brāhmaṇapuri. Betanapreggaḍa, a minister of Prola II (A. D. 1117) [97] caused the construction of a tank and a canal, kūchi-keṛe.

Gangādhara, a minister of Rudradeva and governor of Sabbinadu built a large tank at Dindomṭa.[98] According to the inscription Gangādhara built a large number of tanks, probably at different places and one of them was Gangāciyacéruvu. Malayāla Kāṭa-senāpati[99] built a tank at Koṇḍaparti. In the same village Chauṇḍa, the general of Gaṇapatideva, built a tank called Chauṇḍasamudram, established an *agrahāra* called Chauṇḍapura built a temple for Chauṇḍeśvara and donated to it a *devabhoga* village.[100] Recherla Rudra (A. D. 1213) built a large temple at Nekkoṇḍa and a tank called Nekkoṇḍasamudram.[101] Vennapareḍḍi, a subordinate of the Recherla Reḍḍis, built a tank at Māchāpūr, known as Vennapa Reḍḍicheruvu (A. D. 1217).[102] An undated inscription from Pākhāl mentions that a subordinate of a Gaṇapatideva, Jagadala Mummaḍi built a big tank near Maudgalya *tīrtha.*[103] The Goḍiśāla inscription (A. D. 1236)[104] mentions that Kāṭyanāyaka, a brāhmaṇa officer, built three tanks known as Rājānāyakuniceruvu, Ravvasāni ceruvu, Kāṭayanāuaniceruvu respectively after his father, mother and himself. The Pillalamṛṛi branch of the Recherla Reḍḍi family built a large number of tanks in Nāgulapāḍu Pillalamṛṛi region of the present Nalgoṇḍa district. The Pillalamṛṛri inscription (A.D. 1195)[105] credits Recherla Nāmireḍḍi, a son of Kāmireḍḍy, the founder of the Pillalamaṛṛi branch of Recherla family, with the construction of two *trikūṭa* temples, and digging five tanks Sabbasamudram, Viśvanātha samudram, Gaurasamudram, Gaḍulaceruvu and Aitamaceruvu (A. D. 1202).[106] Eṛukasāni, wife of Beti Reḍḍi, brother of Nāmireḍḍi built a tank at Pillalamaṛṛi called Eṛakasamudra.[107] She also established an *agrahāra* called Eṛakapuram. Her brother, Nūnkanayaka, built a tank, Nāmasamudram, at Annavarm to the east of Nāgulapāḍu.[108] Beti Reḍḍi, brother of Nāmireḍḍi built a tank at Somavaram in the same region.[109]

Tanks built by guilds and professional groups

The professional groups and merchant guilds contributed in providing irrigation facilities and bringing new lands under cultivation. Inscriptions mention tanks like Nāmiseṭṭi ceruvu, Seṭṭikeṛe and Seṭṭiceruvu,[110] which were evidently built by rich merchants or by merchant guilds. The *ekkaṭis* of Ākunūru (A.D.

1172) built a tank at Ākunūru by name Rudrasamudram.[111] The Chittāpūr inscription mentions the building of Sakala samudram by the local guild of *Ayyāvaḷi* 500, headed by Bairiseṭṭi.[112] As the land irrigated by the tank belonged to many individuals, Bairiseṭṭi purchased it from them. Then he gifted 1/3 of the land to the local temple and be gave away the rest as the share of the king. But the nature of the crops that were grown on the temple land, are not known.

Tank-building by individuals

A large number of inscriptions mention tanks whose names suggest that they were either built or owned by individuals. The Govindāpuram inscription (A. D. 1122) mentions 12 tanks,[113] named after indivciduals such as Bollanaceruvu, Guṇḍanaceruvu, Vemanaceruvu and Brammanaceruvu. Some of them were officers. Bollana was a *maneverggaḍa* and Guṇḍana was a *paḍālu*. They gifted land irrigated under those tanks to the local Jain temple. *Sandhivigrahi* Aitarāju joined them in gifting land. The Brammanaceruvu was probably was the work of brāhmaṇas as a group. The Reḍḍis and Seṭṭis were the most prominent among those who got tanks excavated and tanks named as Seṭṭikeṛeya, or Seṭṭiceruvu are numerous in inscriptions.

When a private individual built a tank the land that came under irrigation was apportioned between the individual and the state. It appears that atleast half of the land went to the state. The Annavaram inscription [114] mentions that Nāmireḍḍi built a tank called Nāmasamudram on the eastern side of Nāgulapāḍu. The land that was brought under irrigation was divided in two equal parts; one part wass enjoyed by Nāmireḍḍi and another became the property of the state. The Chittāpūr inscription[115] of Pratāparudra's time records the building of a tank by the local *Ayyāvaḷi*-500 (Vīrabalāñja) community. The land that was irrigated was divided into three parts. Two of them became state property *(Rāchādīnamu)*. This arrangement might have served as an incentive to the private individuals to construct new tanks and bring new lands into cultivation. The share of the individual became evidently his private property. The share of the state was probably distributed among the cultivators of the village.

Aspects of construction of tanks

The contemporary inscriptions from the Telangāṇa region as well as those from other parts of Āndhradeśa give us an idea of some technical details regarding tank-building. In the Telangāṇa region tanks were mainly for storing rain water. For the purpose of storing the rain water, the land or field that was to be converted into a tank was cerefully selected. Where ever possible a site surrounded by hills was selected and the bund was formed by filling the gaps between the hills. The Rāmappa lake was bounded on three sides by a ring of hills and one side by an artificial bund. In other cases, where hills are not available to serve as bunds, a field slightly higher in level than surrounding lands was chosen.[116] Earth was dug out from the neighbouring fields and a high bund was built. The bund was strengthened by pebbles, grantite pieces, sand and other hard meterials. An inscription from Cuḍḍapah district gives a detailed account of the tank building process.[117] One thousand men were engaged and 100 bullock carts were pressed into service for full two years without break. The Pākhāl, Rāmappa and the Ghanūr tanks along with many other tanks have been in use without any repairs till the time of the Asaf Jhani rule in the 19th century.

IRRIGATION CHANNELS

Water was taken from the tanks by means of sluices and canals. Generally, sluices were built on at least four sides of the tank from which canals were eaxcavated to take the water to the fields. In Table VIII a list of canals and the tanks from which they started is given. But no information is available about the drainage facilities.

The large-sized tanks and channels of the period mark a notable improvement in the irrigation technology over the preceding period. The widespread use of stone sluices, single or multiple, was a common feature in the Karṇātaka and Kerala regions. Similar trend is also observed in the Telangāṇa region. The construction of channels connecting the tanks with the nearby river or rivulets was another feature of hydraulic improvemnt in the period. From Urusuguṭṭa inscription we learn that poet Narasimha who was a contemporary of Pratāparudra describes Āndhradeśa as "full of rice fields of golden hue, resembling the dales of the golden mountain with gems and in the country are tanks and thousands of rivulets and they indeed appear to be the ocean and his consorts respectively."[118]

MAINTENANCE OF TANKS

Since tank irrigation was the mainstay of agriculture in Telangāṇa, a system of maintenance of irrigation tanks was evolved. The state as well as the local community took care to maintain the tanks and repaired them whenever necessary. The Bekkam inscription[119] of Tribhuvanamalla dated in the year A.D. 1107, refers to Mahāsāmantha Bejjarasa as *Udagāraposhaṇa*. *Udagāraposhaṇa,* as the name indicates, must be an official incharge of the irrigation facilities or water resources. A later inscription of the Vijayanagara time mentions tenure known as *Daśabandhamānyam,*[120] enjoyed by an officer maintaing the irrigation facilities of the locality. An inscription from Perūr[121] also refers to a Reḍḍi enjoying *Daśavanthamaḍi*. It may therefore be inferred that the Reḍḍi or Pedakāpu of a village was entrusted with the responsibility of maintaining and repairing the tanks, sluices and canals of the village for which he received *daśavandhamānya.*

The words *ceruvu kunca*[122] or *puṭṭi kunca*[123] that are found in inscriptions also refer to the *daśavandha* payment. It is paid to the person specially appointed for this purpose of maintaining tanks and other water resources in the village. They are levied on the cultivatros generally at the rate of one *kunca* per each *puṭṭi* of the gross yield. As such, it is generally called *puṭṭi kunca* or *cheruvu kunca.*

The phrase *daśavanthamānyam*, suggests that 1/10 of the irrigated land or produce was earmarked for the enjoyment of the reḍḍi or pedakāpu or the officer entrusted with the responsibility of maintaining tanks, supervising the distribution and proper utilisation of the water resources of the village.

RECLAMATION OF LAND

The irrigation facilities created by the kings and their

TABLE VIII
Canals

Sl. No.	Place	Name of the canals	Source of the canal	Other information	Reference
(1)	(2)	(3)	(4)	(5)	(6)
1.	Anmakoṇḍa	Kūchikeṛe canal	Betana Taṭākam	The canal irrigates land. 1 ma of that land was granted by Ugravāḍi Meḍarasa to Kaḍalālaya Basadi.	I.A.P. Wl. 22.
2.	Gārla	Ūṭi Kāluva	Ūṭitaṭākam	Bopparāya, a subordinate grants 50 nivartanas of land to god Visvesa. The land is irrigated by the canal and yields two crops in Kārtika and Vaiśākha	C.I.T.D., II pp. 5-8
3.	Kaṭukūr	Iṭṭkālva, Tāṭikālva, Kanti Kālva Vemukālva Betarāju Varanta Kālva	Pedda ceruvu	The canals irrigate land of 10 kunṭas of wet land	C.I.T.D., III, 14-15, 19-21
4.	Kūcimañci	Chintala Kāluva	--	1 ma of wet land	C.I.T.D., III

(1)	(2)	(3)	(4)	(5)	(6)
5.	Upparapalli	Meendi Kālva (Upper canal) Kontepu Kālva Prolakamma Kālva Colubaḍi Kālva Krindi kālva (Lower canal)	Penjeṛvu Kāṭnyāyuni Ceruvu, Ravvasāni Ceruvu. Rājānāyakuni Ceruvu.	Many fields and gardens are irrigated by the canals coming from several tanks	I. A. P. Kn. 30
6.	Chittāpūr (Pariyala)	Ūṭum, kālva Eṭi kālva Tūmu kālva	Canal from a spring, canal from a stream, canal from a tank	The canals irrigated several fields.	I.A.P. Kn. 38
7.	Pedda Kaḍumūr	Brāhmana kālva Hiriya Kālva.	--	--	Tel. Ins. II, 67-73
8.	Amarābad	Buruvuguṇḍāla Kālva.	--	Land cultivated under Progasirivangu kālva was mentioned and new land brought under cultivation was donated to Swayambhu	C.I.T.D., III Mn. 4.
		Paḍumaṭi Kālva			C.I.T.D., III. Mn. 5.
		Pogasirivāngu Kālva			C.I.T.D. III. Mn. 6
9.	Pillala-Maṛṛi	Bommakanṭi kālva	Canal going upto Bommakallu. Lakshmi Samudram Eṛaka Samudram.	Earakapuram, Erakamaṭham are mentioned	Tel. Ins. I. 31-38

(1)	(2)	(3)	(4)	(5)	(6)
10.	Nāgulapāḍu	Nāgulapāṭi Musiḍi Kālva Rāvi kālva	Nama samudram	Majority of the land was irrigated by Nāmasamudram	C.I.T.D., II. No. 29, p. 93
11.	Būrugugaḍḍa	Kūchinenikāluva Lotumgāluva (deep canal) Alugu Kāluva (over flowing canal)	Prola samudram Manḍrāju Ceruvu	Poḍunela, and Devabhoga village Pochapuram are mentioned	C.I.T.D. II. No. 18, 19
12.	Pānugallu	Ādityabhadruni-Kālva,	Udayāditya Samudram	The donor Mallikārjuna is described as 'Royasthāpanā-chārya'.	Tel. Ins. 172
		Uttamagāṇḍa Kālva	-do-		Tel. Ins. I. pp. 75-77.
13.	Ālugaḍapa	Peddatūmukālva	Rāvulaceruvu	Guṇḍapanāyaka is described as Vaḍlūripuravarādhīśvara.	Tel. Ins. I, pp.158-159.
14.	Āgamothukūr	Tippakāluva Rudrama Kāluva Krindi Kāluva (Lower canal) Pykāluva (Upper canal)	Several tanks mentioned	Different types of land are mentioned	K.C.S.C.S., pp.245-248.

subordinates greatly increased the agricultural production. In addition to building tanks, other methods as detailed below were also adopted for improving agriculture.

Forest clearance

The area of the cultivable land was increased by forest clearance and the lands brought under such cultivation was known as *poḍubhūmi*. The Būrugugaḍḍa inscription[124] (A.D. 1258) records a land grant to god Gopīnātha by *Pradhāni* Bollamarāju. The land granted included *poḍubhūmi*. The Anmakoṇḍa inscription of Rudradeva[125] mentions that the king destroyed the fort of Coḍodaya, cleared the surrounding forest and built an irrigation tank there bringing new lands under cultivation.

Water reclamation

When new tanks were built it was natural that some of the waste land was brought under cultivation. It may be observed from Table IV that some of the *agrahāras* created during this period were old villages. For example Vaijanapalli was converted into Śivapura *agrahāra.*[126] The Kundavaram *agrahāra* was formed out of lands belonging to Vemulatomṭa, an old village. The conversion of an old village into an agrahāra was perhaps to bring the land of the village into use. The old village might have been already languishing without any irrigational facility and water resources. Such waste lands were brought under cultivaiton by the establishment of *agrahāras*.

Creation of new villages

Direct epigraphical evidence is not available as to the creation of new villages in the Telangāṇa region except in a few cases. The Pālampet inscription of Recherla Rudra (A. D. 1213) refers to a new town called Ātukūru[127] where Rudra built two temples for gods Rudreśvara and Gaureśvara and built a tank called Nekkoṇḍasamudram. As it has been said earlier, in many inscriptions we find the names of land, not necessarily under cultivation. These names emanated from the geography and topography of the land. These had suffixes like *kuṇṭa, gaḍḍa, meṭṭu* etc. When irrigation facilities were created, a new village developed at these places and these villages derived their names from the old land names. Būrugugaḍḍa, Cintalakuṇṭa, Diccakuṇṭa may be mentioned as such villages.[128]

By these methods large tracts of waste and fallow land were brought under cultivation. However, it cannot be said what extent of land was exactly brought under cultivation in the period under study.

TECHNIQUES OF CULTIVATION

Foreign as well as native historians are critical about the developments in irrigationl facilities and agricultural technology in India. They are generally of the opinion that the methods are primitive without significant innovations over long periods.[129] They argue that there was practically no change in the methods of cultivation and the tools applied in Indian agriculture. By and large, there is some truth in this criticism but it does not contain the whole truth. The methods of agriculture were not completely stagnant over centuries. We do observe certain changes taking place in agricultural technology from time to time.

A large number of inscriptions of early period refer to *rāṭna, embarāṭna,* and *tomṭarāṭna,* used for irrigation. The term *rāṭna* or *embarāṭna* means a water wheel used for drawing water from wells or kuṇṭas (ditches). An inscriptiona Dosapāḍu[130] (A.D. 1190) records the gift of a *rāṭna* to god Tonṭeśvara with necessary wood and bullocks for the cultivation of a garden land. Inscriptions reveal that the *rāṭnas* were generally operated by the members of boya and tammaḍi communities[131] who probably formed a large segment of labour force. The references to the *raṭnas* however become less frequent in the inscriptions of 12th and 13th centuries. The use of *rāṭna* appears to have been confined to the flower gardens and groves of fruit-bearing trees. Thus, we observe a noticeable change in the irrigation practices. The tank irrigation became widespread by the end of 12th century. Notwithstanding the tank irrigation system, certain zones like Adilabad and hilly regions of Nalgoṇḍa depended on well irrigation.

With regard to irrigation and draingage, certain new

developments in agricultural technology were in evidence throughout India. The introduction of animal powered *arghaṭṭa* for deep well irrigaiton and of stone sluices reveal the new developments in irrigation technology. Recent researches have shown that araghaṭṭa, though introduced in the 5th century A.D. became widespread by the end of 12th century A.D. in the northern India.[132] In Telangāṇa where deep well irrigation was a necessity, such devices were widespread from the 11th century.[133]

An important problem associated with agriculture was storage. There were three traditional storage methods that were in use. They were *pātara, puri,* and *gāde. Pātara* was a wide and deep pit dug in the courtyard of the farmer's house. Grain was stored in it with earthen top put on hay stacks. *Puri* was made of coir of hay. Other storage devices were made of bamboo cane such as *gāde,* or *gampa,* and earthern ware *(kuṇḍa)*. But these storage methods were not free from dangers of decay and loss. Rodents are the bitter enemies of the farmer, causing him considerable loss. Especially *puri* and *pātara* were generally exposed to the danger of damage by rains.

LIVE STOCK (CATTLE WEALTH)

Cattle wealth is an important element of the agricultural eco-system. Cattle rearing and agriculture went hand in hand from times immemorial. The former was source of supplementary income to the Indian peasant. In medieval Āndhra, different kinds of cattle are found associated with agricultural and commerical activities. They are : (1) cows and oxen, (2) buffaloes, (3) sheep and goats and (4) donkeys.

The population of sheep and goats appears to have been the largest. They were generally husbanded by the members of the boya and golla communities. Innumerable inscriptions all over Āndhra record the gift of sheep to temples for perpetual lamps. These gifts were entrusted to the boyas who were charged with the duty of supplying ghee to the temple. Common people appear to have made the milk products from sheep a part of their daily food. The refuse of sheep and cow-dung were used as organic manure. There was the practice of keeping flocks of sheep for five or six nights in a field for enriching the soil.

The buffaloes come next to the sheep in importance. These were used not only as milch cattle but also as beasts of burden. They were used in most of the agricultural operation like ploughing, watering and for transporting. A number of inscriptions record the gifts of *Inupa Eḍḍlu* to the temples.[134] There are different interpretations of the word '*Inupa Eḍḍlu*'. The *Sūryarāyāndhra nighanṭuvu* gives the meaning as he-goat.[135] Mallampalli Somasekhara Sarma took the word for cows.[136] Ramachandramurti says[137] that *Inupa Eḍḍlu* means 'milk giving animals' which may be cows, sheep, goats or buffaloes. Thus we understand that *Inupa Eḍḍlu* means milch cattle which include cows, she - goats, sheep or baffaloes. These gifts were also generally entrusted to members of the boya community.

The cow is a sacred animal for the 'Hindus'. killing of cow is a henious crime. At the end of inscriptions, the imprecatory verses say that the violation of the gift recorded would entail the sin of killing a cow at Vāraṇāsi.[138] However, oxen were treated as beasts of burden in agriculture and in transport. The Dosapāḍu epigraph[139] (A.D. 1190) refers to the grant of several *rāṭnas* for the cultivation of a garden to Lord Tonṭeśvara by a chieftain Dosapāti Rudraya. Rudraya made a gift of two bullocks along with the wood for the *rāṭnas*. The bullocks were for drawing water from the well. The ox was also a pack animal. The bullock cart was the chief means of transport. Marchandise was taken over long distances by itinerent merchants in bullock carts. Donkey was also a pack animal used for carrying loads. Trade in cattle was carried on in weekly fairs. Exclusive fairs for cattle trade were also held periodically.

CROPS AND CROP PATTERN

Crops were raised according to the nature of the soil and availability of irrigational facilities. They are generally classified into food crops and money or commercial crops. Jowar, pulses and rice are the food crops. Other crops which are consumed after some processing may be called money crops. These include sugarcane, oilseeds, cotton and jute. These were fed into industry for the manufacture of sugar, jaggery, cloth, packing material etc. These are also called commercial crops.

CROPS

In the macroregion under study, a large number of crops were raised which included both food and money crops.

Food crops : Jowar

Jowar appears to have been the staple food for a large majority in Telangāṇa. Even in the neighbouring district of Palnāḍ, people mainly depended on jowar. Large scale production of this millet was therefore undertaken from the 11th and 12th centuries both in the Karṇāṭaka and Āndhra regions. It was also the cereal produced in the most of the cultivable area. It may be noted that at every trade centre the sale and purchase of jowar are mentioned. (Table IX.)

Jowar is a dry land crop irrigated mainly by rain. The jowar fields were also irrigated by water drawn from wells using water wheels (*rāṭnas*). The crops stood nearly for six months and it was harvested during winter by which time the monsoon retreats. There are three types of this cereal which were cultivated: 1) *jonna*, the yellow-green veriety (2) *bajra* (vajra), the white variety and (3) rāgi, the brown-red variety.

Rice

Rice was wetland crop which needed constant watering. So, this crops was raised in the lands irrigated by the numerous tanks. Rice is a labour intensive crop. Saplings were raised in nurseries and transplanted during monsoon. Harvesting of the crop is done in early winter. One or two weeding operations are necessary between transplantation and harvesting.

COMMERCIAL CROPS

1) *Sugarcane*

Like rice, sugarcane was also raised in wet land. Literary works refer to the cultivation of rice and sugar as a symbol of prosperity. Sugarcane was an annual crop harvested during late

TABLE IX

Agricultural Commodities mentioned at Trade Centres

Sl. No.	*Place*	*District*	*Source with reference*	*Articles of Trade*
1.	Perūr	Nalgoṇḍa	P.I. No.6, (undated)	Jowar, pepper, mustard seed, betel leaf and arecanuts
2.	Pānugallu	Nalgoṇḍa	Pānugal Insn., (A. D. 1124) K.C.S.C.S., Tel. Ins. I, pp. 169-172.	Jowar, pepper, betal leaf and arecanuts, turmeric, paddy, cotton and zinger.
3.	Uppunūtala	Mahaboob-nagar	Uppunūtala Ins. (A. D. 1148) C.I.T.D. - III, Mn.45. pp. 93-94	Cotton
4.	Sirikoṇḍa	Khammam	Sirikoṇḍa inscription (A. D. 1148) K.C.S.C.S. PP. 193-195	Paddy (unhusked rice), betel leaf.
5.	Vardhamā-napuram	Mahaboob-nagar	Vardhamānapuram Ins., (A.D. 1224) C.I.T.D. III, Mn. 46, pp. 94-97.	Jowar, rice betel leaf and arecanut
6.	Warangal	Warangal	Warangal fort insn., (A.D. 1228) IAP wl. No. 63	All kinds o f rice, perpper, cotton, vegetables, betal leaf, arecanuts, coconuts, mango, gingelly, wheat, green-gram, paddy, jowar, mustard gram.
7.	Pammi	Khammam	Pammi Ins., (A. D. 1235)- C.I.T.D. III, pp. 31-35.	Two kinds of rice, gingelly, tama-rind, green-gram, dry-ginger.
8.	Magatala	Mahaboob-nagar	Magatala Ins., (undated) Tel. Ins. II, pp. 161-162	Jowar, fruits, vegetables, rasakala rice, flowers.

winter or early spring (March and April). Large number of the references to the manufacture of sugar and jaggery in the epigraphs and literature suggest wide-spread cultivation of sugarcane.

2) *Oil seeds*

Gingelly was the main source of cooking oil in Telangāṇa during the Kākatīya times. This was raised as a dry land crop. Castor was another oil seed that was raised in the period under study.

3) *Cotton*

The most important commercial crop was cotton. It was produced almost in every village. It is also a dry land crop raised once in a year.

Horticulture

Other important agricultural products were vegetables, fruits and flowers. These were raised in dry uplands, irrigated mainly by rain and occasionlly by water from wells. Mango was the most cherished fruit. Several inscriptions[140] refer to the planting of *māvitonṭalu* (Mango groves). The Bairānipalli (A.D. 1108) record mentions the grant of a mango grove on the banks of Palavalige stream to the Jinālaya of Bekkallu.

The *krīḍābhirāmam* refers to the practice of taking bananas with food.[141] Though inscriptional references are lacking, raising of banana plantations must be a common feature.

Other imporatant groves that were raised in the macroregion were of palmaira and native dates. The favourable drink of the people in this region came from these two trees. This is known as *kallu* (toddy).

Betel leaf and arecanuts

Both these were essential requirements in the temple and household rituals. Besides, the tāmbūla was a popular item of chewing after dinner among the higher classes. The custom of exchanging *tāmbūla* symbolised an agreement or assignment or a courtesy. Betel leaves were grown every where but arecanut plantation was not much practised.

AGRICULTURAL SEASONS

The agricultural operations in Āndhradeśa generally started on the full moon day of the month Jyeshṭa, which is known as *Eṛuvāka Pūrṇima* which comes generally in June.

Generally two crops were raised per year where irrigation was assured and labour available. The Bairānipalli inscription (A.D. 1108) records the grant to a jinālaya of land yielding two crops per year,[142] one harvested in the month of *Kārtīka* and another in *Vaiśākha*. In north India also two crops, khariff and rabbi, were raised during the medieval period. The first is known as the autumn crop and the second the spring crop.

The inscriptional references to agricultural activities including the crops raised indicate that the people in the medieval period showed keen interest in agriculture and were familiar with its different aspects. The production of different articles and their surplus production led to prosperous trade which resulted in the formation of a number of trade centres.

TRADE IN AGRO-PRODUCTS

The Pammi inscription[143] of Devanapregaḍa mentions a number of products like arecanuts, betel leaves, jaggery, dried jinger, green gram, temarind, gingelly, rice, oil and ghee, onion etc., entering the market for sale.

Table IX illustrates the trade activity in various agricultural products. The Table shows that jowar and rice were important articles of trade in every market. They were the major cereals grown. Next in importance were the oil seeds such as gingelly and it appears that the cultivation of groundnut was unknown in Kākatīya times. Cooking oil was taken from gingelly and mustard. There was trade in betel leaf and arecanut at every centre. it indicates the surplus production of these two items and the consumption aptitude of the medieval people for these two items. Another important commodity that was sold at many trade centres is jaggery. This shows that the cultivation of sugarcane was quite popular and most of it was used for producing jaggery. The production of sugar is rarely noted. The next important crop that was raised appears to be cotton especially in the present Warangal, Mahaboobnagar and Nalgoṇḍa distrcts. The other important crops were the black pepper and turmeric. There is no evidence of the production of chillies. Pepper was used for taste instead of chillies. People derived most of the agricultural protein from green gram. Even in hotels, according to the Krīḍābhirāmam,[144] green gram was served with rice. Other types of pulses such as the Black-gram, redgram, and Bengalgram were unknown in Telangāṇa. The fruits that were cultivated are mango and coconut. The Warangal fort inscription[145] refers to the large scale trade of vegetables such as *kanda, peṇḍalum* and onion.

LAND AND AGRICULTURAL TAXES

Land and agricultural taxes generally vary from region to reign. They largely depend upon the nature of soil, availability of irrigational facilities, importance of the crop and at times even on historical traditions. In view of these factors, there is bound to be much divergence between Telangāṇa and particularly coastal Āndhra in taxation. As an example it may be cited that the inscription of Telangāṇa are silent about taxes like *Puṭṭipahiṇḍi*. It may therefore be reasonably assumed that the rulers follwed to a large extent the traditions established by earlier rules and rarely made deviations from them.

The inscriptions of Telangāṇa or Āndhra are not administrative records. They do not contain direct and datailed information about the pattern of taxation in the region. Taxes are mentioned only when they were remitted for the benefit of a temple or a *brahmadeya*. Even regarding the procedure of the collection of taxes, clear picture is not available either in the inscriptions or in the literature of the period. Putting together little bits of information collected form the sources we have to draw reasonable conclusions.

It is already noted that *Dharmaśāstras* enjoined upon the cultivators of land to pay a share of the produce to the state. The share was generally considered to be 1/6th of the yield. In the *Śāntiparva* of Āndhra *Mahābhārata,*[146] it is mentioned that the king got 1/50th of cattle and gold and 1/10th the agricultural produce from the people. The Śāstra literature gives only the picture of an ideal state of affairs.

From about the 10th century A.D. epigraphical data is available about the levies on lands and agricultural yields. *Siddhāyamu*[147] was the term used for the established revenue from a vilage. It appears that a group of villages were taken as a unit for the collection of the revenue. A number of inscriptions mention *Ūḷḷa siddhāyamu*[148] which means *siddhāyam* from villages. A late 10th century epigraph from Sītārāmpalli in Medak district records that the *siddhāya* collected from a group of eight villages in Rāvipolala-80 amounted to 125 gadyāṇas and 125 *khaṇḍugas* of grain.[149] It is clear from the record that the *siddhāya* was collected both in cash and in kind. The headmen of the eight villages were assembled and asked to pay *siddhāya* to the chief of Medak-360 of which Rāvipolāla-80 was a part. The Gaṭṭutummena inscription (A.D. 1116)[150] and the Pānugallu epigraph (A.D. 1132)[151] record the diversion of parts of *siddhāya* to local temples. The Umāmaheśwaram epigraph (A.D. 1320)[152] records a grant of *ūḷḷa siddhāyam* payable by sixteen villages of Munnalūru *sthalam* to god Maheśvara by the *Asankhyāta māheśvarulu* for the merit of the king, Pratāpa Rudra. The Kaṭukūr inscription[153] records the grant of *siddhāya* of the village amounting to 5 *visas* in a *māda* to god Gopīnātha by the *Aṣṭādaśamahāpraja* of the village. The Koṛavi epigraph (C. A.D. 950)[154] records the payment of all types of taxes collected in the region under the chieftain Peddana to king Nirvadya before *Perāmaṇi Punnami*.

The *siddhāyamu*, as it was paid in cash as well as in kind, appears to have included all types of taxes payable by the villagers. These taxes were *pannu, kānika, kaṭnamu, pullari, guddali cinnālu, tāḍlapaiḍi* and others.

The Yelgeḍu epigraph (A. D. 1301)[155] of queen Lakmādevi records the diversion of several taxes on the villagers such as *vennupannu, kānika, kaṭnamu* and *pullari* to god Rāmanāthadeva for the merit of her father, Paldeva Nāyanimgāru.

Pannu

Parabrahma Sastry thinks that Pannu was the general land

tax collected from every landholder of a village.[156] This would mean that *Pannu* was a tax for the possession of a piece of land.

Pullari

Pullari is the general tax collected from the village due from the grazing lands.

Vennupannu

The word *vennu* means 'the ears of corn'. Parabrahma Sastri is of opinion tha tthis tax was levied when the ears of the corn begin to appear. This might have been levied according to the estimated yield of the land.

Guddali chinnālu

The Hasnābād inscription of Rudramadevi's time[157] records the diversion of *Guddali chinnālu* by the ekkaṭis of the village to god Rudreśwara. *Guddali* is an agricultural implement such as a spade or hoe.[158] Thus, this tax appears to have been in cash and was probably levied at the time of beginning the agricultural operations.

Kānika and Katnamu

Kānika and Kaṭnamu were paid in cash when either the king or the *māṇḍalika* visited the village. These taxes were paid by the land holders.

Singanādam pannu

The Magtala inscription (A. D. 1320)[159] refers to the diversion of the *Singanādamu pannu* levied on the soldiers to lord Avubalanātha by Guṇḍayanāyaka. This appears to be a tax levied on the *vrittis* granted to military personnel.

Taxes on groves and gardens

The Hasnābād inscription[160] refers to the diversion of Tāḍla paiḍi to lord Rudreśvara by the local military personnel. The Ākunūru epigraph (A. D. 1172)[161] refers to the payment of 3 *cinnas* per *rāṭna* used in gardens. The same epigraph refers to the diversion of *Boragaṇḍla māḍalu* on the *rāṭnas* as an irrigation facility.

Nīruḍi

The Ākunūru epigraph also mentions a tax called *Nīruḍirūkalu*. This might be a water cess collected in cash (rūkalu) on both wet lands and gardens. The words *paiḍi, māḍa* and *rūkalu* may be taken to suggest that these levies were collected in cash.

The above taxes were collected at appropriate times in the year by the local assembly, headed by the headman, as suggested by the Sītārāmpalli, Umāmaheśvaram and Kaṭukūr epigraphs noted above. The karaṇam maintained the accounts of the different levies. The state share of the grain was collected at the time of harvest. The total amounts thus collected both in cash and kind, were paid before the *Perāmanipunnami* as mentioned in the Koṛavi epigraph.[162] The editor of the epigraph says that the *Perāmanipunnami* means *Vaiśākha pūrṇima*, full-moon day in the month of *Vaiśākha* which generally falls in May. By this time the second crop also would have been harvested.

The term *ūḷḷasiddhāyam*, suggests that the collection of revenue was done with the *sthala* as a unit. As it has been already noted a *sthala* was a group of villages. Within the *sthala* the village formed a unit of revenue assessment. The village assembly, the council of village headmen (*Pabhumukhyas* or *gāvuṇḍas*), the officials of the *sthala* such as the sthalakaraṇam[163] were involved in the tax collection process.

The grain collected in a *sthala* was stored in a warehouse maintained at the headquarters of the *sthala*. An inscription from Umāmaheśwaram[164] mentions *Munnalūrigāde* (granery). Munnalūru, being the headquarters of Munnalūru *sthala*, Munnalūri *gāde* might mean a royal werehouse (*rāca gāde*) at Munnalūr.

REFERENCES

1. The districts are:
   1) Adilabād, ii) Nizāmābād, iii) Karīmnagar, iv) Medak, v) Rangāreḍḍy, vi) Hyderabad, viii) Warangal, viii) Khammam, ix) Nalgoṇḍa, x) Mahaboobnagar.

2. *Āndhra Pradeṣh Year Book* (Hyderabad, 1984).
3. C. S. Picchamuthu-*Physical Geography of India* (Telugu)-Traslation by Mahidhara (New Delhi, 1967). pp. 58-66.
4. *A. P. Year Book* (Hyderabad, 1984).
5. I.A.P. Wl. 58, Tel. Ins. I. pp. 71-72, 88-89, 156-157, etc.
6. Tel. Ins. II. pp. 161-162.
7. Ibid. I, pp. 147-152.
8. Ibid II, pp. 161-162.
9. I.A.P. Wl. 19.
10. P. I. 3.
11. Tel. Ins. I., pp. 31-38.
12. K.C.S.C.S. pp. 245-248.
13. I.A.P., Wl. 17.
14. C.I.T.D. II, pp. 21-23.
15. Ibid, Mn. 31.
16. Tel Ins. I pp. 71-72.
17. C.I.T.D., III pp. 4-5, 19-21, 35-36, Mn. 5, 38-39. Tel. Ins. I., pp. 147-152, tel. Ins. II, 103-107.
18. C.I.T.D. III, Mn., 31, 68-69.
19. C.I.T.D., III, Mn. 31.
20. K.C.S.C.S. pp. 199, tel. Ins., II, pp. 103-107, P.I. 6 C.I.T.D., IV. 41.
21. Tel. Ins., I, pp. 88-89, 158-159, Tel. Ins., II, pp. 103-107, 135-136, C.I.T.D. III, PP. 21-23.
22. C.I.T.D. IV, 11.
23. Tel. Ins., I. pp. 31-38.
24. B. Stein, in *Cambridge Economic History of India* (Delhi, 1984), p. 14.
25. Tel. Ins., I, pp. 31-38.
26. I.A.P. Wl. 19, Tel. Ins, I, pp. 111.
27. Tel. Ins. I., pp. 31-38.
28. V. A. Smith, *Early History of India* (Oxford, 1904), p. 123.
29. *The Laws of Manu* Ed. G,. Bühler, (Delhi, 1984), Chap. VII, pp. 216-252.
30. Gautama, *Institutes of Sacred Law* (The Sacred laws of the Āryas) translated by G. Bühler ed. Max Muller (Delhi, 1962) , Part I, chapter XXI, pp. 227-238.
31. K.C.S.C.S. pp. 181-184.
32. Tel Ins. I., 92, C.I.T.D. II, No. 26.
33. I.A.P. Kn. 38.
34. B. Stein., *Peasant State and Society in Medieval south India* (Delhi, 1980) pp. 141-172.
35. N. Karashima, *South Indian History and Society* (Bombay, 1984). pp. 38-39.

36. I.A.P. Kn. 25.
37. Ibid. 28.
38. Ibid. Wl. 58.
39. P.I. 12, 14, 15, C.I.T.D. IV. 32.
40. Tel Ins. I, 133-136. Tel. Ins. II. pp. 107-114; C.I.T.D. - III. Mn. 47.
41. I.A.P. Wl. 48.
42. Ibid. 16.
43. Tel Ins. I, pp. 145-146.
44. Ibid. II, pp. 161-162.
45. K.C.S.C.S., pp. 181-184.
46. I.A.P. Wl. 37.
47. C.I.T.D. IIi, pp. 19-21. I.A.P., Wl. 90.
48. I.A.P. Wl. 37.
49. I.A.P. Kn. 30.
50. I.A.P. Kn. 38.
51. Tel. Ins. I, pp. 37-38, C.I.T.D. II,, 17.
52. I.A.P. Wl. 48, 50, 51, C.I.T.D. II, pp. 5-8, K.C.S.C.S., pp. 193-195, I.A.P. Kn. 30-34.
52a. 5. I. I. IV, 1048.
52b. E.A.IV, p. 97.
53. C.I.T.D., III, pp. 16-17; 19-21.
54. T. Venkateswara Rao, Local Self-government in Mediecal Āndhra, J.A.H.R.S. XXXI, Parts 1-4, pp. 113-123.
55. I.A.P. Kn. 36.
56. M.L.N. Ācāry, Bhārati, vol. 63. No.9 (1986), pp. 9-13.
57. K.C.S.C.S., pp. 245-248.
58. I.A.P. Kn. 30.
59. I.A.P. Wl. 75, C.I.T.D. II, Mn. 38.
60 Ibid.
61. Ketana, *Vijñāneśvaram* (Nellore, 1977) Vyavahārakāṇḍa Vs. 123. 137.
62. C.I.T.D. - III Mn. 31.
63. I.A.P. Kn. Appendix.
64. Ketana, op. cit. V. 149.
65. Irfan Habib, *Bhāratacharitraloritu* (Tr. by M. Rama Mohana Rao) (Hyderabad, 1985) pp. 1-2.
66. Ibid.
67. Ketana, op. cit. V. 151.
68. I.A.P. Wl. 37.
69. Ketana, op. cit. - Prāyaschittaakāṇḍa v. 14.
70. I.A.P. Kn. 5, 14, 16, 19, 24, 36, I.A.P. Wl. 5, 18, 37, 72, Tel. Ins, I., pp. 85.
71. I.A.P. Kn 25.

72. Tel. Ins. I, pp. 48-50.
73. Ibid pp. 145-146.
74. K.C.S.C.S. pp. 113-146.
75. I.A.P. Wl. No. 29.
76. Ibid 58.
77. Ibid.
78. K.C.S.C.S. pp. 97-99.
79. Ibid pp. 108-119.
80. C.I.T.D. IV., No. 11, pp. 25.
81. Tel. Ins. I, 169-172.
82. Ibid.
83. Tel. Ins I, pp. 73-74.
84. Tel. Ins. I, pp. 75-77.
85. E. I. XII, pp. 188.
86. C.I.T.D. II, pp. 29.
87. *Kākatīya Sancika* App. No. 5.
88. Kāse Sarvappa, *Sidheśvara Caritra*, (Hyderabad, 1960) p. 92.
89. I.A.P. Wl. 36.
90. Ekāmbranātha, *Pratāpacharitra* (Hyderabad, 1960), p. 118-119.
91. Ibid.
92. I.A.P. Wl. 49.
93. E.A., Vol. 1, No. 7, pp. 71.
94. I.A.P. Wl. 57.
95. Ibid.
96. Ibid. 24, 25,.
97. Ibid. 22.
98. I.A.P. Kn. 25.
99. I.A.P. Wl. 485, I.A.P. Kn, 29.
100. Ibid.
101. I.A.P. Wl. 50.
102. Ibid. 54.
103. Ibid. 67.
104. I.A.P. Kn. 36.
105. Tel. Ins. I, pp. 17-19.
106. Ibid pp. 26-31.
107. Ibid pp. 31-38.
108. Ibd pp. 37-38, C.I.T.D. II, 17.
109. Tel . Ins. I, pp. 39-40.
110. Tel. Ins. pp. 111, 169-172,; P. I. 1,2,
111. I.A.P. Wl. 37.
112. I.A.P. Kn. 38.
113. I.A.P. Wl. 26.

114. Tel. Ins. I, pp. 37-38; C.I.T.D. II 17.
115. I.A.P. Kn. 38.
116. D.V. Narayana reddi, 'Techniques of Tank excavations in Ancient and Medieval Andhra' - proc. A.P.H.C. Vol. X, pp, 84-89.
117. I.A.P. C.P. II 11.
118. I.A.P. Wl. 99, 100.
119. Tel. Ins. II, pp. 46-47.
120. I.A.P. Ch. II, 20.
121. P.I. No 6, C.I.T.D. IV, 41.
122. P.V.P Sastry, *The Kākatīyas* (Hyderabad, 1978), pp. 208.
123. Ibid.
124. Tel. Ins. I, pp. 71-72; C.I.T.D. II 18.
125. I.A.P. Wl. 36.
126. Ibid 35.
127. Ibid 50.
128. Ibid 55, 56.
129. Kathleen Gough, *Modes of Production in Southern Indian,* Economic and Political weekly, Annual Number, 1980. pp. 337-354.
130. Tel. Ins. I, pp. 177, C.I.T.D. III.
131. C.I.T.D. III Mn. 31.
132. Irfan Habib in The *Cambridge Economic History of India* (Hyderabad, 1984) vol. I. pp. 48-75.
133. I.A.P. Kn. Nos. 14, 16, 24.
134. S.I.I., IV, 712, 717, 719, 725, 731.
135. *Śri Sūryarāyāndhra Nighaṇṭuvu* (Hyderabad, 1982). Vol. I, pp. 492.
136. Āndhra Patrika Vol. 62, No. 12.
137. S. Ramachandra Murthy, *Andhra Pradesh Devālaya Śāsana Samīkṣa,* (Tirupati 1984), pp. 130.
138. I.A.P. Kn. 30.
139. Tel Ins. I. p. 177. C.I.T.D., III, Ng. 3, III.
140. I.A.P. Kn. 30, C.I.T.D. III, pp. 31-35.
141. Vallabhāmātya, *Krīḍābhirāmam* (Hyderabad, 1960), V. 166. Irfan Habib, *An Atlas of the Mughal Empire,* Map. 15B.
142. I.A.P. Wl. 18.
143. C.I.T.D. III, 31-35.
144. Vallabhāmātya, op. cit.
145. I.A.P. Wl. 63.
146. Tikkana, *Āndhra Mahābhārata,* Śantiparva, (Hyderabad, 1972) Canto II. V. 258.
147. C.I.T.D. III Mn. 10.
148. Ibid.
149. N. Markandeya Sarma, Sītārāmpalli Inscription of Āhavamalla (A.D. 973-997). Proc. A.P.H.C. Vol. X, pp. 114-119.

150. C.I.T.D. III, Mn, 11.
151. Tel. Ins. I, pp. 169-172.
152. C.I.T.D. Mn. 38.
153. Ibid Mn. 18.
154. Tel. Ins. I, pp. 163-165.
155. I.A.P. Kn 37.
156. P.V.P. Sastry, op.cit. p. 214.
157. I.A.P. Kn. 36.
158. C.P. Brown, *Dictionary-Telugu and English* (New Delhi, 1984).
159. Tel. Ins. II, pp. 126-127.
160. I.A.P. Kn. 36.
161. I.A.P. Wl. 57.
162. Tel. Ins. I. pp. 163-165.
163. S.I.I. X 521.
164. C.I.T.D. III Mn. 41.

CHAPTER—III

INDUSTRY

Introduction

Āndhradeśa, including Telangāṇa, has a tradition of industrial activity from very early times. Textiles and diamonds of Āndhra were famous even outside India. Iron and Copper mining and melting and manufacture of metallic tools and utensils formed different aspects of industrial activity in Telugu country. Iron, copper and zinc were found in Guntur district. In Agniguṇḍāla in Vinukoṇḍa Taluq, near Kārempūḍy in Palnāḍ and in several villages to the west of Sattenapalli traces of melting and working of metals are found.[1] In Telangāṇa, at places like Koṇḍāpūr, furnaces belonging to the Sātavāhana period have been discovered.[2] rich iron ore was available at Kūnasamudram near Nirmal.[3] It appears that the iron found here was exported to foreign markets and was used in the manufacture of Damascus swords. Iron mines and steel works are noticed close ot Indūr (now Nizamabad) and Indulavāyi.[4] Gold and silver appear to have been imported from abroad. It is possible that the Kākatīyas revived the old traditions of industrial enterprise in the core region of their authority, i.e., Telangāṇa where trade and industry in metals received tremendous stimulous. The *Maṭṭenakaram* and *Pañcalohālanakaram* were found busy with trade in metals in Telangāṇa. Marcopolo who visited the Āndhradeśa in the 13the century paid a rich tribute to the industrious habits of the people. He praised in particular Āndhra textiles and compared them to the tissue of spider's web.[5] He further gave an interesting description of the diamond industry as well.[6]

Industries may broadly be divided into two categories viz., (1) agro-industries and (2) non-agricultural industries. The agro-industries such as the cotton textiles, jute works, oil pressing make use of agricultural products as raw materials. The raw material for non-agricultural industries is of non-agricultural origion such as metals, precious stones etc., As the workers worked with their hands, through using some tools and mechanical devices, the products are generally known as handicrafts, and the workers are known as artisans. The artisans specialising in an industry had their own tools. The Table X gives the tools and implements used by different artisans. For example the textile workers used the spinning wheel and the handloom. Spinning, weaving and dyeing generally go hand in hand. Therefore, the weaver has to deal with chemicals for producing colours and dyes and with some implements for printing them on the cloth.

AGRO-INDUSTRIES

Cotton Textiles

The most important agro-industry of the period under review, is textile manufacure. Epigraphical evidence reveals intensive cotton growing in the districts of mahaboobnagar, Karīmnagar, Nalgoṇḍa, Warangal, Medak and Adilābād. Cotton was a commodity sold and purchased at almost every trading centre as demonstrated by Table IX. Warangal city appears to be the biggest centre of teaxtile manufacture and trade. The Girmājīpet inscription[7] refers to the guild called *Dharmasālīyajanulu* who built a temple for Sāleśvaradeva. Rich textile merchants like Nijarangāla Mallisеṭṭi and Vennisеṭṭi figure in this record. The record bears ample testimony to the prosperity of textile industry.

Every village produced cloth in small or big measure. The *Basavapurāṇam* states that spinning of cotton thread was household work. Rich and poor, without distinction were engaged in spinning. handlooms were used for weaving the cloth. Dyeing and printing were done on the cloth.[8] Information is not available about the materials that were used in the making of dyes. Perhaps some plant products like the turmeric and minerals like *Ingilīkam* were used to produce colours. *Mañjiṣṭha,*[9] a substance used in producing red dyes was an article of trade in the market of warangal.

Silk Industry

The richer sections of the society used silk cloth and silk sarees especially on festive occasions. Different varieties of silk finds mention in literautre such as *Devāṅga* brocaded silk, *jedara* silk varieties known as *Jedara Matha Jedaradadhimasara* (Pomigranate coloured silk), *Jedarabhatigatu* (patterned silk) *Vichitra* (variegated silk).[10] Another variety was *Sellapaṭṭu* which donates a superior variety of muslin.

Pālkuriki Somanātha in his *Basavapurāṇam* mentions a large variety of silk cloth.[11] The variety was in colour, design and technique of printing. Silk cloth and sarees embroidered with golden thread were hightly prized.[12]

It is not known whether silk thread was produced in Telangāṇa during the period under study. The Moṭupalli charter of Ganapatideva (A.D. 1244) mentions the import of silk cloth and silk thread from far east, especially from China. The Warangal fort inscription (A.D. 1228)[14] mentions the trade carried on in *paṭṭunūlu* (silk thread), *Dāsūripaṭṭu* (perhaps silk from *Dāsūr,* may be Tussore silk) and *pachchapaṭṭu* (yellow or green silk). It appears that trade in silk was carried on by *Ubhayanānādeśi* merchants. This suggests that raw silk was imported into Warangal, where local weavers and artisans produced beautiful cloth out of it with attractive patterns, colours and embroidary. Inscriptions from Āvanca[15] (Mahaboobnagar district, A.D. 1104) and Ālavānipalli[16] (A.D. 1110) mention a community called *Paṭṭasālīlu.* It may be suggested that this *Paṭṭasāli* community was engaged in the silk industry.

About the textiles in Āndhra in general, Morco Polo wrote that in the kingdom of Motufil" are made the best and most delicate buckrams (fine cotton stuffs or fine muslin) and those of the highest price, in sooth they look like tissue of spider's web ! There is no king nor queen in the world but might be glad to wear them. The people have the largest sheep also in the world-----"[17]

Wool Industry

Warangal and its surrounding villages were known for wool industry. As noted above, sheep were reared in large numbers almost in evey district of Telangāṇa and wool was collected from them. The Warangal Fort inscription[18] (A. D.1228) mentions the trade by *Ubhayanānādeśi* merchants in *vūlumalagalu* (bundles of wool) and *Goṛepaḍāla malagalu* (perhaps another variety of wool).

The latter was probably used for producing blankets and carpets. The *Krīḍābhirāmam*[19] refers to the capets woven from sheep wool. Warangal was famous for its carpets in the medieval period. Even today the carpets of Warangal are famous all over the country and abroad.

Oil-pressing

Oil-pressing industry comes next in importance to that of textiles. Oil was essential not only as an article of domestic consumption but also for lighting in houses and in temples. Besides ghee, gingelly oil was used in temples. Many inscriptions refer to donation of oil mills to temples.[20] The workers that specialised in this industry were known as the *Telikis*. They are an old artisan community mentioned in inscriptions of the Satavahana times as the *Śreṇi* of *Telapisakas*.[21] Inscription refer to them as *Telikivevuru or Teliki* 1000.[22] The oil-press was generally made of large stone discs which was worked by animals.[23] It may be said that each village had at least one oil mill. Oil seeds were grown in large areas in Telangāṇa region. Gingelly was the main source of oil. Castor occupied the next place. Trade in oil and oil seeds was common at every centre.[24] The whole-sale trade in oil was also conducted by the *Teliki* community.

Jaggery and Sugar

The production of sugar and jaggary was another agro-industry during this period. In most parts of Telangāṇa, sugarcane was cultivated in wet land with favourable climatic conditions. The *Kriḍābhirāmam* mentions sugar as an article of food served to customers in hotels. Details about the production of sugar and jaggery are not available and it is likely that only conventional methods were adopted in the industry. Jaggery was produced in kilns erected on cane fields. Pānugallu[25] (Nalgoṇḍa district) Perūr[26] (Nalgoṇḍa district) Warangal[27] appear to have been the centres of production of jaggery and sugar.

Jute Industry

The Warangal Fort inscription[28] refers to trade in *Gonesanculu* (jute bags) and *Gone-paṭṭālu* (jute cloth). Jute bags were used to store and transport paddy, rice, jowar and other commodities.

Peṛaka was kind of jute bag which finds mention in many inscriptions. The bags were used for transports of grain and was a unit for taxation. Several records[29] mention *Peṛkavāru*, a community engaged in the manufacture of the jute bags and in transport of goods. Jute was also used for the manufacure of *"nulaka"* (coarse thread) which was used for cots.[30]

NON-AGRICULTURAL INDUSTRIES

Metals

The most important non-agricultural industraial activity was that using metals and alloys. The artisan community that was proficient in this industry was known as *pañcāṇamuvāru*. The artisans viz., *Kamsāli* (goldsmith) Kanchari (alloy worker) *Kammari* (black smith) *Kāśe* (stone carver) and *Vaḍrangi* (carpenter) constitute the *Pañcāṇamuvāru.*

The first three sects of the *Pañcāṇamuvāru* worked in metal where as the fourth worked in stone and the fifth in wood. These artisans too are very ancient but the collective name *Pañcāṇamuvāru* appears to have become current in medieval times. Metal industry was generally controlled by this professional guild. The undated Maṭṭewāḍa inscription[31] refers to a *nakaram* called *Pañcalohāla behārulu* that traded in five metals. The Warangal fort inscription (A. D. 1228)[32] refers to trade in tin and lead by a guild called *tagaramuvāru* and in copper by a guild, *mūsaṛavāru.* These guilds must have been associates of the community of *Pañcāṇamuvāru.*

Iron and Steel

Geologists are of the opinion that iron smelting was widespead in the Deccan and making of iron rods and implements was almost a cottage industry in this part of the country.[33] In Telangāṇa, iron and coal mining was an important industry from early times. These are rich deposits of iron and coal in the Nizāmābād, Nalgoṇḍa, Mahaboobnagar and Khammam districts.[34]

The Jalālpuram inscription (A. D. 1202)[35] in Nalgoṇḍa district mentions a field *Ganimeṭṭakuṇṭa* which may be an iron mine. Traces of lead and iron working are found in Nalgonda and

Mahaboobnagar districts. The present Jaggayyapet area, which was apart of Natavāḍi is well known for iron mining. Ancient copper mines are found at Agniguṇḍāla near Vinukoṇḍa. The area near Sattenapalli in guntur district yielded old iron mines. These must have been the sources for import of these metals into the Telangāṇa. Similarly, lead bearing deposits were also found near Kārempūḍi and Koilkuṇṭla in Palnāḍ, Gājulapally near Nandyāl in Kurnool district, Varikuṇṭa and Jangamarājupalli in the Cuddapah region which were in the Kākatīya territory.[36]

Blast furnaces where iron and steel were produced till the middle of 19th century were found at Kūnasamudram in Nirmal Taluk, Adilābād district. Iron mines and steel works functioning till the Mughal perod were found near modern Nizamābād. Iron and steel were largely used in the manufacture of weapons. Nannecoḍa mentions large number of war weapons in his *Kumārasambhavam* and most of them were manufactured locally. Nirmal and Indalvayi specialised in the manufacture of swords, lances, daggers and other offensive weapons.[37]

Brass and Bronze

The *Kañcaris,* among the *Pañcāṇamvāru,* were experts in casting alloys like brass and bronze and making a large variety of articles in them. This industry was mostly concentrated in the urban and temple centres. Household articles like vessels, tumblers, plates were generally made of these alloys. The Pammi inscription (A.D. 1235)[38] records the gifts made by Devanapreggada to God Prasannavallabha. The gifts included *Piḍigaṇṭa* (bell with handle) *Jayagaṇṭa* (hanging bell) lamp-posts made of bronze and plates. Several inscriptions of the period mention the gift of metal lamp-stands.[39] An undated inscription from Būrugugaḍḍa[40] mentions *Jegaṇṭalavāru* and *Goḍugulavāru* among temple servants who rang the bells and held the umbrellas. These bells and ceremonial umbrellas used on occasions in temples were also made of alloys.

Jewellery

The Moṭupalli inscription of Gaṇapatideva (A.D. 1244)[41] mentions the import of gold, pearls and also metals like copper, zinc, mercury and lead. A later inscription also at the place (A.D.

1358) mentions the import of gold at the port.[42] The import of gold into the country is also corroborated by the literary references especially *Haravilāsa kavya* of Śrīnātha.[43] It sates that Avaci Tippaya seṭṭi imported gold from the far east. Silver was also imported. Marco Polo wrote that silver was imported into south India from Jedda.[44]

Literary works diring this period metion a variety of jewels and ornaments. Pālkuriki somanātha's *Paṇḍitārādhya Charitra*[45] mentions gold umbrellas. Headgear (Helmet) made of iron was used by soldiers.[46] Somanātha refers to bulls adorned with anklets, bells and horns made of gold. Gold ornaments mentioned by him included crowns, bracelets, earrings and finger rings.[47] Children wear ornaments like *puligoḷḷu* and *molanūlu*.[48] Ketana in his *Daśakumāra Caritra* mentions a large number of ornaments.[49]

Maṭṭewāḍa, a suburb of Warangal, according to the local tradition was famous for the manufacture of anklets and *maṭṭelu* (silver rings worn by ladies on their toes) used by married ladies. This led to the suburban village acquiring the name Maṭṭewāda. Usually, silver and lead are traditionally used for the manufacture of *maṭṭelu*. silver lamp-stands, silver flowers, armlets, ear-rings, belts etc., are also mentioned in literature. Mattewada was frequented by the *Pañcalohāla behārulu*,[50] the guilds which traded in five or more metals.

The Telugu poet Manchana writes in the *Keyūrabāhucaritra*[51] that people in the great town for Danadupura (Chandol-capital of Durjayas of Velanadu, Guntur District) did not wear gold ornaments without diamonds. The diamonds of Andhradeśa during the medieval and early modern periods were famous all over the world.

The diamonds and precious stones were mined in the Krishṇā valley.[52] Diamond mining industry greatly flourished during the phase-III of our period. Marco Polo writes, "it is in this kingdom that diamonds are got;—there are certain lofty mountains in those parts and when the winter rain falls—the waters come roaring—in great torrents—when the rains are over—they search the beds of the torrents and find plenty of diamonds. In summer also there are plenty to be found in the mountains and people collect them with the help of kites".[53] But what Marco Polo wrote about diamonds collection appears to have been based mainly on hearsay.

The tools, implements and moulds used by the goldsmith are noted in the *Palnātivīra Caritra*.[54] Some of them are given in the Table X.

Ivory

The Warangal Fort inscription (A.D.1228) refers to trade in ivory by the *Ubhayanānādeśi Pekkaṇḍru*. The Moṭupalli charter of Gaṇapatideva also mentions the trade in ivory. This material was used to manufacture among other articles, caskets used by women to keep jewels and cosmetics.[54-a] The *Krīḍabhiramam* refers to an ivory box. Ivory was also used in ornaments and toys.[54-b]

During the Kākatīya period gold and silver were used for coinage. The gold coin *gadyana*[55] and the silver coin, *ruka*[56] were in circulation and minting of these coins was carried on under the supervision of government. The coinage in use, during the peirod under study is discussed in the Appendix.

Stone work and Building Industry

The Telangāṇa region abounds in granite, dolomite, sandstone and limestone.[57] The *kāśe* community had specialised in stone work including cutting and carving. During this period big tanks were provided with stone bunds and sluices.

The Kākatīya period witnessed vigorous building activity. Temple building was wiedespread all over the land. Even the *māṇḍalikas* and officers built large temples and therefore temple-building became a big industry. Various temple towns witnessed continuous building activity between the 11th and 14th centuries. These included Ālampur,[58] Pānagal,[59] Pillalamaṛṛi,[60] Warangal,[61] Gangāpuram,[62] Perūr,[63] Kollipāka,[64] Pammi,[65] Kaṭukūr,[66] and Būrugugaḍḍa.[67]

A large number of forts were also built during the time. Rudradeva built the fort of Warangal[68] to which Gaṇapati[69] and Rudrama[70]made additional fortifications. The several *māṇḍalikas* and *nāyankaras* built hill and mud forts, using stone and mud at several places in Telangāṇa. The most important forts in the region that were built in the peirod, apart from Warangal, include

Pānugallu,[71] Munnalūru,[72] Vardhamānapuram,[73] Pillalamarri,[74] Allādurg,[75] (Śrīvardhanakoṭa), Sirikoṇḍa,[76] Kūcimañci,[77] Nagurūr.[78]

A number of inscriptions refer to the stone masons as *sūtradhāri (sūtradhāri* Juvapāchārya[79] and *sūtradhāri* Brahmoju[80]) who belonged mostly to Kasevaru. It is interesting to note that Mailambika, wife of *Ēṛuva* Toṇḍaya Coda donated a village Kāsypalli near Pānugallu as *ekabhoga* to *sūtradhāri* Brahmoju.[80] It is not unreasonable to think that Brahmoju gathered around him a group of apprentices and the Kāsypalli *agrahara* might have developed into a school of architects and sculptors.

Wood crafts

Wood crafts was an essential part of agricultural economy of medieval times. The plough was made of wood but had an iron point. The basic transport vehicle, the cart, was made of wood. It was drawn by bullocks or buffaloes. The blacksmith preapared the iron belts to strengthen the wheels. Thus the carpenter and the blacksmith formed essential components of agricultural community.

The carpenter played an important part in house construciton. He prepared the beams, doors, and windows. The household furniture which included chairs, tables, cots and cabinets, was made by him. *Aṭṭakas* and stair railings[90-b] made of wood were mentioned in the contemporary literature.

Pottery

Pottery is an ancient and important craft. Pots were used to store grain and seed. They were also used to carry water to fields. Oil was preserved in Pots. The Nagulapadu inscription[81] (A.D.1303) mentions the potters among the *Aṣṭādaśapraja*. Tikkana refers to the potter's wheel in the *Āndhra Mahābhāratam*.[82]

Brick making is another industry of the medieval period. The Navābpet inscrilption.[83] refers to *iṭakāvamu chenu* (field used for burning bricks). Iṭikāla in Mahaboobnagar district is another place known for the brick industry. This industry was, perhaps, carried on by the kummari (potter) community. Literary sources point to the use of glass mirrors, glass bangles and beads.

Bamboo Cane Industry

Many household and agricultural articles made of bamboo were in use in medieval times. *Gāde*, a large storage vessel made of bamboo, was widely used for the storage of paddy. *Puṭṭi*, made of bamboo, was widely used for crossing rivers and canals. It is a basket with leather covering which is still in use in Rāyalasīma. *Gūḍa*, a device for lifting water from tanks and cannals was also made of bamboo. The *Krīḍābhiramam* refers to cots made of bamboo and cane.[84] Bamboo was also used to make chairs and stools. The *medara community* was engaged in this profession. Medaravāḍa[86] which indicates the large number of workers engaged in the profession.

Leather

The cobbler's craft or leather working also is very ancient in Āndhradeśa. Leather was used in the making of various kinds of articles. Leather buckets known as the *etamu*, were used to draw water from wells for irrigating the fields. Contemporary literary works point to the use of sandals made of leather. These were known as *kiṟṟu cheppulu*[87] made of two layers of leather. These sandals make noise and were used by peasants probably to frighten away snakes and scorpions while working in the fields.

The most popular musical instrument of these times was the drum using leather on both sides. The Telugu literary works Palnāṭi Vīracaritra[87] and Krīḍābhiramam[88] mention variety of musical instruments that were made of leather. They are *naubat*, *Kanakatappeta*, *maddela* and *bheri*. The playing on drum by women was a favourite theme of Kākatīya sculpture.[89] Inscriptions of the time mention that the kings and *sāmantas* were always accompanied by five musical sounds (pañcamahāśabdas).[90] During the war, drums (*yuddha bheri*)[91] were played to rouse soliders. Leather was used in making these different drums.

Miscellaneous Industries

There were many other industrial occupations to which reference is found in contemporary inscriptions and literature. The manufacture of musical instruments was an important industry. The *Vīṇa* was the most popular instrument.[92] In the *Paṇḍitāradhya*

Charitra, Pālkuriki Somanātha gives a list of the types of *Vīṇa*.[93] Other types of musical instruments made of wood and leather were popular among common people as suggested by the *Krīḍābhiramam*.[94] Several hundereds of people were engaged in the manufacture of musical instruments like *vīṇa, tappeta, bheri, naubat, kāhaḷi* and others.

The manufacture of toys was another industry. Nannecoḍa mentions toys made of ivory, glass and wood.[95] Toys made of lac were also mentioned in the literature.[96] Table X summarises the industrial activity.

Taxation on Industry

Just as *kara* or *pannu* was the general tax levied on farmers, *ari* appears to be the tax on artisans. An inscription from Durgi dated in A.D. 1269[97] records the grant of *arisunkamu* collected from every oil-mill at the place of god Gopīnātha by karaṇam Nāmaya, a subordinate of Jannigadeva. The *arisunkamu* amounted to one *visam* in every *gadyāṇa* of oil produced. This would amount to a tax of 1\16 of a *gadyāṇa* on oil costing one *gadyāṇa*. An inscription from Pedaganjām dated in A.D. 1270 records[98] the grant of *ari* on salt pans at Pedaganjām and the neighbouring salt-producing villages by the *pekkaṇḍru* to god Pinneśvara.

An inscription from Velpūru[99] (A.D.1247) mentions the taxes *gānuvula mudra sunkamu, and varusarūkalu*. The former term may be taken to mean a registration fees payable from an oil-mill. We may say that the *mudra sunkamu* was paid by the looms as well. The Pātarlapāḍu inscription A.D. 1300 records the grant of ammounts payable to several communities to the local temple at the instance of Pratāparudra. The *salevāru* (weavers) paid the amount on the basis of the number of the looms held by the community. From this, we may infer that *mudra sunkamu* and *ari sunkamu* were collectlled form the looms as well as from oil-mills.

An inscription from perur (A.D.1119)[101] records the grant of *nelarūka* (a ruka per month) by trade guilds including the *Telivāru* to the local temple. This *nelarūka* might be the same as Varusarūkalu mentionned above.

TABLE X

Industrial Activity

Industry	*Raw Materials*	*Products*	*Tools and implements*	*Community engaged*	*Reference*
(1)	(2)	(3)	(4)	(5)	(6)
Cotton Textiles	Cotton	Coarse cloth, fine cloth, sarees.	Raṭnam (spinnig wheel), Maggam (Handloom)	Salevāru, Saliya-janulu, pattasali.	I.A.P. Wl. 61 Tel. Ins. II
Silk	Silk thread	Silk cloth	--	Paṭṭasali	Tel. Ins. II, 57-62
Oil	Oil seeds (Gigelly, mustard, castor etc.,)	Oil, Oil cake	Oil mill using animal power	Teliki, Tailikulu	Tel. Ins. II, 161-162.
				Telikivevuru-seṭṭis (Teliki-1000)	I.A.P. Wl. 28.
				Siddivāru	I.A.P. Wl. 87
Jaggary + Sugarcane Sugar		Jaggery and sugar	Cane press, kiln etc,	Peasants themselves appear to be manu-facturing these articles on fields.	P.I.No. 6 I.A.P. Wl. 63

(1)	(2)	(3)	(4)	(5)	(6)
Jewellery	Gold and Silver and diamonds and precious stones	Oranaments for men and women and temple-dieties	Iron forcepts, moulds, hammer, scissorse etc.	Kamsāli	Palnati Vira Carita, Chap-42.
(Alloy making) Brass, & Bronze	copper, zinc. Tin and lead	Household utensils, Temple utensils, lamposts, lamps etc.	(Iron smellter)	Kanchari	Ibid.
Iron	Iron	Agricultural implements weapons for war	Vayyandi (iron smelter)	Kammari, Metal workers	Ibid., 4-95.
Wood	All types of wood	Agricultural implements such as the plough etc.	--	Vadrangi	K.C.S.C.S. p. 40
Stone and Building	Stone	Building materi-als, stone for sculpture etc.	--	Kase	Tel. Ins. II, pp. 115-121 C.I.T.D. IV, p. 39

(1)	(2)	(3)	(4)	(5)	(6)
Pottery	Earth	Pots, Jars etc.	Potter's wheel (Sare)	Kummari	Tel. Ins. I, pp. 89-90
Bamboo	Bamboo cane	Cane containers such as putti, Gade, Peruka	Knife	Dommari	Kridabhiramam, v. 70,68
Ivory	Ivory	Caskets, Orna-ments	--	Carpenters	Ibid., v. 77. I.A.P. Wl. 63
Leather	Animal hides	Chappals (padapakshas)	--	Cobbers	Ibid., v. 162
Jute	Jute	Bags, coir, Thin coir	-- --	Perikavaru	S.I.I.K. pp. 304.
Toys	Ivory, Wood, Glass	--	--	--	Kumara-sambhavam, canto III, v. 36.
Glass	Earth	--	--	Potter	S.I.I. X, p. 274.
Musical instru-ments	wood, iron wire etc.	--	--	--	Kridabhiramam, v. 136.
Brick and tiles	Earth	Moulds and kiln	--	Kummari	S.I.I. X, 274.

Other taxes on artisan products included *Kolapoḍuvu* and *Kaṛṛakūli*.[103] These two taxes were paid by the wood craftsmen (*vadrangi* community). Similar taxes might have been levied on other artisans. *Gāṇḍsunkamu*[104] and *buṛṛasunkamu*[105] appear to be such levies.

REFERENCES

1. Mackenzie, G. *Manual of Kisina District* (Madras, 1883) pp. 77-247.
2. G. Yazdani, A.B.O.R.I., Vol. XXII, pp. 171-185.
3. K. satyanarayana - *A Study of the History and Culture of the Andhras* vol. II (New Delhi, 1982), p. 50.
4. Irfan Habib, An Atlas of Mughal Empire, Sheet 15 B.
5. K.A.N Sastri, *Foreign notices of South India, From Megasthanese to Ma Huan* (Madras, 1939), p. 175.
6. Ibid. pp. 174-175.
7. I.A.P. Wl. 63.
8. Palkuriki Somanātha, *Basavapuranam* (Hyderabad, 1969) canto 3. ll. 100-130.
9. ·I.A.P. Wl. 63.
10. Vijaya Ramaswami, Indian Historical Review, VI, Nos. 1-2, (1979-80) p. 123.
11. Palkuriki Somanātha, op. cit. (Hyderabad, 1969). Ibid.
12. Ibid.
13. E.I., XII, pp. 188.
14. I.A.P. Wl. 63.
15. Tel. Ins. II. pp. 60-62.
16. Ibid. pp. 57-59.
17. K.A.N. Sastry, op. cit. p. 175.
18. I.A.P. Wl. 63.
19. Vallabhāmātya, *Krīḍābhirāmam* (Secunderabad, 1969), v. 232.
20. I.A.P. Wl. 18, I.A.P. Kn Nos. 22, 24.
21. K. Gopalachari- *Early History of the Andhra Country* (Madras, 1976), pp. 118-119.
22. I.A.P. Wl. 28.
23. Vallabhāmātya, op. cit, v. 103.
24. Refer Table XIII.
25. Tel. ins. I, pp. 169-172.
26. P. I. No. 6.
27. I.A.P. W. 63.
28. Ibid.
29. S.I.I., X pp. 304.
30. Mancana, *Keyūrabāhucaritra* (Hyderabad, 1966) Canto I. V. 26.

31. I.A.P. Wl. 68.
32. Ibid. 62.
33. G. Kurian, *India - A general survery* (National Book Trust) (New delhi, 1970), pp. 105.
34. Andhra Pradesh year book (Hyderabad, 1984).
35. Tel. Ins. II, pp. 103-107.
36. *Memoirs of the Geological Survery of India* vol. VIII, 10.
37. Irgan Hbib - *An Atlas of Mughal Empire* (Delhi, 1986) sheet 15 B, p. 62.
38. C.I.T.D. III, pp. 31-35.
39. Ibid.
40. Tel. Ins. pp. 83-84.
41. E.I. XII, pp. 188.
42. S.I.I., X. 556.
43. Śrīnātha, *Haravilāsam,* Canto I, v. 26.
44. Marco Polo II, pp. 389-390, quoted by K. Sundaram, in *Studies in Economic and social conditins of Medieval Āndhra* - Machilipatnam, 1968 - Page 18.
45. Pālkuriki Somanātha - *Paṇḍitāradhya Caritra, Parvata Prakaraṇam.*
46. Ibid.
47. Tikkana, *Āndhra Mahābhāratam, Virāṭaparvam* (Hyadrabad, 1970) cont. 5, vv. 133. 237, 272.
48. Gona Budha Reḍḍi, *Ranganātha Rāmāyaṇam, Bālakāṇḍam.*
49. Ketana - *Daśakumāracaritra* (Hyderabad 1967) III. v. 77.
50. I.A.P. Wl. 68.
51. Mañcana, op. cit. Canto I, v. 19.
52. K.A.N. Sastri, op. cit, p. 174.
53. Ibid.
54. Śrīnātha, *Palnāṭivīri caritramu, Bālachandruni Yuddham.*

54a. Vallabhāmāṭya, op. cit. v. 77.

54b. I.A.P. Wl. 63.

55. S. Dasarathi, Proc. A.P. H.C. Vol, X, 'Numismatic References in Nannaya's Mahābhārata', pp, 117-119.
56. Vallabhāmātya, op. cit. v. 116.
57. Ch. Lilanandam, Building stones in Andhra Pradesh, Journal of the Deccan Geological and Mining society-I, 1 pp. 27-32.
58. M. Radha Krishna Sarma-*Temples of Telangāṇa* (Hyderabad, 1972) p. 39.
59. Ibid, p. 84.
60. Ibid., p. 100.
61. Ibid. p. 105.
62. Ibd. p 77.
63. P.I. No. 6, 9.
64. Op. cit. p. 66.
65. C.I.T.D. III, 31-35.
66. C.I.T.D. III, 16-17.

67. Tel. Ins. I, pp. 83-85.
68. Kāse Sarvappa - *Siddheśvaracaritra* (Hyderabad, 1960). p. 108.
69. Ibid p. 113.
70. Ibid. p. 129.
71. B. N. Sastri, *Kandūru Coḍula Sasanamulu Caritra Sanskṛiti.* Introduction pp. 5-44.
72. Ibid.
73. Ibid.
74. Tel. Ins. I., Miscellaneous Inscriptions No. 11.
75. Tel. Ins. I, pp. 143-144.
76. B. N. Sastri, op. cit.
77. C.I.T.D. III, pp. 19-21.
78. I.A.P. Kn. 25.
79. Tel.Ins. I, 169-172.
80. K.C.S.C.S. pp. 166-173.
81. Tel Ins. I., 89-90.
82. Tikkana, op. cit. *Udyogaparvam* (Hyderabad, 1970) canto. IV, vv. 116-117.
83. S.I.I. X 274, pp. 141-142.
84. Vallabhamatya, op. cit. v. 70.
85. Ibid.
86. Ibid. 68.
87. Ibid. v. 162.
88. Ibid. v. 147.
89. S. Gopalakrishna Murthy, - *The Sculpture of the Kākatīyas* (Hyderabad, 1964). Plate-45 B.
90. Sringa, Mridanga, Śamkha, Bheri, Ghana - Śāsana Śabdakośamu, K. Isvaradatt, (Hyderabad, 1967) p. 172, S.I.I. IV 811.
91. Śrīnātha, *Palnāṭi Vīracaritra* - op. cit.
92. Vallabhamatya, op. cit. v. 136.
93. Pālkuriki Somanātha, *Paṇḍitārādhya caritra, Parvataprakaraṇam.*
94. Vallabhamatya, op. cit. v. 147.
95. Nannecoḍa, *Kumāra Sambhavam* (Hyderabad, 1968), canto III, v. 36.
96. Ibid. canto II, v. 46.
97. S.I.I., X 422, p. 225.
98. S.I.I. X. 427.
99. S.I.I. X. 314.
100. P.V.P. Sastri - *The Kākatīyas* (Hyderabad, 1978) pp. 230.
101. P.I. No. 6.
102. S.I.I. X. 314.
103. K.C.S.C.S. pp. 138-140.
104. Tel Ins. I., pp. 79-80.
105. Ibid.

CHAPTER—IV

TRADE

The expansion of agriculture in the plains and in forest zones and the growth of industries on the basis of agricultural and other prouducts and the surplus in both the fields of economic activity led to a spurt in internal and external trade. Trade being a rich source of state income, the rulers, the Rāṣṭrakūṭas and following tnem the Later Cālukyas encouraged trade and commerce, and Deccan once again, as during the time of Sātavāhanas, began to bristle with commercial activities. The Rāṣṭrakūṭas are known to have encouraged Arab merchants[1] to settle down in their kigdom and carry on trade. The Cālukyan inscriptions from about the beginning of the 11th century contain references to rich merchants—*behāri* and *seṭṭi* and merchant orgainsations like *Ayyāvaḷi 500* and *Nānādeśis.*[2] Telangāṇa which formed part of the Rāṣṭrakūṭa and Cālukyan empires felt the impact of and made its own contricution to the growing mercantile enterprise.

TRADE ORGANISATIONS

From the eleventh century onwards epigraphs of Telangāṇa contain references to merchant organisations. But there is a marked difference between the eastern and western parts of the region. In the west, the records from places like Āvanca[3] and Gangāpuram[4] refer to *Samayas*. An inscription from Gangāpuram (A. D. 1079) refers to *Āśakasamaya*[5] among other marchant organisations. An inscription from Avanca (A.D. 1104)[6] records the remission of certain taxes by Kumāra Tailapadeva, payable by *Paṭṭasāligam, Angaḍiseṭṭigar, Sāliseṭṭigar* and *samaya*. The virtual absence of the *samaya* in the contemporary epigraphs o f the eastern Telangāṇa is striking contrast to the west. The inscriptions from Chilkur (A.D. 1067)[7] and Anmakoṇḍa (A.D. 1090)[8] in the eastern districts mention *nakaram* organisations. Kenneth Hall has pointed out[9] that *Samaya* denotes an itinerant trade guild whereas the *Nakaram* denotes a guild of local merchants. It is therefore clear that in western Telangāṇa, a region adjucent to Karnāṭaka and ruled directly by the Cālukyan monarchs, local merchant guilds did not develop till the beginning of the 12th century A.D. Kannaḍa merchants formed into Samaya guilds and carried on local as well as itinerent trade. However, as the *Sāmantas* such as the Coḍas of Kandūr and Kākatīyas of Warangal became powerful, *nakaram* guilds began to grow all over the region. As the authority of the Cāḷukyas declined in the middle of the 12th century, the *nakaram* became the most significant basic unit that set the pattern as an agent of integration in the trade of rural markets in the entire Telangāṇa region. The trend continued with greater vigour in the 13th century. The *samaya*, as an organisation of traders, was probably integrated into the *nakaram* network as the latter organisation became diversified into several specialist trade guilds such as *Ponkanakaram, Pañchalohala nakaram* etc.[10] Moreover, itinerant trade guilds like the *Ayyāvaḷli* 500[11] and *Mummūri-daṇḍas*[12] played a dominant role in serving the royal centres and temple towns, meeting their demand for variety of consumer goods. Thus, it may be said that the emergence of the *nakaram* network drew the itinerant trade linking the intraregional with interregional commerce.

Samaya

In Telangāṇa, during the early times of Cālukyan rule the organised commerce was carried on by *samaya* guilds. This is attested by the epigraphs of Āvanca,[12] Gangāpuram[13] and *Paṭāncheruvu*.[14] The Kannaḍa inscriptions from the Mahaboobnagar district[15] refer to trade guilds with the suffix *samaya* and *Samayam*. The Gangāpuram inscription (A. D. 1079) refers to *Samastaseṭṭi-kāraru* and *Āśaka Samayagalu*.[16] The Āvanca inscription (A. D. 1124) mentions the remission of certain taxes by Tailapa on merchant guilds such as the *Paṭṭasāligam* and the *Samayam*.[17] The Paṭāncheruvu inscription (A. D. 1127)[18] mentions that the *seṭṭikārasamayas* of four villages were entrusted with the execution of Bhūlokamalla Someśvara's charity to a Brāhmin Nannaya-bhaṭṭa. However, it may be said that with the disappearence of the Cālukyan hegemony and the rise of Kākatīyas, the *Samaya* type of trade organisations slowly disappeared. It appears that these *samayas* operating in the Telangāṇa region were mainly composed of Kannaḍa marchants and that the term *Samaya* generallydenoted an itinerant merchant guild. The epigraphical evidence quoted above from Telangāṇa supports Hall's definition of *samaya*. Howeve, the Telugu word *Pekkaṇḍru*[19] was in greater use to denote itinerant trade guilds. Thus, we may conclude that the *samaya* organisations of earlier times (before c 1126 A.D.) developed into (a) the *Nakaram* at the local level and (b) the *pekkaṇḍru* as the supra local level.

Growth and Diversification

With the establishement of semi-independent *sāmanta* states at Koḍur, Anmakoṇḍa and Polavāsa and with the expansion of trade, a number of guilds came into existence. These may be classified into (1) *Nakaram* network (2) Artisan-cum-mercantile guilds and (3) Itinerant trade guilds.

Apart from these, there was another significant organisation frequently mentioned in contemporary epigraphs. That is *Pekkaṇḍru*. This organisation appears to be inclusive of the members of the above three types and was a corporation of the guilds.

Nakaram

The *nakaram* is the most frequently referred trade guild in Telangāṇa between the 11th and 14th centuries A. D. The word *nagaram* was also used in inscriptions with the same import. In Tamilnāḍu in the age of the Colas, *nagaram* was the standard term.[20] Hall defines nagaram as a "physically defined area inhabited by a group of people known as *nagarattar*" an assembly of merchants.[21] Thus, *nagaram* of the Cola timers denoted two things at the same time: (1) an area and (2) an assembly or guild. The *nagaram* organisation in the Cola domain represented town—hinterland ralationship. The members of the body are known as a *nagarattar*[22] and participated in the transactions of interregional, intraregional and overseas trade. They were closely associated with the temple institutions in the management of grants and gifts. Membership was secular in character. The *nagaram* organisation assumed the character of a local body maintaining local markets, supervising the flow of goods, and providing a regular link between *nāḍus* and itinerent traders.[23] Increase of *nagaram* centres within the *nāḍus* and diversification in trading activity giving rise to guilds like *sāliya nagaram, śankarappādi nagaram* was due to the spurt of commercial activity.[24]

The sustained effort in agricultural expansion and growth of rural economy during the 11th-13th centuries in Telangāṇa led to the growth of *nakarams*. The distribution of *nakarams* listed localitywise in Table XI demonstrates the factors for such increase. Temple towns and royal and administrative capitals became the centres of growth for the *nakaram* organisation.

The diversification of *nakaram* in particular trade items is also evidenced where the richness of the merchandise was available.

After A. D. 1090, both the words *nagaram* and *nakaram* are used in the inscriptions only to denote a merchant guild and not a market town or a city. Two inscriptions from Kaṭukūr[25] of Khammam district include *nagaram* among the *aṣṭādaśamahā-praja* of the village along with the *mahājanulu, kāmpulu* and others. The *nakaram* organisations, as they are noticed in inscriptions, are given in Tables XI and XII.

As it has been pointed out, *nakaram* is the most basic trade guild of the medieval Talangāṇa. The basic definition of *nakaram* of this time can be given basing on the Khājipet inscription (A.D. 1090).[26] The inscription records that *"Anumakoṇḍapurada seṭṭi pramukha nakaramu"* donated an oilmill to Lord Beteśvara. This trade guild, as it is suggested by its name, is a group of leaders of trading communities (*seṭṭi pramukha*) of Anuma-koṇḍapura. *Pura* means a capital city. Evidently, this *nakaram* consisted of the *pramukhas* or leading member of the trading community. As such, it was not a general body. It was like an executive council. *Nakaram* may therefore be defined as a small body of elders or leaders elected by the general community of traders.

The rural towns that developed as a result of agricultural expansion as well as royal camps, administrative centres (head-quarters of *nāḍus, sthalas* etc.,) and temple towns witnessed the growth of *nakarams*. The 11th and 12th century epigraphs of Telangāṇa region reveal that Paṭāncheruvu, the secondary capital of the Cālukyas of Kalyāṇi; Anmakoṇḍa, the early capital of the Kākatīyas; Pānagal and kandūr, the capitals of the Kandūri Coḍas and Perūr as the main centres of commerce around which the trade network developed in the later centuries. The major temple centres like Alampūr, Vemulavāḍa and Bodhan were important nodal points in the trade network.

At the apex level, the urban centres where the most influential and wealthy *nakarams* were located played a dominant role. The *nakaram* organisation as revealed form the above-noted records of Anumakoṇḍa, Warangal and Paṭāncheruvu was a body of merchants of all categories known as pramukhaseṭṭis. It was local in character integrating all the commerce. Although inscriptions from Anmakoṇḍa do not provide indormation on the organisation aspect, the data from Paṭāncheruvu shows tha the *nagaram* was presided by a *nagaramukhya*.

The structure and functions of nakaram

Kenneth R. Hall [27] gives an account of the *nagaram* as an administrative institution in the age of imperial colas.

According to him, the *nagaram* was an assembly, having administrative functions over a physically defined area (*nāḍu*) . The *nagaram* assigned parts of tax revenues to the local temples and held administrative rights over agricultural lands in the area. The guild administered the affairs of the market place.

Burton Stein[28] holds the view that the *naṭṭār* of the *nāḍu* assembly and the *brahmasabha* members of the *brahmadeya* villages held a large number of administrative responsibilities. However, Hall thinks that the three organisations—*brahmasabha naṭṭār* and the *nagaram* discharged all the major adninistrative functions of a *nāḍu*. While the *sabha* administered a *brahmadeya* village and the *ūrār,* an agricultural village, the *nagaram* administered all the affairs of a market town.

During the perid and in the area under study, it seems that *nagaram* or the *nakaram* lost most of its administrative function and control on the agricultural land. In only one inscription we find the *nakaram* donating agricultural land at the instance of the local ruler. The Bānājipet inscription (A. D. 1082)[29] records that at the instance of Kākatīya Betarasa, a subordinate of Tribhuvanamalla Vikramāditya VI, the *nakaram* of Bānājipt donate wet land on all sides of the village and also residential plots and a flower garden to *Vīrakamalajinālaya*. From this inscription it appears that the *nakaram* was in possession of the land. Such large scale land grants by a *nakaram* organisaiton are not to be found in later inscriptions. It may therefore be inferred that after 11th century A.D., *nagaram* organisations lost exclusive control on agricultural land. The kaṭukūr inscription (A.D. 1303)[30] records a gift of land yielding two crops per year to Gopīnāthaswāmy temple by the *aṣṭādaśamahāpraja* which included the *mahājanulu, kāpulu, balañjiseṭṭigāṇḍru, nagaram* or *nakaram* became a part of the village or local assembly, *aṣṭādaśamahāpraja* which administered the lands of the village and gifts to the temple institutions. This might also suggest that there were no exclusive maket towns in the area in the period under study. Srinivasachari[31] has also expressed the view that *nakaram* of the period did not denote a market town but only an organisation of merchants.

The *nagaram* was generally composed of merchants from a small territorial division such as a town, a *sthalam* or a *kampaṇa*. The Khājīpet inscription (A. D. 1090)[32] cited above suggests that the *nakaram* was composed with the merchats from the city and as such its jurisdiction was confined to the city. Two inscriptions from Chilkūr (A.D. 1096)[33] record a *nakaram* of Chikūrupalli and refers to Chilkūr as the chief town of Lombālika-70, a subdivision of sabbi-1000. From these two inscriptions it may be understood that the jurisdiction of the *nakaram* at Chilkūr extended all over Lombalika-70. An undated inscription[34] from Maktal refers to the town as *Magatala nagaram*. The same inscription refers to it as *Magatala sthalam* consisting of at least eight villages. This indicates that Magatala was a trade centre having a *nakaram* operating in the *sthala*. Table XI gives a list of trade centres where *nakaram* organisations were functioning in a territorial unit consisting of a number of villages. It may be said that all the merchants belonging to that area were general members of the *nakaram*. Here it may be said that the guild functioned integrating the rural areas with the chief town.

The Chilkūr inscription (A. D. 1067)[35] records that the chief of the local nakaram, *Polisetti* was granted certain amounts of money from three classes of shops. An inscription from Paṭāncheruvu[36] refers to a *Nagaramukhya*. These suggest that a *nakaram* had a head or chief marchant. The *Nagaramukhya* collected the amounts from the members and used the money as directed by the *nakaram*. The chief coordinated the affairs of the guild with the ruling classes and other guilds. He presided over the guild meeting and implememted the decisions of the guild.

CLASSIFICATION OF NAKARAM

An examinatin of the records mentioning the *nakarams* shows that the guild can be classified into four categories as follows:-

1. Locality-wise *nakarams*
2. Commodity-wise *nakarams*
3. Composition based *nakarams* and lastly
4. Function-wise *nakarams*.

Locality-wise nakarams

The growth of rural economy gave rise to emergence of several *nakarams*. The Table XI gives the distribution of locality-wise *nakarams*. The Anmakoṇḍapura *nakaram* cited above, as its name suggests, functioned in the city as a market locality. An inscription from Perūr (A.D. 1119) mentions Perūri-*nakaram*.[37] Another inscription from Pānugallu (A. D. 1124)[38] refers to Pānugallu-*nakaram*. These *nakarams* must have been guilds of merchants belonging to either the town or a small territorial division such as a *sthala* or *kampaṇa*. These, along with other *nakaram*

TABLE XI

Locality-wise (Nadu/Sthala) Nakarams

Sl. No.	*Place*	*District*	*Name of the nakaram*	*Locality/territory*	*Ref. with date*
1.	Poṭlapalli	Karīmnagar	Nakaramu		I.A.P. Kn. No 16. A. D. 1066
2.	Chilkūr	(Rangāreḍḍi) Medak	Nakaramu	Lombālika - 70	C.I.T.D. - IV No. 6, p. 39, A. D. 1067.
3.	Khājīpeṭ	Warangal	Anumakoṇḍaseṭṭi Pramukha nakaramu	Anmakoṇḍapaṭṭa-nasthala	I.A.P. Wl. No. 15, A. D. 1090.
4.	Ujjili	Mahaboobnagar	Aśeṣhanakaramu	Kaḷḷakelagunāḍu	Tel. Ins. II, pp. 66-67. A.D. 1097.
5.	Ālavani-palli	"	Nagaramu	Koḍūru-300	Tel. Ins. II, pp. 57-59. A. D. 1110.
6.	Paṭānche-ruvu	Medak	Nagaramu	Paṭancheruvu town	C.I.T.D. - IV, pp. 18-23. undated.
7.	Sirikoṇḍa	Khammam	Nakaramu	Koṇḍavīṭināḍu	K.C.S.H.C. pp. 193-195 A. D. 1148.
8.	Perūru	Nalgoṇḍa	Perūrinakaramu	Perūri Kampaṇam	C.I.T.D. IV, No. 41, undated
9.	Pānugallu	Nalgoṇḍa	Pānugallu nakaramu	Panuganṭisthalam	K.C.S.H.C. p. 166, A. D. 1124
10.	Vardhamāna-puram	Mahaboobnagar	Nakaramu	Attapi-90 in Vaḍḍavaṇa-500	C.I.T.D. III, Mn. 46. pp. 94-97. A. D. 1224.
11.	Warangal	Warangal	Nakaramu	Waragal city	I.A.P . Wl. 63, A. D. 1228.
12.	Magatala	Mahaboobnagar	Magatalanagaram	Magatala sthalam	Tel. Ins. II, pp. 161-162. undated
13.	Kaṭukūr	Khammam	Nagaramu	Kaṭṭukūr sthalam	C.I.T.D. III, pp. 16-17. A. D. 1303.

organisations having no prefixes, traded in all types of commodities. For example, the *nakarams* of *Vardhamānapuram*[39] (Mn. dist.), Sirikoṇḍa[40] (Km. dist.), Ālavānipalli[41] (Mn. Dist.), Kaṭukūr[42] (Km. dist.), Chilkūr[43] (Kn. dist.), Rāchūr[44] (Mn. dist.) traded in almost all commodities like grain, oil, arecanuts, betal leaf, cloth and metals.

Commodity-wise nakarams

Another type of *nakaram* organisation was based on the commodity in which the merchants traded. For example, the Girmājipet inscription (A.D. 1228)[45] mentions *Chīramaṭṭi-nakaram*, traded exclusively in cloth. The Maṭṭewāḍa inscription[46] (undated) mentions Gandha *aśesha nakaramu* which traded in sandal. The same inscription refers to *Ponkanakaramu* which exclusively traded in arecanuts. The Kushmahal inscription[47] mentions *Pañchalohāla nagaramu* whose merchandise was evidently metals. The Govindāpuram inscription (A. D. 1122)[48] mentions a guild of horse traders known as *Ghoṭakabhyu-vyavahārulu* of *vājikula*. The inscription does not call it a *nakaram* though it was a trade guild exclusively trading in horses. The members of the *Vājikula* called thesmslves *Vaiśyakulavardhanulu*[49] which denotes that they were *vaiśyas*.

Another corporate body having a number of branches engaged in the trade of metals and alloys was the *Pañchalohāla nakaramu*. This guild is also referred to as *Pañchalohāla behārulu*. The maṭṭevāḍa inscription (undated, Ganapatideva's regnal period)[50] records some gifts made by this *nakaram* to Maṭṭiyawāḍa somanāthadeva. The metals and alloys traded in by this *nakaram* might be copper, tin, iron, lead and zinc. The Warangal fort inscription (A. D. 1228)[51] mentions *tagaremvāru* as a guild trading in tin and lead and *mūsaravāru* as a guild trading in copper. These guilds might be branches of *Pañchalohāla nakaram* .

The trade in gold and silver appear to have been carried on by the *Bacchumaṭṭe nakaram* discussed below.

Miscellaneous nakarams

There are certain other *nakarams* which discharged specific

TABLE XII

Commodity-wise & Function-wise Nakarams

S. No.	Place	District	Name	Commodity/Function	Ref. with date
			A. Commodity-wise		
1.	Pānugallu	Nalgonda	Nibaramanakaram	Cloth of fine variety	Tel. Ins. I. pp. 169-172 A. D. 1132.
2.	Girmājīpet	Warangal	Chīramaṭinakaram	Cloth and silver	I.A.P. Wl. 61. A.D. 1228.
3.	Warangal	"	Gandhyaaśeshanakaram	Sandal	I.A.P. Wl. 62, undated
4.	Maṭṭewāḍa	"	1) Panchalohāla-behāramāḍeḍi nakaram	Metals	I.A.P. Wl. 68, undated
5.	Warangal	"	2) Gandhaaśesha nakaram	Sandal	-do-
			3) Pomkhanakaram	Arecanuts	-do-
6.	Warangal	"	1) Panchalohālanakaram	Metals	-do-
			2) Gandhaaśeshanakaram	Sandalwood	-do-
			3) Pomkanagaramu	Arecanuts	-do-
7.	Warangal	"	Nūnebehārulu	Oil	I.A.P. Wl. 63. A. D. 1228.
8.	Warangal	"	Kūragāyabehārulu	Vegetables	I.A.P. Wl. 63. A. D. 1228

(1)	(2)	(3)	(4)	(5)	(6)
			B. Functin-wise		
9.	Bānājipet	Warangal	Savaṭunakaram	Exchange of goods	I.A.P. Wl. 14 A. D. 1082
10.	Maṭṭewāḍa	"	Santanagaram	Administration of weekly market	I.A.P. Wl. 68, undated
11.	Warangal	"	Santanakaramu	Same as above	I.A.P. Wl. 63, A. D. 1228
12.	Warangal	"	Maṭṭeaśeshanakaram	Charged with maintenace of clock	I.A.P. Wl. 63. A. D. 1228
13.	Meṭṭewāḍa	"	Bachchumāḍanakaram	Exchange of money	I.A.P. Wl. 68, undated
14.	Warangal	"	Bachchumaṭṭenagaramulu	-do-	I.A.P. Wl. 68, undated

functions. The inscriptions from the Warangal fort (A. D. 1228), Maṭṭewāḍa (undated) and Kushmahal (undated) mention *Santanagaram* or *Santanakaram*. *Santa* in Telugu means a fair held periodically. It appears, therefore, that the function of the *Santhanakaram* was to make arragements for the holding mentions *Maṭṭteaśesha-nakaram*. Another inscription from Ujjili (A.D. 1097)[52] mentions *aśeshanakaram*. The phrase "*aśesha*" might mean "all inclusive". It might be either a apex body of all the *nakarams*. The *maṭṭeaśeshanakaram* of Warangal fort was entrusted with the maintenance of a clock at the market place. The Kushmahal inscription refers to one *bachchumaṭṭenakaram*. The Maṭṭewāḍa inscription mentions *bacchumāḍa nagaram* whose functions were not specified. This *bacchumāḍa* may be a mistake of the scribe for *bacchmaṭṭe nakaram*. This *nakaram* finds mention in one of the inscriptions at Pāṇem (A. D. 1319)[53] in kurnool district. The function of this *Bacchumaṭṭenakaram* is considered to be exchange of money of different types.

COMPOSITION OF NAKARAM

An inscription from Perūr (A.D. 1119)[54] refers to *Aruva-nakaram* and *Telugunakaram*. These names indicate the composition of the guilds, the former consisting of the merchants from Tamilnād and the latter of Telugu seaking merchants. The *samayamupēmṭa* mentioned in the same epigraph might indicate a market conducted by Kannaḍa merchants.

ARTISAN-MERCHANT GROUPS

During the 11th and 12th centuries, the *nakaram* guild appears to be composed of a number of communities as it replaced and substituted for the *samaya* organisation. But, as the trade guilds became diversified in industrial *nakaram* guilds appear to have been dominated by the *komaṭi* community. While mentioning the components of the *aṣṭādaśamahāpraja*, some records[55] note the *nakaram* along with *sālevāru, akkasālevāru, telikavāru* but not *komaṭis* as a caste. This leads to the conclusion that the *nakaram* was composed of one homogeneous community i.e., the *komaṭivāru*.

The second kind of trade guilds operating in a locality are

the artisan-mercantile groups such as the *Telikivevuru* and *Dharmasāliyajanulu*

Telikivevuru

An undated inscription[56] from *Anmakoṇḍa* during the time of Vikramditya VI recoards the gift made to the local temple by *Telikivevuru seṭṭis* on the day of *Uttarāyaṇa sankrānti*. An undated sanskrit inscription from Maktal[57] refers to the gifts made to God Svamyambhu Mallinātha of the Magatala by *vaiśyas, telikis* and other communities of Magatala *nagaram*.

An undated inscription from Konakanchi[58] of Krishna district of the time of Potarāju (Konakanchi is in the present Jaggayya-peṭa-Nandigāma region which was known in medieval times as Natavadi and is contiguous with Telangāṇa and was ruled by the subordinates of Kākatīyas) mentions one Kuṛṛiseṭṭi of teliki community who presented two lamps of the local temple. This inscription also mentions Bejawāḍa *telikivevuru*. Two inscriptions from Nādenḍla[59] also mention Bejawāḍa *Telilkivevuru*. In these inscriptions *Telikivevuru* are referred to as *Bejawāḍa śāsanulu*. The Ṭeki inscription[60] mentions the Teliki community as having thousand branches with names like *Velumanūka, Pallipālu Naṛillu, Kumudallu, Maṛṛruḷḷu, Povanḍlu, Svavākulu, Undrāḷḷu, Anumagunḍalu* and *Aḍḍalanūḷla*.

From the above account it is understood that the *Telikivevuru* were a corporate body consisting of number of branches whose main occupations were manufature of oil and wholesale and retail trade in it.

The Nādenḍla inscription refers to the *Telikivevuru* as Bejawāḍa *śāsanulu*. Sundaram remarks[61] that the member of the communityhad met at Bejawāḍa and gave themselves a charter of trade and a code of conduct.

Sālevāru

Another important corporate body who were engaged in both manufacture and trade was the *sāle* commuity. The Girmājīpet inscription (A. D. 1228)[62] mentions that on instructions from *Dharmasālīyajanulu*, Nijarangāla Malliseṭṭi and his son Veniseṭṭi built three temples for saleśvara, Gaṇapeśvara and Sakaleśvara. The *Dharma sāliyajanulu* directed that one *vīsa* in each *gadyāṇam* on sales of cloth be donated to these temples. They also directed the *Chīramaṭṭi nakaram* to grant some amounts to Lord Nakareśvara in *Chīramaṭṭi* from each cloth shop.

The *sālīyajanulu* mentioned in the above inscription are same as the Sālevāru mentioned as one of the 18 communities of a village or town and were engaged in production and trade of cloth.

An inscription from Āvanca (A. D. 1104)[63] and another record from Ālavānipalli (A.D.1110)[64] refer to *Paṭṭasāle* community. This appears to be a branch of the sāle community. This community apears to have engaged themselves in the manufacture and trade of silk cloth.

From the above, we may say that in the period there functioned organisations which were engaged both in trade and idustry. The *Telikivevuru* and *Sālīyajanulu* were such organisations. It is also interesting to note that each of these organisations had several branches.

ITINERENT TRADE GUILDS

Itinerant trade guilds played an important role in the trade activity of medieval Telangāṇa. Although the trading activity individually and collectively by the early organisations like *Ayyāvaḷi* 500 was in evidence before the eleventh century, the growing needs of royal and temple centres in different agrarian regions and political expansion of the Colas and the Cālukyas brought the region into larger commercial net-work.

The Telangāṇa region was noted for its iron and steel products, textiles and diamonds. The growth of rural economy was significant feature of this period. Being a landlocked country, it depended for many commodities such as salt on the itinerent merchants. As the local production was mainly agricultural, it depended for many non-agricultural commodities on the neighbouring lands such as Karnāṭaka, coastal Āndhra and Tāmilanāḍ and therefore itinerent trade existed form very early times. some of the members of this itinerent merchant communities slowly settled down at various market centres. But they referred to themselves as affililates of the original communities in many inscriptions.[65]

The itinerent merchants were generally called *nānādeśi*, which means that the members of the guild belonged to several countries or regions. An early inscription from Polasa (A.D. 1108)[66] records gifts made to Lord Polesteśvara of Polavāsa in the Jagityal taluk of Karimnagar district by three merchant guilds namely *Vīrabalāñja*, *Ayyāvaḷi* 500, *Mummūridaṇḍa* of 36 bidus and Samastha Ubhaya Nanadesi Pekkandru. These three appear to have different origins and different compositions. A Kannaḍa inscription from Perūr[67] (A. D. 1119) refers to nine trade guilds meeting at the temple of Lord Svayambhu Somanātha and gifting two the temple of Lord Svayambhu Somanātha and gifting two *Hagas* in evey hundred *Hires* of all the varieties of articles traded at that centre. These are.

1) *Gangaramuvvatār* (Gangaras of 36 towns)
2) *Ghaṭaraharu Padunenṭi bīḍu* (Ghatarahus of 18 towns)
3) *Tulila Sandavāru*
4) *Allavajjiyavāru*
5) *Balāñjiyavāru*
6) *Ṛāmaḍuvāru*
7) *Nallarumaḍuvāru*
8) *Śankarapādivāru*
9) *Māḍuvalavāru*

These merchant guilds appear to have been coming from the neighbouring Kannaḍa country. The Govindāpuram inscription (A. D. 1122)[68] records the gift of an itinerent guild of horse-traders known as *Ghoṭakabhyu vyavahārulu* to Jaina Pārśvanātha. They remitted one pair of China silk cloth per each horse they sold. The Warangal Fort inscription (A. D. 1228) refers to *Deśi*, *Paradeśivāḍalavāru* and *Svadeśi paradeśi behārulu* engaged in the trade of indigo and betel leaf.

Table XIII gives alist of inscription recording the itinerent trade guilds operating in Telangāṇa. The areas to which their operations spread and the commodities in which they traded are also given in the Table wherever such information is available.

Ayyāvaḷi 500

Among the itinerent trade guilds, the *vīrabalāñja* community affiliated to *Ayyāvaḷi* 500 is the most significant in Telangāṇa.

The *Ayyāvaḷi* 500 was perhaps the largest and the most powerful and richest itinerent trade guild of south India whose operations extended to entire Deccan and south India. The Ayyāvaḷi stands for "Aihole" a town near Badami in Karnataka. However, the Ayyāvaḷi 500 was not a single body and the headquarters did not remain at Aihole permanently. Subsequent to the 9th and 10th cneturies, *Ayyāvaḷi* 500 represented various mercantile groups of different regions and communities. In the inscriptions of 11th century, we come across the terms *nānādeśi, ubhaya nānādeśi, svadeśi* and *paradesi, vīrabalāñjas, mummūridaṇḍas* along with *Ayyāvaḷi* 500. The later two terms denote the militant character. Thus the common interests and unity of the guild are reflected in their *praśastis* and naming several towns as southern *Ayyavoles* in the 11th and 12th centuries.

Sundaram[69] Champakalakshmi[70] and Hall[71] have said that this guild first met at Aihole and gave themselves a code of merchantile conduct known as *vīrabalāñja samaya*. The word *Samaya* means a code of condust to be followed by the members of the community. The phrase *vīrabalāñja* is a corrupt form of *vīravaṇija* meaning a heroic merchant. Their *praśasti* contains phrases like *vīrasahasra, virājitāsāhasra*[72] etc., It may be said that this trade guild was well-armed. The members were ready to fight to protect their caravan and merchandise. Most probably, they had a small division of an army following them. Hall finds[73] similarities between *Ayyāvaḷi Ainnūruvār* and *"Tichaiyayerattainnūrruvār"*, an it intenerent merchant organisation operating in the Tamil country during Cola times. *Ticaiyayerattainnūrruvār* means the 500 merchants of the thousand directions. It may be said that the original founders of this corporation numbered five hundred. The *Ayyāvaḷi* organisations had members from the four linguistic groups of south India. Their territory of operation was divided into two zones of 18 cities each (1) north of Kāveri river and (2) south of the Kāveri.

The inscriptions of Telangāṇa region reveal that Ayyāvaḷi 500 were associated with Alampūr, a temple town, and Peddakaḍumūr, Polasa, Peddapariyāla the market centres in the

TABLE XIII

Itinerent Trades Guilds in Telangāṇa (A. D. 1000-1325)

Sl. No.	*Place/Territorial division*	*Name of the trade guild*	*Articles of trade*	*Remarks*	*Ref. with date*
(1)	(2)	(3)	(4)	(5)	(6)
1.	Alampūr (Yāje-300)	1) Ayyāvaḷi - 500 2) Mummūridaṇḍas of 36 bīḍus 3) Nālsāsi Renum.	-- --	--	Tel. Ins. II, p. 87. A. D. 1182
2.	Gangāpuram (Kodur-300)	Seṭṭlis of 36 bīḍus	--	--	Tel. Ins.I, pp. 105-106. Mahaboobnagar dt.
3.	Gangāpuram (Koḍur-300)	Samastasethikāra samaya	--	--	Tel. Ins. I, pp. 118-119.
4.	Āvanca	Samaya	--	--	Tel. Ins. II. pp. 60-62. (A. D. 1124)
5.	Paṭāncheruvu	Seṭṭikāra samaya	--	--	C.I.T.D. IV, No. 21. (A. D. 1127).
6.	Perūru (Perūru Kampaṇamu) (A. D. 1119)	1) Gangarumuvvāttāru 2) Haṭarahas of 18 towns 3) Tulila Sanduru 4) Ālavajji 5) Balānjigas 7) Nallas 8) Maḍuvas 9) Śankarapādis	--	--	C.I.T.D. IV No. 12. pp. 27-28 (A. D. 1119)

(1)	(2)	(3)	(4)	(5)	(6)
7.	Peddakaḍumūr	1) Ayyāvaḷi - 500 2) Mummūridanḍas of 36 bīḍus 3) Kannaḍanālkusāsira	--	--	Tel Ins. II. p. 87. A. D. 1181.
8.	Polasa (Ugravadi) (A. D. 1108)	1) Vīrabalāñja Ayyāvaḷi-500. 2) Mummūridanḍas of 36 bīḍus	--	--	I.A.P. Kn. 75. (A. D. 1108)
9.	Govindapuram (A. D. 1122)	Ghoṭakabhyuvaharibhihi	Horses	The guild donated one pair of China Silk per each horse	I.A.P. Wl. No. 26 A. D. 1122
10.	Kucimanchi	Vīrabalāñja	--	--	C.I.T.D. III. Kn. 9, pp. 19-21. (A. D. 1260) Khammam dist.
11.	Pedapariyāla (Chinapariyala sthala, Karim-nagar dist., (undated)	Vīrabalāñja Ayyāvaḷi-500	Paddy, betel leaf, Arecanut, oil.	(An. itine-rent merchants guild that settled down at Pariyāla)	I.A.P. Kn. No. 38. (Undated) (Pratāparudra's time)

Godāvari valley. From the 11th century or even prior to that, the presence of *Ayyāvaḷi*-500 was in the Telangāṇa region controlling the trade that connected the hinterlands of Krishna-Tugabhadra valleys from Alampūr, Gangāpuram, Peddakaḍumūr, Kūcimanchi i n the central part of Telangāṇa on the trade route connecting Warangal. Vāḍapalli was another important centre in the Mūsi valley.

The merchandise of Ayyāvaḷi-500 included elephants, horses, precious stones, diamonds, cardamom, cloves, sandal, musk , camphor, salt and perfumes and drugs.

It was necessary fo the itinerent merchants to have cordial relations with the local merchant guilds like the *nakaram* and therefore some members of this community appear to have settled down at various trade centres throughout the Āndhra country including Telangāṇa. Moreover, they forged alliances with local merchants and formed bigger organisations known as the *Pekkaṇḍru*. The *pekkaṇḍru* organisations such as the *sthalamu-samastha pekkaṇḍru*[74] and the *cālumūla samasta pekkaṇḍdru*[75] were associated with *vīrabalāñja* community of *Ayyāvaḷi*-500. Thus it may be said that this community formed bigger organisatiuon with local merchants as well as itinerent merchants from other coutries.

Mūmūridaṇḍas-36

The Kannaḍa inscription[75a] from Peddakaḍumūr of Kālachūri Āhavamalla (A.D. 1181) mentions the trade guild *"Muvvattār Bīḍu Mummūridaṇḍa* along with *Vīrabalāñja Dharma Ayyāvaḷi Ainnūrvāru svāmi*. The inscription records a number of injuctions for the welfare of these guilds. Another Kannaḍa inscription from Alampūr[76] of the time of the same monarch refers to the grant of certain taxes to Lord Gaureśvara. The inscription mentions the areas in which these guilds traded which was styled as *mahānāḍus*. These are Tumbula *Sthalavu,* Gobbura *Sthalavu*, Nayikalla *Sthalavu,* and Dakshinavārāṇāsi (Alampūr). Here *mahānāḍu* denotes groups of villages of different localities as they are referred to as *sthalas*. The Gangāpuram inscription of Jagadekamalla's time[77] mentions the grants made by some *seṭṭis* belonging to *muvvattāra biḍanaseṭṭi kararu*. The Polasa inscription[78] in Karimnagar district (A. D. 1107) refers to the *Mummūridaṇḍas* of *36 bīḍus*.

The word *bīḍu* means a market town. This *muvvattārubīḍu mummūridaṇḍas* must have been an itinerent trade guild having an army of its own, called *Mummūridaṇḍas*. It may be said that this trade guild had its major mercantile ooperations in 36 market towns of South India. Somasekhara Sarma expresses the view that the *Mummūruidaṇḍas* were an advance guard of the trading caravan and bore the flag staff with three bands. The trade guild might have got its name from its army.

Thus the south-western part of Telangāṇa particularly the Krishana-Tungabhadra valley formed an agrarian zone in which several markets were organised. The supralocal Character of *Mummūridaṇḍas*-36 is revealed by an inscription from Alampūr[79] according to which its activities extended from Gobbūru in the west to Alampūr which constituted the main zone of the integrated market. Their spread from this zone to places like Polasa in the north Telangāṇa in the Godāvari valley further reveals the extended activities of the guild.

Another itinerent guild mentioned along with Ayyāvaḷi-500 and *Mummūridaṇḍas of 36 bīḍus* is the Kannaḍa *nālkusāsira*.[80] This trade guild may be called Kannaḍ-4000. It was perhaps commposed of Kannaḍa merchants. The Gangāpuram inscription[81] mentions another guild known as *nālvaruseṭṭi*. among these various guilds, it was the *Ayyāvaḷi*-500 which existed till recent times. The last epigraphical reference to the guild comes from the inscription from Bangalore dated in the year A. D. 1706.[82] It is said that the other itinerent trade guilds got incorporated into the *Ayyāvaḷi*-500 and the latter became a federal corporation of itinerent trade and overseas commerce.

The Pekkaṇḍru

Generally the members of itinerent trade guilds settled down at different places with a view to have cordial relations with the local guilds such as the *nakaram*. Such settlements are found in various trade centres throughout the Āndhradeśa including Telangāṇa. The itinerent merchants forged alliances with local traders and formed bigger organisations known as the *pekkaṇḍru*. These are given in Table XIV.

Ther term *pekkaṇḍru* in Telugu means many. As such, the *pekkaṇḍru* organisation constituted by a large number of merchats from the local and itinerent merchants. It was a joint corporation comprising the local guilds, artisan organisations and itinerant guilds. The itinerent merchants brought several kinds of merchandise from far-off lands and exchanged them with local guilds. In turn, the itinerent merchants purchased the locally available surpluses. Thus, the *pekkaṇḍru* organisation provided the means for exchange of local goods for non-local goods and vice-versa.

The *pekkaṇḍru* organisations are found with a variety of suffixes. These suffixes define the nature of the corporation. The heirarchy of *Pekkaṇḍru* organisations as mentioned in inscriptions of Āndhradeśa as pointed out by R. Narasimha Rao[83] are : (1) Town based *Pekkaṇḍru*, (2) *Sthala Pekkaṇḍru* (3) *Nāḍu pekkaṇḍru*, (4) *Nānādeśi Pekkaṇḍru* , (5) *Ubhayanānā Deśi Pekkaṇḍru (6) Cālumūla Ubhayanānādeśi Pekkaṇḍru* (7) *Mahānāḍu Pekkaṇḍru*.

Sthalamu Pekkaṇḍru

The Yanamadala inscriptrion[84] dated in the year A. D. 1260 mention *Yanamadala sthalam pekkaṇḍru* as an affiliate of *Ubhaya-nānādeśi pekkaṇḍru* of the *vīrabalāñja* dharma and were the chiefs of Pākanāḍu-21,000, Vēṅgi-16,000 and Anmakoṇḍa Paṭṭana sthala. The *pekkaṇḍru* collected a fee from its members called "*magama*". The Alampūr inscription[85] (A. D. 1299) records the grant of 5 *marturs* of black soil by the *sthalamu samastha pekkaṇḍru*, who were associates of *Ayyāvaḷi*-500 of the *vīrabalāñja samaya dharma*. The prefix *sthalamu* indicates that the jurisdiction of the *pekkaṇḍru* was over a *sthalam* in which the *pekkaṇḍru* undertook exchange of goods.

Sthalam pekkaṇḍru are mentioned in inscriptions from places of great commerical importance like Anumakoṇḍa and Alampūr. Therefore, it may be taken that the *pekkaṇḍru* functioning as a unit at the *sthala* division, must have existed at the temple and administrative centres where several *nakarams* existed. As the inscriptions describe *pekkaṇḍru* as the *prabhumukhyas* i.e., the

TABLE XIV

Pekkaṇḍru Organisations in Telangāṇa

Sl. No.	*Place*	*Prefix of the Pekkaṇḍru*	*Other guilds mentioned*	*Articles of trade/remarks*	*Rerence*
1.	Polasa	Samastha Ubhayanānā-deśi	1) Ayyāvḷi-500 2) Mummūridaṇḍas of 36 bīḍus	--	I.A.P. Kn. 15
2.	Warangal	Ubhayanānādeśi	1) Svadeśiparadeśi-behārulu	Camphor, Sandal musk, silk thread, Ivory, precious stones, pearls, many agricultual products and industrial products	I.A.P. Wl. 63,
3.	Alampūr	Sthalam Samastha	Ayyavole-500	--	C.I.T.D. II,
4.	Peddaka-ḍumur	Ubhayanānādeśi	1) Ayyavole-500 2) Mummūridaṇḍas of 36 Bīḍus. 3) Kannaḍanālkusā-sira	--	Tel. Ins. II, p. 87.
5.	Alampūr	Ubhayanānādeśi	1) Ayyavole-500 2) Mummūridaṇḍas of 36 Bīḍus. 3) Nalsāsi Revum.	--	Tel. Ins. II, p. 88
6.	Gangāpuram	Nānādeśi	--	--	Tel. Ins. I, p. 128.

royal fovourites, they had a dominant role in the commercial transactions of the area, as buyers and sellers of a region. In the epigraphs of Telangāṇa, the town based *pekkaṇḍru* appear only at Anumakoṇḍa.[86]

Nānādeśi pekkaṇḍru

Two inscriptions from Tripurāntakam (A.D. 1270[87] and A. D. 1292)[88] and one from Gangāpuram[89] (undated) refer to *nānādeśi pekkaṇḍru* trading in rice, greengram and other agricultual products. The *nānādeśi* directed the members that *magama* at the rate of 2 *vīsas* per *māḍa* of all articles sold at Tripurāntakam *pēmṭa* be remited to Lord Nagareśvara.

The prefix *nānādeśi* means that the merchants belonged to or coming from several countries and they formed a *pekkaṇḍru* corporation including local guilds.

Ubhayanānādeśi

Ubhayanānādeśi pekkaṇḍru was the most prominent of the *pekkaṇḍru* organisation. The Peddakaḍumūru inscription[90] and the Alampūr inscription[91] of the time of Kālachuri Āhavamalla mention the *Ubhayanānādeśi* as consisting of the *Ayyāvaḷi*-500, *Mummūridaṇḍas* of 36 *bīḍus* and Kannaḍa *nālkusāsira* guilds. The Warangal fort inscription (A.D. 1228)[92] mentions that a variety of luxury articles like sandal, musk, silk thread, silk cloth, wool, pearls, etc., besides agricultural products like turmeric, vegetables, wooden furniture and cotton thread in which the guild traded. Trade in indigo[93] and other articles by *deśi, paradeśivāḍalavāru, svadeśi paradeśi behārulu* is mentioned along with the trade by the *ubhayanānādeśi*.

The name *ubhayanānādeśi pekkaṇḍru* indicates that this organisation consisted of the stationery local merchants and itinerent merchants. It was conposed of *vīrabalañjas* of Ayyavole, *nānādesi, ticaiyāyirattaiññūṟṟuvar* and the wealthy merchants like *Deśi-paradeśi-vāḍalavāru, paradeśi-behārulu* might also be members of *ubhayanānādeśi*

From a comparison of the inscriptions available in Telangāṇa region and those in coastal Āndhra and Rāyalasīma, it may be said that the *pekkaṇḍru* corporations were more active in the latter regions. The Ṭanguṭūr inscription (A. D. 1315)[94] refers to the donation of *magama* to Lord Somanātha by *Cālumūla samastha pekkaṇḍru*. This guild was mentioned i n the Ūṭukūru inscription of the same district[95] (A. D. 1370) as affiliated to *Ayyāvaḷi*-500 along with *Ūṭukūrinagaram* and *Vīrapurāntakulu*. This *cālumūla samastha pekkaṇḍru* might mean a guild of merchants coming from various countries from all directions. An inscription form Tangeḍa,[96] a river port in Guntur district, mentions a guild called a *cālumūla ubhayanānādeśi pekkaṇḍru* with titles-*virabalāñja dharma pratiṣhṭāpaka, garuḍadhvaja virājita, kadanapra-chaṇḍra, Ayyavāḷi puravarādhīśvara*. This guild might have included armed intinerent merchants coming from all the directions and the local merchants. The Moṭupalli inscription (A.D. 1358)[97] mentions *paradeśi vyavahārulu* and *dvīpāntara-vyavahārulu*. Evidently these were merchants from countries across the ocean.

STATE POLICY TOWARDS TRADE

Though the entire trade was conducted by the guilds which enjoyed considerable freedom, the state exericised its power through the bureaucratic machinery.

Contemporary or near contemporary literery works such as the *Vijñāneśvaram*[98] and the *Sakalanitisammatam*[99] describe the policy of the state towards trade. It was policy of encouragement and control. The *Vijñāneśvaram* states that it was the responsibility of the state to see and the correct weights and measures were used by traders and take measures against hoarding and arbitrary pricing.[100] Again, the king was to take steps to coordinate the activities of merchants, collect taxes and punish the mischievous traders.[101] The *Sakalanītisammatam* states that the king should encourage foreign merchants by giving them permission to trade in his kingdom.[102]

Inscriptional evidence shows that the textual injunctions were followed to the possible extent by the rulers of the period. There were officers functioning at the trade centres. Some of the officers had troops under them. This was perhaps necessitated by the fact that itinerant guilds had armed men accompanying them. The Cālukyas had officers like *vaḍḍarāvula daḍanāyaka*.[103] Two tax officers at Jaḍcherla as mentioned in an inscription dated A. D. 1162 were *daḍanāyakas*.[104]

While following the same policy, the Kākatīyas took great interest in imporoving trade. Gaṇapatideva's *abhayaśāsana* at the port town of Moṭupalli[105] is an example evidence for the same. Most of the trade cntres became the capitals of *māṇḍalikas* and *nāyankaras*. Tax officials like *sunkādhikāri*,[106] *sthala karaṇam*[107] and *tīrpari*[108] functioned at these towns. The names of the officers reveal that they not only collected the levies but settled disputes between probably different trade guilds and between the officers and guilds.

Articles of trade

The table XV shows different trade organisations and the items of trade that entered the markets. The items of trade can be classified as:- (1) agricultural products, (b) industrial products (c) forest products and (d) minerals and metals. The Warangal Fort inscription classifies trade articles as *Ettubhāṇḍālu, Būsibhāṁḍālu* and *Maṇibhāṇḍālu*.

a) *Agrilutral Products*

Grain, mostly jowar, paddy, rice and wheat and among pulses greengram were the agriculturl products that made their way into almost every market. These are called as the *būsibhāṇḍālu*. Cotton, pepper, betel leaf and arecanuts, were the other agricultural products that entered the markets. Cotton and betel leaf were produced locally. It appears that pepper and arecanuts were imported into the Telangāṇa markets from Karnāṭaka. Turmeric, gingelly, indigo are the other important agricultural products that were marketed. Wool is another item sold in the market.

b) *Industrial products*

Among the products of agro-industrial activity, cotton and silk textiles, cotton and silk thread and jute articles found their way into markets. Oil was the most marketed agro-industrial product. Salt was an important product marketed in Telangāṇa by itinerent merchants.

It is signifincant to note that metallic objects like measures, plates, lamp posts, tools and utensils are not found at trade cntres. Perhaps they were made to order or sold and purchased locally.

c) ***Forest Products***

Among the forest products, sandalwood and its powder are the most significant items sold and purchased. The *Gandha aśesha nakaram*[109] specialised in their trade at Warangal. Woodcrafts such as carts, cots, boxes and caskets were sold at many markets.

Tamarind is another forest product sold at many trade centres.

d) ***Metals and Minerals***

The *Pañchalohāla nakaramu* was the guild that traded in metals. The metals that were traded included copper, tin, zinc, iron and lead. It is not certain that gold and silver were traded at markets. The *mūsaravāru* mentioned in the Warangal Fort inscription might be making and selling metal moulds as suggested by the word "*mūsa*" which in Telugu means a mould. Alloys such as brass, bronze and steel were also articles of trade as suggested by the mention of articles made of them in inscriptions and literary works.

The trade in precious stones is mentioned in the Warangal fort inscription.[110] These precious sstones included *ravva* (diamond) and glass beads.

Other items of trade are camphor, musk, ivory, and pearls. It is probable that these were imported and carried into the area under study by itinerant traders.

The Moṭupalli charter of Gaṇapatideva (A. D. 1244)[111] mentions several items of trade and the rates of duties levied on them. However, the items included both exports and imports, But the items of import are clear in the list. The articles mentioned in the epigraph are sandal, camphor, pearls, rosewater, ivory, civet, copper, zinc, mercury, lead, silk-thread, corals, perfumes, pepper, silk, cotton textiles, pepper and arecanuts. Elephants and horses were imported whereas gems were among the exports. Some of the items mentioned in the Moṭupalli charter are found at the markets in the Telangāṇa area.

TRADE CENTRES

The surplus agricultural production and industrial activity gave rise to a large number of trade centres all over the Telangāṇa region. Table XV gives a list of trade centres and the commodities that entered the markets there. The Table makes it clear that many of the trade centres such as Warangal, Sirikoṇḍa, Vardhamāna-puram, Alampūr, Gangāpuram and Pānugallu were also political headquarters of either the Sovereign or a *sāmanta* chief. Warangal became a large trade centre with three trading places viz., Warangal, Anmakoṇḍa and Mattewāḍa. The Warangal Fort inscription (A. D. 1228) refers to specific markets like *nuvvulapēmṭta* and *uppupēmṭa*.[112]

In addition to the trade centres that developed at the centres of political power, each *sthalam* had its own market place. These were known as *sthalamupēmṭas*. As had been discussed earlier, the *sthalamu* is a territorial unit of a group of villages. Some of the *sthalams* mentioned in inscriptions are market towns like *Anmakoṇḍa paṭṭaṇa sthalam,* (Anmakoṇḍa) *Magatala sthalam* (Magatala) *China Pariyāla Sthalam* (Peda periyāla).

Trade centres also developed at places where a good number of temples came up. Some examples are Alampūr, Gangāpuram and Govindāpuram.

The following Table illustrates the classification of trade centres.

TABLE XV (A)

S. No.	*Type of trade Centre*	*Examples*
1.	Sthalam markets (Rural trade centres)	Chilkūr,[113] Tekumbeḍḍa[114]
2.	Temple towns	Alampūr,[115] Govindāpuram[116]
3.	Administrative Centres	Paṭāncheruvu,[117] Pānugallu[118]
4.	Industrial Centres	Ālavānipalli,[119] Maṭṭweāḍa[120]
5.	Cantonment towns	Ujjili,[121] Magatala[122]
6.	River ports	Vāḍapalli,[123] Yeleśwaram[124]

TABLE XV (B)

Trade Centres

Sl. No.	Name of the Trade centre	Guilds trading at the centre	Articles of Trade, etc.	Reference
(1)	(2)	(3)	(4)	(5)
1.	Bānājipeṭ	Savaṭunakaram		I.A.P. Wl. 14.
2.	Govindāpuram	1. Ghoṭakatabhyuvyavahari	Horses	I.A.P. Wl. 26,
		2. Vāji-Kula		" "
3.	Hanumakonda	Telikivevuru	Oil	I.AP. Wl. 28
4.	Girmājipeṭ	1. Dharmasāliyajanulu	Cloth	I.A.P. Wl. 61
		2. Chīramaṭṭinakaramu	"	"
5.	Warangal Fort	Gandhya Aśeshanakaramu	Jute Bags, Cotton-thread	I.A.P. Wl. 62
6.	Warangal Fort	1. Maṭṭiyanakaram	Cloth	I.A.P. Wl 63
		2. Deśiparadeśi vāḍalavāru	Indigo	
		3. Ponkamaṭṭiya (Svadeśi Paradeśi)	Arecanut, Betel leaf	
		4. Kūragāyabehārulu	Vegetables	
		5. Nūvulapēmta	Pulses, Paddy etc.	
		6. Upppupēmṭa	Salt	
		7. Nūnebehārulu	Oil	
		8. Aśeshanakaramu	Maintainance of clock	
		9. Santhanakaram	Rice	
		10. Gandhyamvāru		

(1)	(2)	(3)	(4)	(5)
		11. Tagaramvāru 12. Mūsaravāru 13. Ubhayanānādeśi	Variety of goods including luxury items	
7.	Maṭṭewāḍa	1. Pancalohāla behārulu 2. Gandha Aśeshanakaram 3. Babumadanagaram 4. Pomkanagaram 5. Santhanagaram	Five metals Sandal powder	I.A.P. Wl. 68
8.	Ākunūru	No Nakaram is mentioned. But it appears to be a trade centre	Measures like Ettu-bhaṇḍam, Koluchu Bhaṇḍam and Gadyāṇamu, Rūka, Māḍa, Cinnamu are mentioned.	I.A.P. Wl. 37
9.	Pedapariyāla	Vīrabaliñja	Paddy, Arecanut, betel leaf	I.A.P. Kn. 38
10.	Polasa	1. Vīrabalāñja 2. Mummūridaṇḍa (Belonging to 36 bīḍus) 3. Samasta Ubhayanānādeśi		I.A.P. Kn. 75
11.	Chilkūr	Nakaram	Dramma and Angaḍi Siddhāyamu is mentioned Uttama, Madhyama and Kanishṭa Angaḍi are mentioned	C.I.T.D. IV, No.6 pp. 6-11

(1)	(2)	(3)	(4)	(5)
12.	Mellaceruvu		The term cinna is mentioned and Komaṭivaru, Sālevāru,	C.I.T.D. Part-II pp. 88-90.
			Gollavaru are mentioned. Black soil, white soil and wet land is mentioned	Tel. Ins, Vol. I. No. 50, p, 92
13.	Nāgulapāḍu	--	Komaṭlu, Īdaravaru. gollalu, Akasālevāru are mentioned	C.I.T.D. Part-II pp. 94-95.
14.	Perur	1. Gangara Muvvattār 2. Ghataraharu of 18 towns 3. Tulila Sanduru 4. Ālavajjiyalu 5. Balāñjigas 6. Rāmaḍuvāru 7. Nallarumaḍuvāru 8. Śankarapādivāru	Items of trade are not mentioned. But Devamanya, Achala, Mudraāṇada, Gadyaṇa, Sahavasi are mentioned. Vaḍḍarāvula Daṇḍanāyaka, Hersumkādhikari are also mentioned	P. I. Nos. 4,5,6.
15.	Vāḍapalli	Komaṭlu	--	C.I.T.D. IV, No. 60 pp. 114-115.
16.	Pānugallu	Nibarama nakaram	Salt, Jowar, betal, leaves Arecanut, ginger, turmaric, cotton, jaggery, pepper, Nibaramasrees-Angaḍi Sidhāyamu is mentioned.	

(1) (2)	(3)	(4)	(5)
17. Alampūr	Vīrabalañja Samayadharma Samastha pekkaṇḍru, [Camphor, Cotton, Thread, Śrikaṇḍham, salt, dry ginger etc.]	Paṭṭanasvāmi is mentioned. Trade item is not mentioned. Sunkavergeḍa.	C.I.T.D. Part-II pp. 167-168. Tel. Ins. II, pp. 20-21.
18. Jaḍcherla	--	Maḍiga Sunkamu, Sthalamu sunkamu are mentioned	C.I.T.D. Part-III pp. 43-44.
19. Matkal	Vaiśyas Tailikas Vārtākas	The chieftains of Matkala are mentioned, singanādampannu is mentoined Matkala is a Sthalam headquarters.	C.I.T.D. III pp. 49-50, pp. 56-58.
20. Vardhamānapuram	Nakaramu	grain, oil, Betel leaf, Devamānika, Gidda are mentioned. (Nakaramu-nandu Intisaṭṭigam mentioned)	C.I.T.D. III Mn. 46.
21. Āvania	Samaya, Seṭṭis are mentioned	Removal of Aputrika Seṭṭigam tax is mentioned.	Tel. Ins. II, pp. 60-26
22. Peddakaḍumūr	Ayyovole Inūrvārsvāmi, Muvvattārubīḍu mummūridandas, Kannaḍanālkusāsira Ubhayanānādeśi	Injuctions for the welfare of the guilds are mentioned.	Tel. Ins. II, p. 87

(1)	(2)	(3)	(4)	(5)
23.	Alampūr	Ayyāvaḷi - 500 Mummūridanḍa Ubhayanānādeśi Kannaḍa Nālsāsirevum	Trade controller Vaḍḍerāvula daṇḍanayaka is menioned	Tel. Ins. II, p. 88 Tel. Ins. I, pp. 113-114.
24.	Gangāpuram	Samastaseṭṭikāraru Āśakasamayamgaḷu	--	Tel. Ins. I, pp. 118-119
25.	Kaṭukūr	-- Nagaramu Kāmpulu Balāñjiseṭṭigāṇḍru	--	C.I.T.D. III, pp. 16-17.
26.	Kūcimañci	Vīrabalāñjayas	An itinerent trade guild associated with a capital town ruled by a chieftain.	C.I.T.D. III, pp. 19-21.
27.	Paṭānceru	Seṭṭikāra Samayas of four villages	The king donated to jyosigam the income on Kolaga)	C.I.T.D. IV. pp. 36-39

These trade centres are connected by roads used not only by trading caravans, but also by armies and pilgrims.

TRADE ROUTES

The frequent military operations and the increased trade led to the development of means of transport. But sources are silent about the interest shown by the state in improving and maintaining roads. Nor is there any evidence that the trade guilds took special measures for maintaining the local roads.

The chief means of transport was the cart drawn by bullocks or buffaloes over long distances. For short distances, animals such as the donkey were used. The *peṛika* community supplied not only the gunny bags but also the pack bullocks (peṛike eḍḍlu) to carry them. [125]

The existence of a few long distance high ways is menitoned in some literary works of the age. These routes were not only used for trade but also became pilgrim routes. These roads therefore connected market towns, capital cities, sea and river ports and pilgrim centres. They were known as *baṇḍi teruvu* or *śakaṭa mārga* (cart tracks).[126]

These routes were used for the movement of armies in times of war and are therefore popular as *daṇḍubāṭa*. The *Āndhrabhā-ṣābhūshaṇam* of Ketana refers to a high way from Kanchi to Ayodhya through Vikramasimhapuram (Nellore) and Orugallu (Warangal).[127] As Warangal was the capital city of the Kākatīya Kingdom it must have been connected by a number of routes. The *Krīḍābhirāmam*[128] describes a route from palnāḍ to Warangal through Nalgoṇḍa and Nakrekal. This route must have extended upto Tripurāntakam as the latter was an important provincial headquarters and a temple town. The *Palnāṭivīracharitra*[129] refers to a route from Mācherla to Pānugal through Chityāla and describes the thick jungles of Chityāla which was a riverport on the Krishna. However, it is doubtful whether this Panagal is the Panugal in Nalgoṇḍa District or the one in Mahaboobnagar District. Generally people crossed the river krishna at the ports like Chityāla, Eleśwaram, Vāḍapalli, Amarāvati and of course, Bejawāḍa. In the *Paṇḍitārādhya charitra,*[130] Somanātha describes the journey of Mallikārjuna paṇḍita from Amarāvati to Kalyāṇ. Paṇḍita left Amarāvati crossing the river at Amarāvati and visited Niruguḍumula which is identified by Prabhakara Sastry as Naḍigūḍem in the Nalgoṇḍa district and by Lakshmana Rao as Vaḍḍigūḍem in the Nandigama taluq of Krishna district. From there, the Paṇḍita proceeded to Pānugallu, the capital town of Choḍodaya. There is a difference of opinion about Pānugallu also whether this is the Pānugallu in the Nalgoṇḍa district or the one in the Mahaboobnagar district. As the Paṇḍita was travelling towards the west, Pānugallu must be the one in the Mahaboobnagar district. From Pānugallu, the Paṇḍita went to Vaṇipura, the present Vanaparti in Mahaboobnagar district. At Vanaparti he received the news of Basava's death. From Vaṇipura he turned south towards Śrīśailam and reached Vellaṭūr where he died. Thus, there must have been a route from Amarāvati across Krishna to Kalyāṇ, the capital of the later Cāḷukyas through the present Nalgoṇḍa and Mahaboobnagar districts. If we put these pieces of information from *Paṇḍitārādhya Charitra* and *Krīḍābhirāmam* together, we understand that there was highway between Warangal and Kalyāṇ through Nalgoṇḍa and Mahaboobnagar districts. Parabrahma Sastri[131] mentions another route from Warangal to Kalyāṇ through Kolanupāka, Paṭṭancheru and Bīdar. During the period of later Cāḷukyas the route between Raichur in Karnāṭaka and Kolanupāka in Telangāṇa was a highly traversed route. There must have been a road from Warangal to Devagiri (Daulatābad) through Vemulawāḍa, Polasa (Polavāsa) near Jagityala and Bāsar which was used for the movement of army and by traders and pilgrims. The river Godāvari was crossed at Bāsar, Manthena and Mahādevapūr.

Inscriptions also refer to several small routes. The Āgāmotukūru inscription (A. d. 1282)[131a] of Rāmanātha Coḍadeva refers to a road to Pānugallu (panugaṇṭi teruvu). Āgāmotukuru is near Māḍuvula on the Nalgoṇḍa-Miryālaguḍa road.

Perūr is a big trade centre where merchants from Karnāṭaka, Tamilnāḍu and Āndhradeśa carried on brisk trade. Moreover, Perūr is on the ahalya (present Hāliya) river which is a tributary of the river Krishna. Inscriptions refer to Perūr as a meeting point of several routes.[132] The trade centres and trade routes are as shown in Map III. a list of trade centres is given in Table XIII.

The rivers Krishna and Godāvari must also have served as arteries of trade. But definite information is not available about the Godāvari as a trade route. But the Krishna had a number of ports on its either side, which are mentioned in inscriptions and literary works. Bejawāḍa, Amarāvati, Vāḍapalli, Boppūḍi, Eleśwaram, Chiṭyāla are some of the ports.

Means of Transport

The chief means of transport was the bullock cart. More often peasants and petty traders carried the merchandise on head in bags known as *peṛka* or *peṛika* made of coarse jute thread. *Peṛka, Ettapeṛka, Talamopu* (head load) are referred to in a Perūru inscription.[133] Bamboo cane baskets were also used. *Kāvaḍi* with two loads suspended at the two ends of a bamboo stick and supported on the shoulder of a person was another common means of transport. Loads were also carried on the backs of beasts like oxen, bullocks, horses and donkeys. Inscriptions refer to traders dealing in horses and at times they were known to have belonged to *Vājikula.*[134] Carts drawn by bullocks or buffaloes were also used for transport. Cotton, oil-seeds and paddy are transported in bags *(peṛaka)* by carts. The palanquin was another means of domestic transport used by richer sections of people. These were carried by the Boyas.

It is interesting to note that carts and beasts of burden were available for merchants on rental basis. An inscription from Tripurantakam (A.D. 1245)[135] registers the remission of *sunka* on 300 *peṛika Eḍlu* (bullocks used for transport) in the town of Tripurāntakam. These animals belonged to the temple of Tripurāntakeswara.The Kampus *(kāpus)* that lent these beasts for hire were known as Perikavāṛu. It is clear from this that big temples maintained carts and beasts of burden not only for temple services but also for lending them to the needy merchants by collecting rent from them.

TAXES ON TRADE

Like industries, trade was an important source of state income and there were different taxes on trade which were generally known as *Sunkams.*[136] During the rule of the Cālukyas of Kalyān, tax on trade was called *vaḍḍarāvula Sunka,*[137] which term during the Kākatīya times was replaced by *aḍḍapaṭṭu*, or *aḍḍaveṭṭu* or *aḍḍagaṭ ṭu sunka.*[138] It was also calleld *angaḍi sunkam.*[139] But the sources are not clear about the rate of sunkam levied on different items of trade. However, inscription from Gunṭūr and Prakāśam districts belonging to the Kākatīya period give us some information about the general rate of *sunka*. The Tangeḍa inscription (A.D.1308)[140] records the gifts of *māḍabaḍivīsamu* i.e. at the rate of one *vīsa* per *māda* of sales by the *Ubhayanānādeśi pekkaṇḍru* of the Tangeḍa *sthalalm*. The Tripurāntakam inscription[141] (A.D.1296) records the gift of *Ubhayanānādeśi pekkaṇḍru* to Śri Tripurādevi, the *uppusunkam* (tax on salt) at the rate of *māḍabaḍicinnamu*. Another inscription[142] refers to Vilchuvīsālu. Vilchu in Telugu means purchase. An inscription from Perūru (A.D. 1130)[143] records the remission of two *sunkas* on salt bags payable by the local *nagaram*.

The inscriptions cited above make it clear that sunka was levied both at the time of purchase and at the time of sale. The terms *vīsam* and *cinnam* help us to calculate the rate of *sunka*. *Vīsa* is a fraction equal to 1 in16 whereas the value of cinnam varied from 1 in 8 to 1 in 14. Thus, the *sunka* comes to about 6 to 7 percent.[144]

Pēmṭa sunkamu

The Uppunūtala inscription (A.D. 1149)[145] refers to the diversion of *pēmṭa sunkam*, among other taxes, by Kandūri Somaāthadeva to Gods Kedāreśvara and Keśavadeva. From this, it may be infered that in addition to the general *sunka* levy, a market cess was also collected. An inscription from Jaḍcherla (A.D. 1162)[146] mentions sthalamu sunkam. Thus might be the same as *pēmṭa sunkam* collected at the *sthalam pēmṭa* or the weekly market held at the headquaters of a sthala. The rate of this tax is not clear.

Maḍiga Sunkamu

The maḍiga sunkam or *maḷiga sunkam* is another tax levied on traders. The word maḍiga or maḷiga means a shop with stores. An undated epigraph from Perūru[147] classified the shops into three types as *uttamam, madhyamam* and *kaniṣṭa*. An inscription from Rāchūr (A.D.1157)[148] also classifies the shops at the market into three classes whereas the Jaḍcherla[149] inscription cited above mentions *maḍiga sunkam*.

The Perūr epigraph makes it clear that the rate of the tax as two *rūkas,* on and a half *rūka* and three quaters of a rūka on the first, second and third classes of shops respectively.

Kolaga

The Bairānipalli inscription[150] mentions the tax named *kolaga*. It might be a tax levied on articles measured and weighed such as oil and sandal. The rate of this tax also is not known.

Prattimalaga

The Uppunūtala inscription (A.D.1148)[151] mentions a tax called *prattimalaga*. The name indicates that it was a levy on cotton bales.

MACHINERY OF TAX COLLECTION

There was an efficient machnery of officers for the assessment and collection of taxes. The inscriptions of the Cālukyan times refer to *Sunkavergaḍa*[152] and *Vaḍḍarāvula Daṇḍanāyaka*.[153] The Perūr inscription (A. D. 1130)[154] records that the māṇḍalika or Perūru *Kampaṇam,* Ambanāthadeva Paṇḍanāyaka diverted several *sunka* leives to God Keśavadeva and entrusted the execution of the grant to the *Sunkādhikāri*. From this record we can deduce that at Perūr, a big trade centre, a *Sunkādhikāri,* an officer in charge of commercial taxes was stationed. Further the record makes it clear that the *māṇḍalika* of the place enjoyed the right of diverting the levies through the officer. The *Sunkādhikāri* might be responsible for remitting the levies to the royal treasury.

Most of the taxes appear to have been collected at the market place itself. Such of the taxes were known as *aḍḍavaṭṭu sunkam*.[155] Parabrahma Sastri interprets the words as to mean 'to hold at the place'. Parabrahma Sastri finds support to his view in the words *Sunkari* and *sunkamānya gāṇḍru* of the Tripurāntakam inscription (A.D. 1296)[156] and concludes that there was the practice of auctioning the right of collecting levies to contractors. But, the Telugu word *Paṭṭu* has another simple meaning i.e. at. Accordingly, the term *"Aḍḍapaṭṭu sunkamu"* means only "the tax collected at the market". The compound *"aḍḍavaṭṭ"* becomes meaningful if *paṭṭu* is taken to mean only 'at the place'. If *paṭṭu* is to mean to hold, the compound that would form out of the two words *Aḍḍa (addan)* and *Paṭṭu* is *aḍḍabaṭṭu*. Moreover, the term *Aḍḍagaṭṭu sunkamu* means only the levy payable at the place. It may further be added that the collection of tax through contractors was very rare during the Kākatīya period.

When taxes were diverted as gifts to brāhmaṇas or temples by a member of the ruling class, the local merchant guild was entrusted with the responsibility of executing the decision. Someśvara III made a grant to a brāhmaṇa,[157] Nannaya Bhaṭṭa, and directed the *Seṭṭikārasamayas* of Paṭtancheruvu to implement the grant. We have many instances when the merchant guilds like the *Samaya, Nakaram* and *Pekkaṇḍru* made grants to temples out of the taxes payable by them to the royal treasury either with the consent of the king or his local deputy. Hence, it may be said that the guilds themselves collected the taxes from the members and paid the king's share through the *Sunkādhikāri*.

During the Kākatīya period, the machinery for tax collection became more elaborate. In addition to the *Sunkādhikāris,* we find the mention of such officials as *karaṇam* and *tīrpari*[158] at trade centres . Evidently, *Karaṇam* was a tax accountant. The *tīrpari* resolved any disputes that arose between officials and traders. These officers assisted the *Sunkādhikāri* in the discharge of his duties.

In view of the existence of well-organised trade guilds and elaborate state machinery, tax contractors appear to be superflous. However, the sunkamanyagandru are mentioned only in a single inscription of Tripurantakam and therefore they might have been connected with the sunkas payable to the temple.

The levies were collected both in cash and in kind. It may be interest to note that the levies on agricultural products were mostly in kind. The taxes on most of the industrial products were collected in coin.

From the Chālukya phase (A.D. 973-1126) to the Kākatīya imperialist phase (A.D. 1199-1323) there is thus a gradual increase in taxation on agricultural goods and artisan products. The machinery for tax collection also become more elaborate with a number of officials. Moreover, there are numerous references to the markets, to the classification of shops and to a variety of levies. This reveals the growing marketisation of rural economy as we move into the 14th Century A.D. This is well-born out by the evidence of inscriptions from places like Rachur, Bairaipalli, Uppunuatala, Duddeda etc. which were mostly rural centres. These were gradually brought into the network of market economy. It is also noticed that the growing tendency of donars gifting the revenues from commercial levies to temples. Suggest that the state was receiving substantial revenue from commercial taxes.

REFERENCES

1. P. B. Desai, *A History of Karnāṭaka* (Dharwar,1970), p. 146.
2. I.A.P. Kn. 75.
3. Tel. Ins,. II, pp. 60-62.
4. Ibid., I. p. 108. p. 128.
5. Ibid., p. 118-119.
6. Ibd., II. pp. 60-62.
7. C.I.T.D. IV, No. 6.
8. I.A.P. Wl. 15.
9. Kenneth R. Hall, *Trade and Statecraft in the age of the Colas,* New Delhi, 1980, pp. 147-155.
10. I.A.P. Wl. 71.
11. I.A.P. kn. 75.

12a. Ibid.

12b. Tel. Ins. II., pp. 60-62.

13. Ibid., I. pp. 118-119.
14. C.I.T.D. IV, No. 29.
15. Tel. Ins. I, p. 108, p. 128.
16. Ibid., pp. 118-119.
17. Tel. ins. II, pp. 60-62.

18. C.I.T.D. IV, No. 21.
19. Table XV.
20. Kenneth R. Hall, op, cit. p. 51 ff.
21. Ibid., p. 52.
22. Ibid., p. 130.
23. Ibid., pp. 141-146.
24. R. Champakalakshmi, Section I, Presidential Address, Proc. I.H.C., Srinagar, 1986. pp. 45-107.
25. C.I.T.D. III, pp. 16-17.
26. I.A.P. Wl. 50.
27. Hall, Kenneth, op. cit, p. 61.
28. Burton Stein- *Peasant State and socitey in Medieval South India.* (Delhi, 1980) pp. 90-172.
29. I.A.P. Wl. 14.
30. C.I.T.D. III, pp. 16-17.
31. Ibid., II, pp. 201-212.
32. I.A.P. Wl. 15.
33. C.I.T.D. IV, No. 6, Ibid., No. 10.
34. Tel. Ins. II, pp. 161-162.
35. C.I.T.D. IV, No. 6.
36. Ibid., No. 9.
37. P. I. No. 6.
38. K.C.S.C.S., pp. 170-173.
39. C.I.T.D. III, Mn. 46.
40. K.C.S.C.S., pp. 193-195.
41. Tel. Ins. II, pp. 57-59.
42. C.I.T.D. III, pp. 16-17.
43. C.I.T.D. IV, Nos. 6, 10.
44. K.C.S.C.S. pp. 191-201.
45. I.A.P. Wl. 61.
46. I.A.P. Wl. 68.
47. I.A.P. Wl. 71.
48. Ibid., 26.
49. Ibid.
50. Ibid., 68.
51. Ibid., 63.
52. Tel. ins. II, pp. 66-67.
53. S.I.I. X No. 526.
54. P.I. No. 6.
55. C.I.T.D. III, pp. 16-17.
56. I.A.P. Wl. 28.
57. Tel. Ins., II, pp. 161-162.
58. S.I.I. X, 514.
59. S.I.I., IV 812, S.I.I., X 221.
60. E.I. Vol, VI, p. 334 ff.

61. K. Sundaram, *Studies in Economic and Social conditions In Medieval Āndhra* (Machilipatnam 1968), pp. 44.
62. I.A.P. Wl. 61.
63. Op. cit.
64. Op. cit.
65. I.A.P. Kn, 38, Ibid., 75.
66. I.A.P. Kn. 75.
67. P.I., No. 4.
68. I.A.P. Wl. 26.
69. K.Sundaram, op. cit. p. 69 ff.
70. Champakalakshmi, R. Op. cit. p. 70.
71. Kenneth R. Hall, op. cit. pp. 150-155.
72. I.A.P. Kn. 38.
73. Kenneth R. Hall, op. cit. pp. 147-151.
74. C.I.T.D. III, pp. 167-169.
75. I.A.P. Cp. Part I, p. 156.
76a. Tel. Ins. II, p. 87.
76b. Tel Ins. II, p. 88.
77. Ibid., I, pp. 105-106.
78. I.A.P. Kn. 75.
79. Tel. Ins. II, p. 88.
80. Ibid., p. 87, Ibd., I. P. 128.
81. Ibid., I. p. 108.
82. M.A.R. 1927, PP. 33-34.
83. Narasimha Rao, R. *Corporate Life in Medieval Āndhradeśa* (Secunderabad, 1967) p. 11 ff.
84. S.I.I., IV, No. 935.
85. C.I.T.D. III, pp. 167-169.
86. S.I.I., IV,No. 935.
87. S.I.I. , X 429.
88. Ibid., 473.
89. Tel Ins. I, p. 128.
90. Ibid., II, p. 87.
91. Ibid., p. 88.
92. I.A.P. Wl. 63.
93. Ibid.
94. I.A.P. Cp. Part I, p. 156.
95. Ibd., Part II, No. 13.
96. S.I.I. X, 567.
97. Ibid., 556.
98. Ketana, *Vijñāneśvaram* (ed) C.V. Ramachandra Rao, (Nellore, 1977).
99. Maḍiki Singana, *Sakalanītisammatamu* (ed) Venkat Rao, N. and Appa Rao, P. R. (Hyderabad, 1970).
100. Ketana, Op. cit., Prayaschittakanda, vv. 65-85.
101. Ibid.

102. Maḍiki Singana, op. cit. vv. 218-219.
103. Tel. Ins. I, pp. 113-114, P. I. No. 4.
104. K.C.S.C.S., pp. 202-204.
105. E.I. XII, p. 188 ff.
106. P.I. No. 9. K.C.S.C.S. p. 202-204.
107. S.I.I., X 521. Ibid., V 211.
108. N.D.I. 1. p. 340.
109. I.A.P. Wl. 62, and 68.
110. Ibid.
111. E.I. XII, p. 188 ff.
112. I.A.P. Wl. 62.
113. C.I.T.D. IV, No. 6 and No. 10.
114. Tel. Ins. I, p. 91, C.I.T.D., II, pp. 166-167.
115. Ibid., pp. 113-114.
116. I.A.P. Wl. 26.
117. C.I.T.D. IV, pp. 32-35.
118. K.C.S.C.S. pp. 170-173, Tel. Ins. I, pp. 169-172.
119. Tel. Ins. II, pp. 67-69.
120. I.A.P. Wl. 68.
121. Tel. Ins. II, pp. 66-67.
122. Ibid, pp. 126-127, pp. 161-162.
123. C.I.T.D. IV, No. 6.
124. Ibid., 43.
125. S.I.I. X, 304.
126. Tel. Ins. I, pp. 71-72, Ibid., II, pp. 123-125. Tel. Ins. II, pp. 161-162.
127. Ketana, *Āndhrabhāshābhūshaṇam*, p. 4, v. 12.
128. Vallabhāmatya, *Krīḍābhirāmam* V. 121 (Hyderabad, 1960).
129. Śrīnatha—*Palanāṭivīracarita* (Vijayawada, 1961) (ed) Pingali Lakshmikantam, pp. 74-78 (Palnāṭi Rājya bhāgam).
130. K. Lalitamba—*Vīraśaivism in Āndhra* (Guntur, 1976), p. 31.
131. P.V.P. Sastry, *The Kākatīyas,* (Hyderabad, 1978). p. 250.
131a. K.C.S.C.S., pp. 242-248.
132. P.I. No. 3.
133. Ibid., No.6.
134. I.A.P. Wl. No.26.
135. S.I.I. X, 304.
136. Ibid., pp. 79-80, Tel. Ins. I, pp. 144-145, Ibid., pp. 157-158, I.A.P. Wl. 57.
137. P. I. No. 4, C.I.T.D. IV, No. 12, 27.
138. K.C.S.C.S., pp. 138-140.
139. C.I.T.D. III, pp. 166-170.
140. S.I.I. X, No. 495.
141. Ibid., No. 480.
142. S.I.I. X, 527.
143. P.I. No. 9.
144. See appendix for Fractions of Visa and Cinnamu.

145. K.C.S.C.S., pp. 138-140.
146. Tel. Ins. I, 157-158; C.I.T.D. II, Mn. 12.
147. P.I. No. 6.
148. K.C.S.C.S. p. 199.
149. Ibid., pp. 202-204.
150. C.I.T.D. IV, No. 8, 14, Ibid., pp. 36-39.
151. K.C.S.C.S., pp. 138-140.
152. Tel. Ins. II, pp. 20-21.
153. Ibid., pp. 161-162, Ibid., 113-114.
154. P. I. No. 6.
155. K.C.S.C.S., pp. 202-204.
156. S.I.I. X, No. 480.
157. C.I.T.D. IV, pp. 36-39.
158. S.I.I. X, No 480.

CHAPER—V

SOCIAL STRUCTURE

As in economy, there was no stagnation in the society of Āndhra. As a result of the impact of the economic developments outlined in earlier chapters there were several social changes and the society of the medieval age in Telangāṇa presents a complex picture. Generally, historians of India attempt to explain the society of a period against the background of the *Cāturvarṇa* order i.e. divison of the "Hindu" society into four *varṇas*, *brāhmaṇa, kṣatriya, vaiśya and śūdra.*[1] But it must be said that the *Cāturvarṇa* system only a atraditional and theorotiacal concept, derived from the condition of the Vedic Āryans. In course of time, the Indian society has undergone several changes and departed from the *Cāturvarṇadharma*. There occured a process of acculturation as Āryans expanded eastwards and southwards in the sub-continent.[2] They came into contact with various non-Aryan races and attempted to *āryanise* them and integrate them into their own social order. Besides, the *anuloma* and *pratiloma* marriages between Āryan and non-Āryan groups resulted in the rise of mixed castes. The *Dharmaśāstras* of Vaśiṣṭha and Bauddhayana tried to fix the positon of these mixed castes and tribes in the Āryan social order.[3] *Varṇasankara*[4] became a common feature in the society from very early times. Buddhism and Jainism, the two non-vedic religions also contributed to the process of acculturation.

By the 11th and 12th centuries, Buddhism and Jainism declined and there was a resurgence of "Hinduism" in the form of purāṇic theism which supported the caste system.[5] The king and the brāhmaṇapriests began to uphold the *Cāturvarṇadharma*. In the Āndhra country the brāhmānical revival began in the Vēṅgi kingdom during the reigon of Rājarājanarendra (A.D.1022-1063). Nannaya, the first great Telgu poet translated *Mahābhārata* with a view to uphold the *Varṇāśramadharma*. Nannaya states that

Rājarājanarendra upheld the *Varṇāśramadharma*.[6] Many literary works came in the wake of *Mahābhārata* and most of them, except those by the śaiva poets like Pālkuriki Somanātha, propagated the *Cāturvarṇadharma*. Even among and the Śaivities the followers of Mallikārjuna, known as the Āradhyas reconciled with the brāhmānical social order.

Several inscriptions of Telangāṇa during the Cālukya and Kākatīya periods refer to the theoretical concepts of the order of four varṇas. The Māṭeḍu inscription (A.D.1120)[7] of mahāsāmanta Vemabola Boḍḍama Mallenāyaka, a genral and feudal chief under Kākati Prola II refers to the creation of the four orders by Brahma. The Kundavaram inscription of Kundamāmbika[8] refers to the emergence of Brahma from the navel of Viṣṇu and the four orders from Brahma. The kings of the period took titles like *Cāturvarṇa-dharma pratiṣṭāchārya* and *Cāturvarṇadharma pratipālitulu*.[9] However the *Varṇāśramadharma* was upholds only in principle by the rulers of the period. The *praśasti* titles noted above are merely traditional and they should not be taken seriously.

Although the above titles were taken by the kings, the Cāturvarṇadharma could not be maintained. Though the concept of four *varṇas* remained, the castes based upon occupations increased in number since very early times. We find from the medieval inscriptions that the contemporary society was characterised by the *aṣṭādaśa mahāpraja*.[10] As its name indicates, the aṣṭādaśa mahāpraja was a general assembly of 18 major communities. The basis of the classification of the society into 18 communities appears to have been occupational. Actually, the medieval records mention more than 18 castes. Like the *cāturvarṇa* system, the concept of *aṣṭādaśa mahāpraja* also became purely traditional. It may be said that even in the time of the Sātavāhanas, eighteen *śreṇis*, each being an occupational group, were mentioned in contemporary inscriptions.

An occupational group may be called a *Jāti*. The *Dharma-śātras* have defined *jāti* as a group into which a person is born and as occupations were mostly hereditary, each occupational group came to be called a *jāti*.[11] These occupational groups had their own codes of conduct known as *Samaya and samaya daṇḍana*[12] meaning the punishment for violating the code of the community. Each *jāti* or *kula* had its own rules and regulations. If any member violated the *jāti* regulaltions *(kuladharma or jātidharma* or *samaya)* he was liable for punishment. Some inscriptions refer to "*aṣṭādaśasamayāla samastapraja*"[13] meaning all the people belonging to 18 self-regulating communities. It is therefore, more realistic to keep in mind the concept of *aṣṭādaśapraja* rather than *cāturvarṇadharma* while attempting an analysis of the social conditions of the period under study.

The Aṣṭādaśamahāpraja

The *aṣṭādaśamahāpraja* which is mentioned in several records was a representative assembly of the major communities of a village or town or a *sthala*. It discharged several administrative functions and played an important role in the economic and social life of the people. The *aṣṭādaśamahāpraja* genrally consisted of:[14]

(1) *Mahājanulu,* (2) *Nakaramu* (3) *Kāmpulu* (4) *Balañja seṭṭigāṇḍru* (5) *Komaṭis* (6) *Īdaravāru* (7) *Gollavāru* (8) *Akkasālijanulu* (9) *Sālevāru* (10) *Śrīvaiṣṇavulu,* (11) *Velamaveguru* (12) *Illaris* (13) *Gaṇḍavāru* (14) *Nāyakulu* (15) *Reḍlu* (16) *Karṇālu* (17) *Telikivevuru and* (18) *Nāyilu.*

Some other records mention them as

(1) *Brāhmaṇa* (2) *Kṣatriya* (3) *Vaiśya* (4) *Śūdra* (5) *Vyavahārika* (6) *Pāñcāla* (7) *kumbhakāra* (8) *Tantuvāya* (9) *Vastrabhedaka* (10) *Tilaghāṭika* (11) *Kurantaka* (12) *Vastrara-kṣaka* (13) *Devānga* (14) *Peṛeka* (15) *Gorakṣaka* (16) *Kirāṭaka* (17) *Rajaka* (18) *Kṣuraka.*

Actually we find many more communities mentioned in the inscriptions and literary works of the period. The Table XVI represents the communities, their profession and the guild they formed. Those professionals who have not organised into a guild are also mentioned.

The causes for the emergence of a large number of communities by the early medieval period are discussed by several authors. The major causes are discussed below :

Ethnic factor

Long before the medieval age, the process of drawing the hill and forest tribes like the śabaras, boyas, puḷindas, and others into the mainstream of society began. These tribes were warlike in nature and did heavy physical work. These features helped them to a large extent. As the constant warfare increased the military requirements of the rulers of the age, the more hardy of the tribes were recruited into military services, and other took to the cultivation of land. In the Māṭeḍu inscrilption (A.D.1120)[15] of Mahāsāmanta Vemabola Boḍḍama Mallenāyaka, a vassal under prola II, mentions that he beloged to puḷinda vamśa which was created by Brahma for the protection of brāhmaṇa, kṣatria, vaiśya and śūdra order. The originator of his family, Būchena of vemabolakula had the title koṭamalla which means 'destroyed of forts'. Būchena should have distinguished himself in wars and thus elevated his family's position at the kākatīya court.

Another important tribe that became slowly integrated into the society was the boyas.[16] The boyas were engaged in agriculture and animal husbandry. As they were war-like and known for their marksmanship, they were recruited into military service.[17] Moreover, most of the cattle grants to temples were entrusted to the members of the boya community with an obligation to supply ghee for the temple lamp.[18] They operated hydraulic machines like the rātṇam.[19] Gradually, the boyas were integrated into the social mainstream and rose to high positons at the court and in the camp. On the basis of the Gaṇapeśwaram record, it seems that Jāyapa the Gajasāhiṇi of Gaṇapati descended from Nāraboya, the ruler of Divi.[20]

The process of assimilation of various ethnic groups into the society multiplied the number of castes. As noted above the *Dharmaśāstras* facilitated the absorption of the aboriginals into Cāturvarṇa order through the concept of *Varṇasankara*. An inscription at Mellaceruvu mentions beṭṭevāru in samastapraja.[21] The word beṭṭe or beṭṭu means fighting temperament, adventurism and cruelty[22] and as such it signifies aboriginls and hunters. The above noted record make it clear that aboriginals and hunters were absorbed into the society as beṭṭe caste *(jāti)*.

While enumerating the castes in the city of Warangal it is interesting that Vallabhāmātya mentions *turakas* (Turks=muslim) and their *masjid*.[23] There is reason to beleive that the turn of fourteenth century Muslim population in Telangāṇa was sizable and its presence significant. It is learnt that from about the last quarter of the 13th century, muslim, especially Sūfi saints and their disciples, made their way into the south. A certain muslim saint by name Baba Fakr-ud-din established his Kankah at Penugoṇḍa[24] where he died in A.D.1294. The Sufi brothers shaik Baba Sharaf-ud-din and Shaik Baba Shaib-ud-din are said to have settled at a place near the present city of Hyderābād.[25] Latter, at the instant of the famous saint khwaza Nizam-ud-din Auliya of Ghasipur, a band of sufis left for the south. Again in A.D.1309 another band of sufis led by Burhan-ud-din Gharib shah came to the south. Many of these sufis settled down in Telangāṇa, built *Masjids* and by their pious life attracted both Islamic and Hindu devotees.[26] The muslims known to the Hindus as Turks gradually became a part of the local social order, being looked upon almost as one of the śūdra subcastes.

Economic Factors

From early times, occupational groups graduallysettled down in the "Hindu" society as castes or subcastes. Agriculture, being the mainstay of the economy during medieval Āndhra, led to the growth of a number of subsidiary supporting industries each of which give rise to a subcaste. Even among the agriculturists, there were several subcastes such as the *reḍlu, tammaḍlu, gollas, boyas, īdara* and others.

The textile industry which is next in importance to agriculture also led to the rise of subcastes based upon the specialised skills. *Vastrabhedaka* (dyer), *devānga* (spinner), *tantuvāya* (weaver), and *vastrarakṣhka* (sewer) are mentioned in the records of the period. These four groups, evidently, were involved in the cloth making and cloth manufacturing.

Religious movements

The new religious movements of the 11th and 12th centuries

within the fold of 'Hinduism' also led to the rise of new castes. The *vīraśaiva* movement led by Bâsava in Karṇāṭaka[28] had its echoes in Telangāṇa where the kālāmukha[29] system of śaivism was popular. In Āandhradeśa, Śrīpati Paṇḍita and Mallikārjuna Paṇḍita also preached a militant form of Śaivism which was developed into the *Ārādhya* system.[30] All these śaivite systems were opposed to caste or anti-caste in general. The Vīraśaiva movements had opposed the traditional brāhmānical order and Basava is described as an axe to the root of the tree of caste. The followers of Basava did not follow any rules regarding ceremonial pollution, though at a later date, the sect began to develop social exclusiveness based on privilege of birth and cleanliness of profession. The followers of Basava were mainly the trading communities, potters, shoe makers, tanners, weavers and untouchables. On the other side, during the 11th and 12th centuries, Rāmānuja led the Śrī-vaiṣṇava movement in Tamilnāḍu. Rāmānuja observed, "If we descend below the four castles and come to the Caṇḍālas who, however lacking in virtue, are true worshippers of .... Viṣṇu, their servants are my masters and their feet are mine to worship".[31] The idea of caste negation, in the early phase of the movement was entertained by the *ācāryas* and the Tengalai or *prabandhic* school was dominated by mostly śūdras who enhanced their status and tried to establish their superiority over the orthodox vaiṣṇavites who gave preference to the sanskrit texts among other things. Śrīvaiṣṇava movement had made deep impact on Āndhra and Telangāṇa regions which brought into its fold, the śūdras enhancing their status regardless of pollution and caste privileges. These movemnts led to the rise of new sects among brāhmaṇas and castes among the śūdras. The brāhmaṇa followers of Mallikārjuna and Rāmānuja formed into the subsects of ārādhyas and Śrī-vaiṣṇavas respectively. Among the śūdras the *jangamas* and *balijas* were śaivite sects[32] where as *dāsarlu* and *sātānis*[33] were vaiṣṇavities.

Political factors

The period under study witnessed the decline of the traditional ruling caste, generally claiming to belong to the kṣatriya *varna*. The kṣatriyas were slowly replaced by tribal chiefs and peasant warriors. In the Rāṣṭrakūṭa army, which invaded Vēṅgi, there were several Śabara chiefs[34] whereas in the court of Velanāḍu many boya chiefs held very high positions including those of maṇḍaleśvara.[35] The names of the early Kākatīyas such as Eṛṛa, Guṇḍa and Prola are very common among tribals. These names ssuggest that they too were tribals who were recruited into the army of the Rāṣṭrakūṭas. The early Kākatīyas called themselves as belonging to *sāmanta viṣṭi vamśa*,[36] and viṣṭi is the sanskritic form of veṭṭi which means a slave or servant. In later inscriptions they claimed to have belonged to the fourth caste.[37] But in some instances, they are described as Kṣatriyas.[38] But Vidyānātha describes that their fame excelled the fame of the solar and lunar families.[39] It may be taken to imply that they did not belong to either. We have already noted the case of the Puḷindas.

Another important development during this period is the rise of peasent warrior groups. The reḍḍis, velamas and other kāpus who were mainly agriculturists entered the military services under various ruling families. This was necessitated by frequent wars of the age. Moreover, war gave an opportunity to plunder and become rich and powerful quickly, though at the risk of life. These factors helped the recruitment of young peasants into armies. The *nāyakulu*[40]and *ekkaṭlu*[41]are two such groups mentioned in several inscrilptions. Gradually, they rose to the position of military chiefs daṇḍanāyaka and senapati) and that of governors *(maṇḍalikas)* and *sāmantas*. The *nāyankara* system under Pratāpa Rudra helped further development and increase in number of these militarychieftains. Immediately after the fall of the Kākatīyas, the Āndhra country witnessed, the establishment of several independent kingdoms. Prolayanāyaka of the Musunūri family who is considered to belong to the kamma caste established an independent kingdom at Rekapalli.[42] The reḍḍi chief, Prolaya Vemāreḍḍi became independent at Addanki[43] and the velama chief Singamanīḍu became independent at Rājukoṇḍa.[44] These peasant-warrior nāyakas liberated the Telugu country from the muslim rule and resisted the Bahamani incursion,[45] This period is generally known as the Reḍḍi-Nāyaka age in the history of the Āndhras.[46]

TABLE XVI

Social Groups

Sl. No.	Community/ sub group	Guild	Occupation	Reference
(1)	(2)	(3)	(4)	(5)
1.	Brāhmalu	Mahājanulu	Priesthood	I.A.P. Wl. 89. T.I., II, 161-162.
2.	Kṣatriyulu	--	Warrior Class	I.A.P. Wl. 42.
3.	Komaṭlu	Nakaram	Trade (mainly local)	K.C.S.H. C.pp. 199. T.I.I., 89, 90, 92, P.I. No. 6. I.A.P. Wl. No.87
4.	Sālevāru	Dharmasālī-yajanulu	Cloth manufa-cture	I.A.P. Wl. No. 61. T. I. II, pp. 57-59. 60-62, etc,
5.	Teliki or Tailikulu	telikivevuru	Oil pressing and Oil trade	T.I. II, pp. 161-12. P.I. No. 6, I.A.P. Wl. No. 87.
6.	Vīrabaḷāñjulu	Bālañja seṭṭi-gāndru, Ayyāvaḷi 500	Itinerent and local trade	C.I.T.D. - III, pp. 19-21.
7.	Tammaḍlu	Kāmpulu	Agriculture	I.A.P. Wl. Nos. 57, 85, 89, C.I.T.D., IIpp. 68-69.
8.	Gollavāru	Kāmpulu	Animal husban-dry, agriculture	I.A.P. Wl. Nos., 37,87, T. I. No. 92

(1)	(2)	(3)	(4)	(5)
9.	Ídaravāru	Kāmpulu	Horticulture, toddy trade	T.I. I pp. 89-90
10.	Mangalulu	"	Temple service barber	I.A.P. Wl, No. 37. T.I.I., 89-90
11.	Kummarulu	"	Potters	T.I.I., 89-90.
12.	Akasālivāru	Pañchāṇamuvaāru	Metal work	Ibid.
13.	Reḍḍlu	Kāmpulu	Agriculture and administration	I.A.P. Wl. No. 89 and 53.
14.	Nāyakulu	Solidiers (Ekkaṭi vīraparivāramu)	Peasent warriors	T.I.II, pp. 73-74.
15.	Vasadivāru	Jains	Priesthood and teaching	I.A.P. Wl. Nos. 37, 87.
16.	Damarivāru or Medara	--	Bamboowork	I.A.P. Wl. No. 87. *Kriḍābhirāmam* V.
17.	Velamalu	Kāmpulu (Velamaleguru)	Agriculture	T.I.I. p. 92.
18.	Sankaṭelu	--	--	I.A.P. Wl. No. 37.
19.	Garagalu	--	--	T.I., I, pp. 40, *Krīḍābhi rāmam* v. 43.
20.	Karaṇālu	Karaṇālu	Small govt. officials, clerks, accountants.	T. I., II 60, 62.
21.	Boyalu	Kāmpulu	Agriculture and Animal Husbandry	K.C.S.C.S. p. 223.

(1)	(2)	(3)	(4)	(5)
22.	Puḷindas	--	warfare	I.A.P. Wo. No. 24.
23.	Sidivaru	--	Trade in castor oil (mainly local trade)	I.A.P. Wl 87
24.	Mālakarulu	--	gardeners	I.A.P. wl. 37.
25.	Mācharāsi	--	Fishermen	Ibid.
26.	Beṭṭevāru	--	Hunter	T.I.I. pp. 89-90
27.	Mere (Kuṭrapuvāru)	--	Tailor	*Krīḍābhirāmam*, v. 106
28.	Peṛikevāru	--	Basket making and Transporting	*Pratāpa Carita*, p. 151.
29.	Kāsevaru	Pañcāṇamvāru	Stone work	Ibid.
30.	Turakalu	--		*Krīāṇbhirāmam*. v. 149

T. I. = Telangana Inscriptions.

A large number of government officials began to be appointed to discharge administrative functions in the Kākatīya period. Thus, a bureaucracy, loyal to the ogvernment developed both in towns and villages. These government officials at different levels (*grāma* and *sthala*) were referred to in inscriptions as *karaṇālu*.[47] These were mainly drawn from the brāhmaṇa caste who gradually developed into the separate sect of *niyogis*.

REFERENCES

1. Pandharinath H. Prabhu, *Hindu Social Organisation* (Bombay, 1961) pp. 284-335.
2. R. S. Sarma - *Material culture and Social Formation in Ancient India* - Delhi (1983) p. 146.
3. *Sacred Laws of the Aryas*, Tr. G Buhler (Delhi, 1984) Part B. *Vaśiṣṭha dharmaśāstra*, Chapter XVII and XVIII and *Baudhāyana Dharmśāstra*, Praśna I, Adhyāya 9, Khaṇḍika 17.
4. Pandharinath H. Prabhu Op. cit. P. 296 ff.
5. B.S.L. Hanumantha Rao, *Religion in Andhra*, (Guntur 1973) pp. 212-227.
6. Nannaya, *Āndhra Mahābhārata*, (Hyderabad, 1970) *Ādiparva*, Canto IV.6.
7. I.A.P. Wl. 24.
8. I.A.P. Wl. 58.
9. S.I.I. X 400, 473.
10. Tel Ins. I. pp. 83-84 C.I.T.D. III pp 16-17
11. V. S. Apte, *Sanskrit-English Dictionary* (Delhi, 1965) p. 219.
12. C.I.T.D. III Mn. 38.
13. Tel. Ins. I. pp. 89-90.
14. Tel. Ins. I. pp. 83-84 Ibid pp. 89-90, C.I.T.D. III pp. 16-17, S.I.I. X. No. 395.
15. I.A.P. Wl. 24.
16. B.S.L. Hnumantha Rao, 'The Boyas in Medieval Āndhra History', J.A.H.R.S. Vol. XXXVIII, Part-IV, pp. 77-91.
17. Ibid
18. S.I.I. IV. 673.
19. K.C.S.C.S. pp. 223-225, C.I.T.D. III Mn. 31.
20. Tel. Ins. I pp. 89-90.
21. B.S.L. Hanumantha Rao, op. cit.
22. *Śrī Sūryarāyāndhra nighanṭuvu* - Vol. V, p. 1061.
23. Vallabhāmatya, *Krīḍābhirāmam* (Secunderabad, 1960) V. 149.
24. M. Somasekhara Sarma, *Āndhra Vijñāna Sarvasvamu* (Madras, 1959) III, p. 565.
25. John Brigg's Ferishta, I. pp. 163-175.

26. Sherwani, H. L. and Joshi P. M. *History of Medieval Deccan* (Hyderabad, 1974), Vol. II, p. 178.
27. A.R. 1918, p. 174.
28. P.B. Desai, *Basaveśvara and his times* (Dharwar, 1968), pp. 199-219.
29. B.S.L. Hanumantha Rao, *Religion in Andhra (Guntur, 1973)* pp. 276-278 I.AP. Wl. 25.
30. K. Lalitamba, *Vīraśaivism in Āndhra* (Guntur, 1976) p. 69.
31. B.S.L. Hanumantha Rao, Op. cit. op. 254-257.
32. S. Pratapa Reḍḍy, *Āndhrula Sānghika Caritra* (Hyderabad, 1982), p. 426 ff.
33. Ibid.
34. N. Venkataramanaiah, *Eastern Cālukyas of Vēṅgi* (Madras, 1950) p. 31.
35. S.I..I. X, 90.
36. I.A.P. Wl. 15.
37. C.I.T.D. II, p. 25 ff. Ibid III. Mn. 17.
38. C.I.T.D. II, p. 82, E. I. XIX pp. 247 ff.
39. Vidyānātha, *Pratāparudrīyam, Nāṭakaprakaraṇa* V. 13 'Atyarkendukula Praśastimabhijadyam kākatīyānvayam'.
40. Tel. Ins. II pp. 73-74.
41. I.A.P. Wl. 37. I.A. P. Kn. 36.
42. M. somasekhara Sarma, *A Forgotten Chapter of Āndhra History* (Madras, 1945) pp. 25 ff.
43. Ibid.
44. Ibid.
45. Ibid.
46. B.S.L. Hanumantha Rao, *Āndhrula Caritra* (Guntur, 1983) pp. 297-353.
47. Tel. Ins. II, pp. 73-74.

CHAPTER—VI

SOCIAL GROUPS

Neither the ancient theory of Cāturvarṇa nor the medieval concept of *aṣṭādaśa mahāpraja* can give a satisfactory picture of the society in Telangāṇa of the period under study. Both the concepts are basically occupational. But as economic activity in different fields viz., agriculture, industry and trade increased, new soical classes or castes emerge out of 'functional necessity',[1] and the result was gradual multiplication of castes. The castes in medieval Telangāṇa may be broadly classified into four major social groups, viz, priestly, ruling, agricultural, artisan and trading classes

PRIESTLY CLASS

The brāhmaṇas are, in general, known as the priestly class and enjoyed high ritual purity and occupied the first place in society. A careful study of the available evidence would reveal a change in lthe condition of the brāhmaṇas in society. In general, they enjoyed the same old ritual purity and commanded respect as itellectuals and learned members of the society. Among the *aṣṭādaśamahāpraja*, the brāhmaṇas were referred to as mahājanulu. The name mahājana was deriuative of *mahāyanjana*. A brāhmaṇa was ordained to perform five *yajnās everyday.*[2] i.e., 1) *devayajña* 2) *brahmayajña* 3) *pitṛyajña* 4) *bhūtayajña* and 5)*manuṣyayajña.*

The performer of these five *yajñas* and who followed six duties[3] (*yajana, yājana, adhyayana, adhyāpana, dāna* and *pratigrahaṇa*) was known as *mahāyajña or mahāyajana or mahājana.*

The brāhmaṇas are generally mentioned with their *gotras* as in the inscriptions of Perūr,[4] Budāpūr[5] and Kundavaram.[6] The brāhmaṇas used the suffixes like *Bhaṭṭlu,*[7]*Peddi,*[8] *Pinni,*[9]*Appa*[10] and *Sūri.*[11]

The brāhmaṇas were widespread in society. Baddena, the author of *Sumatī śataka*[12] says that a village without a brāhmaṇa was not a fit place to live in. Mārana, the author of the Telugu *Mārkaṇḍeyapurāṇam*,[13] also says that a village must have at least one *śrotriya* brāhmaṇa family. However, there are exclusive brāhmaṇa villages, known as *agrahāras* and *brahmādeyas*. Besides, there were *brahmapuris*. Generally, *brahmapuris* are known to have been schools of brāhmānical learning. So, they were attached to even temple complexes or *devabhoga* villages. We come across Koḍūra brahmapuri[14] and Gokarṇa *brahmapuri*[15] in inscriptions.

The status of a community is two-fold, ritual status and the actual status.[16] The ritual status is as outlined in the *Dharmaśāstras*. The actual status is determined by the contemporary political and economic conditions. The brāhmaṇa community enjoyed a high ritual status during the period under study. They were priests to kings as well as to the common people. They occupied high positions such as *rājaguru*, *rājapurohita*, *purohita* at the courts of kings and their *sāmantas*. The *rājagurus* were generally drawn from the brāhmaṇa community. Manchibhaṭṭopādhyāya of Manthena epigraph[17] (A.D.1199) describes himself as *purohitas* to king Gaṇapatideva.

Political status of the brāhmaṇas

Several members of brāhmaṇa community were recruited into both civil and military services by the kings and their subordinate chiefs. They occupied high positions such as the *pradhāni* and *mahāpradhāni* in civil service and those of daṇḍanāyaka and senāni in the army. Gangādhara,[18] a brāhmaṇa of Ātreya *gotra* hailing from Vellankipura agrahāra in the Vēṅgi country was recruited by Prola II as an official to look after various works in the palace. Gangādhara served under Prola and Rudra as a civil and military officer. He obtained the five niyogi Vṛttis and the title *amātya* from Rudra and was appointed governor of Sabbi *sahasra maṇḍala* (Sabbināḍu-1000) with Nagarūru as its headquarters. After he obtained such a high political status Gangādhara appears to have taken the suffix "*rāju*."[19]

The Goḍiśāla (Upparapalli) inscrption[20] records the building of templels, tanks and gift of lands and gardens by a brāhmaṇa chief kāṭayanāyaka, son of Rājānāyaka. The latter was a general under Recherla chiefs. The inscripiton gives an account of the military exploits of Rājānāyaka.

The Induluvi family of brāhmaṇas served the kākatīya dynasty with distinction.[21] The family originally belonged to village Indulūr in the Kolleru lake region. They belonged to the kauṇḍinya *gotra* of the ārādhya sect. According to the śivayogasāram, written by Kolani Gaṇapati, a later descendent of the family, the ancestor of the family Nanna Gauraya, migrated to Anmakoṇḍa. His sons, Pedamalla and Pinamalla entered the court as officials. Pedamalla entered the army where as Pinamalla entered the civil service. Somanamantri, son of Pedamalla led many expeditions during the region of Kākati Gaṇpati. Another member of the family, Kolani Rudra was a great scholar and administrator. He served the king Rudradeva as *mudrāpaka* (incharge of royal seal) and he became the governor of eastern provinces extending between Orugallu and Simhāchalam. He possessed the titles *"rāya cauhattamalla" māṇḍalika cauhattamalla" "kalingarāyavibhāḷa", "pañcha pāṇḍya rāja marda"*. Kolani Rudra was a great scholar in grammar and philosophy. The author of Śivayogasaram attributes to him the title *vyākaraṇabrahma* and he is credited with the authorship of a commentary on *Ślokavārtika* called "Rājarudrīya".[22] The closeness and the nature of service to the royal family rendered by Indulūri chiefs can be understood by the fact that Rudramadevi gave one of her daughters, Ruyyama, in marriage to Indulāri Annaya, son of Pedagannamantri.[23]

The *Siddheśvara caritra*[24] narrates the tradition that Gaṇapatideva appointed several brāhmaṇas as officers. In the Kākatīya polity, karaṇams appear in the village and at *sthala*. The word karaṇam literally means an assessor of taxes (kara=tax, ṇa=count) or an accountant. The Moripirāla inscription (A.D.1181)[25] refers to one Malaparāju as "iṇṭakaraṇam" who was probably the family accountant of the Viriyālas. It is a matter of interest that during the Kākatīya period only a few brāhmaṇas are found holding high positons at the court and in the camp. With the exception of the three or four members mentioned above, no other brāhmaṇa officer of high rank is known from the inscriptions of the Kākatīyas. It is doubtful whether there were any brāhmaṇas among the *nāyankaras* during Pratāpa Rudra's time. But the karaṇam in the village was almost invariably a brāhmaṇa. The reasons may be that 1) the brāhmaṇa was the onlyl learned person in the village and (2) as the brāhmaṇa was still respected by all including the reḍḍis and velamas, the village administration, which is the basis of all administration, would be safe in the hands of brāhmaṇas. An efficient trust-worthy brāhmaṇa as village *karaṇam* therefore, made for the stability of administration.

Brāhmaṇas as scholars and teachers

Though they lost their monopoly over learning, the brāhmaṇas of the period continued to be the highly intellectual and widely learned section of the society. Epigraphical records of the 11th to 14th centuries belonging to the Telaṅgāṇa region refer to a large number of brāhmaṇas as embodiments of learning and scholarship.[26] The composers of the records of the Kākatīyas and their subordinates were mostly brāhmaṇa scholars. The brāhmaṇas living in *agrahāras* persued vedic learning and handed it over to the succeeding generations. They were also engaged as teachers at *ghaṭikas,* temples and *maṭhas.*

It has been noted that during the period many agrahāras were established and the receipients were generally scholars of eminence. They mastered and gave instruction in a variety of subjects like *Vedas, Vedāṅgas, Itihāsa, Purāṇa, Dharmaśāstra* as well as secular subjects like astrology, *rājanīti*, warfare and logistics. Probably by the side of agrahāras there appear to have developed *brahmapuris.* The Māṭeḍu inscription of Mallenāyaka (A.D. 1120)[27] records a land grant to a *brahmapuri*. Other inscriptions refer to Koḍūra *brahmapuri* at Gangāpuram[28] and Gokarṇa *brahmapuri* at Pānagal.[29] A *brahmapuri* may be defined as "a settlement of learned brāhmaṇas who included poets, philosophers, orators ans similar advanced scholars".[30] They might have developed as appendix to *agrahāras,*[31] each specialising in a particular branch of learning.

Besides, there flourished institutions of advanced learning

known as *ghaṭikas*. The Alampūr[32] and Perūr[33] inscriptions give some details about the management of a *ghaṭika*. There were as many as 30 teachers in the Perūr *ghaṭika* who included 19 *Upādhyāyas*, six *Shaḍangis* two *paṇḍitās*, a *Jyotiṣa* (astrologer) and a *Ghaṭiyaśāsi* (Principal). In addition to the *Ghatiaśasi* the Perūr *ghaṭika* had a *nāyaka*. At Alampūr, the *mahāsthānadhipati* of the temple appears to have been the administrative officer. In the *ghaṭikas*, instruction was given not only in the traditional subjects like *Vedas* and *Vedangas* but also in *Āyurveda*, Dhanurveda, Gandharva and Arthaśāstra. The temple and *maṭhas* also served as centres of education.

These educational institutions must have catered to the needs of expanding bureaucracy under Cāḷukyas and Kākatīyas. The administrative machinery especially under the Kākatīyas was dominated by the śūdras including the newly absorbed aborginals. For efficient discharge of their duties they must have received training in civil and military arts in the *ghaṭikas* and *maṭhas*. It is interesting to note that there were several non-brāhmaṇa scholars and poets of great merit in Sanskrit and Telugu like Rudradeva,[34] Jāyapa,[35] Baddena,[36] and Gona Buddha Reḍḍi.[37] The gates of knowledge were thus opened before the members of the śūdra caste probably under the influence of Jainism and radical śaivite sects.

Sectarinasism

The brāhmaṇa community gradually lost its solidarity. By the 10th and 11th centuries, regionalism became a feature of politics which reflected in social life. In the major communites in Āndhra, several endogamous groups formed generally on the basis of occupation and territorial division. Brāhmaṇas too came to be divided into sects such as *Kammanāṭi, Kāsalnāṭi, Velanāṭi,* and *Āruvelanāṭi* brāhmaṇas. In the earlier stages, religious beliefs and practices also contributed to such group formation. These groups during the Kākatīya period when compared to earlier ages. The major sects which can be marked out are (1) *Smārtas* (2) *Ārādhyas* and (3) *Śrīvaiṣṇavas*.

The Smārtas

The smārtas are those who followed the *smṛtis* in their daily rituals and other religious practices. They worshipped both Śiva and Viṣṇu on equal footing. However, rituals formed the mainstay of this sect. Most of them followed the Śaṅkara school of *Advaita* and offered daily worship to *Pañcāyatana.*[38]

Gradually, there arose the *Vaidika* and *Niyogi* sects among the *smārta* brāhmaṇas. As the names imply a *vaidika* is one who made out a living by officiating at and conducting vedic rituals and functions whereas a *niyogi* is one who held an administrative or military post. The *niyogis* had to their name the suffixes like *mantri, preggaḍa, herggaḍa, amātya, rāju* etc, whereas the *vaidikas* has *bhaṭṭu, peddi sūri* etc., as suffixes. But, before the Kākatīya time this bureaucratic class of brāhmaṇas did not develop into a strictly separate sect. Though the differentiation between the two classes of brāhmaṇas had its beginnings in the Cāḷukyan period,[39] it did not grow rigid even during the Kākatīya times. An inscription from Pānugallu[40] (A.D. 1121) records that the government of Māḍuvula village in Kukkaḍam-30 was granted to Bhīmana *preggaḍa* while a village in Aḍḍalūru-70 was granted to Doḍḍaya *bhaṭṭu* as estates. Doḍḍaya *bhaṭṭu* was referred to as the son of the above Bhīmana *preggaḍa*. This shows that the *vaidika* and *niyogi* sects were not clearly seperated or not crystallised as endogamous groups or sects in the early Kākatīya period. The life of Gangādhara shows how an *agrahāra* brāhmin became a *niyogi*. His Karīmnagar inscription records Gangādhara's receiving *niyogi vrittis* (insignia of office) from king Rudra along with the title *amātya*. At the end of the inscription he is referred to as Gangarāju.[41] This shows hows *niyogis* were formed out of *agrahāra* brāhmaṇas.

The Ārādhyas

Some sections of brāhmaṇas, who were not satisfied with the *smārta* system, were attracted to the devotional cults of Śaivism and Vaiṣṇavism. Radical Śaivism, as it appears, develped as a protest against the brāhmānical rituals and exclusiveness and to counteract the influence of Jainism.This movement was led by

Śrīpati Paṇḍita and Śivalenka Mancana. Medieval Śaivism attracted large sections of people. Meanwhile, the echoes of vīraśaivism started in Karnāṭaka by Basaveśvara reached Āndhra including Telangāṇa. Mallikārjuna, the most famous of the *paṇḍitas,* developed a system of Śaivism as a compromise between devotionalism and brāhmānism that came to be known as the *ārādhya* system. The *ārādhyas,* according to K.A.N Sastri, are semi-lingāyats, half-converted *smārtas* who were the sacred thread and the *liṅga* and worshipped Gaṇapati. They do not take *prasāda* from a temple. They bury their dead, and have no *śrāddha* proper but only *ārādhana* with no *apasavya.*[42]

Śrīvaiṣṇavas

The śrivaiṣṇavas appear in the coastal Āndhra as early as A. d. 1023.[43] During the Cālukya-Cola period many Śrivaiṣṇava families migrated to the coastal Āndhra[44] and some of them might have spread to Telangāṇa. The established *vaiṣṇava samayas*[45] and *maṭhas*[46] and propagated Vaiṣṇavism. Magatala in Mahaboobnagar district appears to have become a Śrīvaiṣṇava centre under the Gona chiefs.[47] In the Nalgoṇḍa district, Būrugugaḍḍa appears to be another Śrīvaiṣṇavite centre.[48] The chieftain of Būrugugaḍḍa, Pradhāni Bollamarāju called himself *"Devakīputradāsa"*. Another inscription from Ālugaḍapa records[49] the consecreation of god Varada Gopīnātha by Rāmānujadāsa of Kauṇḍinya *gotra*, Perumāḍidāsa of Bhāradhvāja *gotra,* Pimbhanivillidāsa of Kauśika *gotra*. Evidently, these were brāhmaṇas who accepted Śrīvaiṣṇavism through *Dīkṣa* i.e., a mechanism of conversion, which consists of five items : 1) *puṇḍra* 2) *Mudra* 3) *prasāda* 4) *ekādaśī* 5) *dāsa* suffix to the names.[50] The *'dāsa'* suffix to their names therefore, clearly indicate their conversion to vaiṣṇavism. Incidentally, Komaṭi Bhaṇḍāri Śrī Lakṣmanadāsu of *Chenakula gotra* was also associated with the consecreation of the Varada Gopīnātha temple. Mahāpradhāni Rāyasthāpanācārya Kannāra Devanāyaka, perhaps a velama official, was the chieftain of the place. A large number of Śrivaiṣṇava brāhmaṇas appear to be living at Būdāpūr in Mahaboobnager district. However, it may be added that Śrīvaiṣṇavism was limited to a small section of brāhmaṇas in Āndhradesa in general.

RULING CLASSES

The kṣatriyas were the traditional ruling class. The *cāturvarṇa* system, entrusted them with political power. According to the *Dharmaśāstras,* they occupy the second place in the social heirarchy. There is a strong view that, in south India, there was no kṣatriya community as such.[51]

The caste of the early dynasties namely the Sātavāhanas, Ikṣvākus and Viṣṇukuṇḍins that ruled over Āndhra is a matter of serious debate. They too did not claim as *Kṣatrias*. The Sātavāhanas and Ikṣvākus did not mention their *gotra* whereas the Viṣṇukuṇḍins claimed ot have possessed the splendour of the brāhmaṇa and kṣatriya castes.[52] However, the Cālukyas described themselves as having belonged to lunar race and of mānavyasa *gotra*.[53] The Cālukyas of Mudigoṇḍa and Vemulavāḍa, being the branches of original Cālukya family claimed to have been kṣatriyas of lunar race. The Chodas of Kandūr claimed that they belonged to the kṣatriya family of the solar race and *Kāśyapa gotra*.[54] But most of the historians had the view that these ruling families were local people who claimed *kṣatriya* descent after attaining political power.[55]

By the time of the Kākatīyas, the Cālukya and Coḍa families declined all over Āndhradeśa. The history of the *kṣatriya* community in Telangāṇa during the Kākatīya period is a story of decline. With the loss of political power, they lost social status and moved downward in heirarchy. The thousand pillar-temple inscription (A. D. 1163)[56] refers to the existence of the *kṣudra kṣatriyas*. This means that the *kṣatriyas* of ancient lore began to lose their social status. The declining *kṣatriya* families became anxious to same the little power they had by cementing matrimonial alliances with the rising warrior communities. But, there were sove proud families who refused such alliances and they disappeared from political stage. The Polavāsa chief, Meda, is said to have preferred to surrender his kingdom than to giving his daughter in marriage to Rudra.[57] On the other hand, there is a strong view that Udayana Coḍa made peace with Rudradeva by offering his daughter in marriage.[58] The marriage of Rudramadevi with prince

Vīrabhadra of the Cālukya family shows the steady rise and upward mobility of the Kākatīyas and the decline of the Cālukyas.

There were a few kṣatriya families ruling in various parts of Telangāṇa as vassals of the Kākatīyas. The Bekkalu inscription (A. D. 1195)[60] records the building of several temples by members of a Ranjana *kṣatriya*, who were feudatories of Rudra. The *nāyankara* of Pariyāla, Chinni Rudradeva is referred to as belonging to the solar race of the *kṣatriyas*.[61] Ketaya nāyaka, the ruler of Sirikoṇḍa, claimed descent from the great Pallava family.[62] Kandūr Rāmanāthadeva Coḍa was ruling over parts of Nalgoṇḍa district as a feudatory of Rudramadevi.[63]

It must be said that the palce of the *kṣatriyas* as rulers and warriors was occupied by the rising peasant warrior communities who invariably belonged to the fourth caste. The Kākatīyas were śūdras and their court and camp were dominated by the śūdras. The caste of the Kākatīyas is not known. Attempts ara made to show that they were kammas. But it seems that they did not identify themselves with any of the castes. The śūdra castes that dominated the politics of the period were the velamas and reḍḍis. The velamas might have been the kāpus of Velanāḍu who rose to prominence at the court of the Durjayas of Chandol and after the war of Palnāḍ migrated to Telangāṇa seeking service at the Kākatīya court.[64]

The reḍḍis were widespread in Āndhra. They too were originally kāpus but probably rose ot the position of headmen in villages during the Rāṣṭrakūṭa hegemony.[65]

AGRICULTURAL COMMUNITIES

The people who were generally grouped under śūdra denomination in the *varṇa* order were engaged in agriculture and animal husbandry. These people formed into several endogomous groups castes or *kulas*. According to Somasekhara Sarma, "two important factors seem to have chiefly operated in giving rise to those divisions" in the fourth *varṇa*.[66] They are (1) geographical divisions whose boundaries are formed into several factors such as rivers or rivulets and hills. These prevented easy mobility form one division to another and, as such, endogomy in the same division became a salient feature.The regional kingdoms and the semi-independent principalities in each of these sub-divisions strengthened the sectarian differences. These physical and political conditions gave rise to several branches or *śākhās* like the *Velanāṭi, Kammanāṭi. Pākanāṭi* and *Vēṅgināṭi* sects among the two major communities of the medieval period viz., the brahmaṇas and the śūdras.

The second factor for endogomous group formation in the same geographical division is occupation. The corporate activity of a people pursuing an occupation or a trade resulted in marriage and kinship alliances being confined to the same occupational groups.

Some of the members of the *śūdra varṇa* who entered royal service either in the court or in the camp became politically powerful and entered into marital alliances with old ruling families. The non-vedic religions, Jainism and radical Śaivism, helped these families to gain even ritual purity and they claimed to be *satśūdras*, equal in status to the Kṣatriyas. This is a case of social mobility up on the vertical scale. Suvira Jaiswal says that among the śūdras of the south there are two sections, *satśūdras* and *asatśūdras* and the former were almost equal to *kṣatriyas* of the north in social status.[67]

The other section of the śūdras took to agriculture and allied occupations and remained'in their original status. The *balāñjas,* the *telikis* and the *sālevāru* were also of the śūdra community as memrchant-artisan groups.

Tammaḍlu

Tammaḍlu figure as a major agricultural community in Telangāṇa during the period under study. The Warangal Fort inscription (A.D. 1313)[68] refers to *guḍi tammaḍlu.* This might mean that this community were engaged in the cultivatiom of temple lands. The above record of Pratāpa Rudra's time registers certain land grants to *guḍi tammaḍlu,*[69] whose names end in the suffix *Jiyya*. The suffix *Jiyya* is generally held by temple priests, and the cultivaters of the temple land took the suffix out of their respect towards their masters. Gradually, some of them began to discharge the duties of priests, especially in the Śaivaite atemples. At present, the community of priests functioning as *arachakas* in Śaiva temples are known as *"Tambaḷe"*. This word *"tambaḷe"* may be the result of metamarphosis of *"tammaḍi"*

Gollavāru

Thurston has observed that the *gollas* were a pastoral class of Telugu people whose hereditary occupation was tending sheep and cattle and selling milk.[70] Their social status was fairly high and they were allowed to mix with the *kāpus* and *balijas* as they acquired land and took to tilling of the soil also.

Telagas

A.A. Stuart writes that the *telagas* are a Telugu caste of cultivators who were forrmerly soildiers in the armies of the 'Hindu' soverigns of Telangāṇa.[71] Somaśekhara Sarma bracket *telagas* along with other two subcastes, *onṭarulu* and *kāpulu.*[72] *Onṭarulu* were soldiers who were experts in the combat of singles known as *"ekkaṭi kayyamu"*. Several inscriptions of the Kākatīya times refer ot the *ekkaṭis* and *ekkaṭivīra parivāramu.*[73] They are associated with land grants also and they became big landholders. They were called upon to take up weapons at the time of war but during peace time they took to agriculture.

Reḍḍis

Reḍḍis appear to be the most singnificant agricultural community in Telangāṇa from very early times. The origin of the word *reḍḍi* and its meaning have generated a lot of discussion among scholars and historians. Dr. Fleet,[74] Rao Saheb H. Krishna Sastry[75] and Somasekhara Sarma[76] were some of the scholars who contributed largely to the understanding of the word reḍḍi. The consensus among these scholars is that the word evolved from *raṭṭaguḍi* which gradually metamorphosed into *raṭṭodi, raṭṭaḍi,* and then *raḍḍi* and finally *reḍḍi*. But the word *raṭṭa* is the *deśi* equivalent of *rāṣṭra*. The word *rāṣṭra* mean two things: government and province. Somaśekhara Sarma[77] holds the view that *raṭṭa* meant a people of an ethnic stock living all over the central Deccan, clans of which were known as *aratta, suratta* and *maratta*. The earliest imperial kings of this region (the central Deccan) were the Sātavāhanas. They divided the empire into provinces called *rattas* and the name *ratta* was derived from the tribal names of the people who lived in the regions.[78]

The early inscriptional evidence about *rattagullu* comes from the Cuḍḍapah district. The Rāmeśwaram epigraph[79] of the time of Renāṭi Cola chief Puṇyakumāra (A. D. 625-650) records the grant of 300 *marturs* of land and two gardens in the village Viriparti to god Vasantīśvara by the queen Vasantipori Cola mahādevi for the merit of Puṇyakumāra Pṛidhvī vallabha Cola mahārāja and the grant was made with the consent of the local *rattagullu*. The Chimakūru epigraph[80] of Vikramūditya Cola mahārājaś time (A.D. 700-725) records the gift of a garden land with the consent of certain Tolpakāmi *rattagullu*, Choliya *rattagullu* and Atiśaya *ratt agullu*. Krishnasastry was of the view that *"rattaguḍi"* connected with the later sanskrit word "Rāṣṭrakūṭa" meant the headman of the village.[81] The mention of the *rattagullu* in the land grant epigraphs only means that they were to supervise the execution of the particular grant.

An inscription from Drākṣārāma (A. D. 1281)[82] mentions *rattaḍam* meaning the office of a *rattaḍi*. As it appears *"rattaḍam"* or *reḍḍigam* was the authority and responsibility bestowed upon the leading member of the agricultual community with the title *grāmakūṭa*. The term *grāmakūṭa* transformed into *grāmaguṇḍa, gāmuṇḍa, gāvuṇḍa* and then *gauḍa*.[83] An inscription from Sanigaram (A. D. 1051)[84] states that Nārāyaṇayya, son of Vaijarāja *preggaḍa* of *mahāsāmanta* Kākatīya Beta renovated the Duddhamalla Jinālaya of Sanigaram and endowed it with a *rāṭna* with the consent of local *gāmuṇḍas* named Muppaḍayya and Punni reḍḍi. Another epigraph at the same place (A.D. 1053)[84] records the gift of land and a *rāṭna* to god madhupīśvara of Khaṇḍiśanigara in the villages Sanigaram and Baejavānka with the consent of the local *gāvuṇḍas* and Kāṭreḍḍi of Bejavānka. Thus the terms *reḍḍi* and *gāvuṇḍa* meant one and the same thing viz., the village headman who was generally the leading member of the agricultural community *(kāmpulu)*. As Somaśekhara Sarma rightly observed, "all reḍḍis are kāpus but all kāpus may not be reḍḍis".[85]

The reḍḍis or *panṭa kāpus* (protectors of harvest) as they are known are divided into fourteen sects with the following prefixes:[86] (1) Pākanāṭi (2) Velanāṭi (3) Moṭāṭi (4) Morasa (5) Cāngalunāṭi (6) Munnūṭi (7) Panṭa (8) Nāreṭi (9) Bhūmanci (10) Desaṭi (11) Ayodhya (12) Oruganṭi (13) Kuricheṭi and (14) Ganḍikoṭa.

These names make it clear that these divisions are mostly based on the region where the *panṭa kāpus* settled.

Īdaravāru

Īdaravaru or *īndulavāru* were a community associated with the maintenance of the toddy-yielding trees. The Pratāpacaritra[87] mentions that there were several *īnduvala* houses in Warangal city. Some inscriptions of this period also mention the *īndula* community. We may say that this community was looking after horticulture especially of the palm trees *(tāṭi)* and the native date plam trees *(īta)*. It may be added that this community was entrusted with the responsibility of maintaining and guarding of the flower and fruit gardens and groves as well. The Nāgulapāḍu inscription (A.D. 1303)[88] refers to *īdaravāru* as one of the *padunenimidi samayāla samasta praja*.

Upparavāru

The *Pratāpacharitra*[89] mentions that many families of *uppara* community lived in the Warangal city. The *upparulu* worked with earth and mud. This was an important occupation connected with agriculture and especially with the tank buillding and canal digging. The Būrugugaḍḍa inscription[90] mentions *uppara* as one of the 18 communities.

MERCHANT AND ARTISAN COMMUNITIES

1. Komaṭis

The traditional merchant class among the Āndhras claimed that they have belonged to the *vaiśya varṇa* or the third order of the *varṇa* system. In the Vedic times, agriculture, animal husbandry, industry and trade were the occupations of the *vaiśyas*.[91] But after the emergence of the *śūdra* caste. the *vaiśyas* almost monopolised trade and commerce. In medieval times, the local traders in south India identified themselves with the *vaiśyas* of the Vedic Āryan order. But the community was known in the Telugu country as *komaṭis*. In the inscriptions of Telangāṇa, during the period of our study, the word *komaṭi* occurs more frequently than the term *vaiśya*.[92] Thus we may say that the term *komati* was more popular than the term vaiśya which is only Sanskritic adoption in the wake of Āryanisation. The preference of the *komaṭis* for the name *vaiśya* might be the result of the general desire found among the rich sections of people for higher social status.

The origin of the word *komaṭi* is a subject of controversy. Some scholars believe that the word *komaṭi* is a derivate of Gomaṭha.[93] They argue that the *komaṭis* were Jains from early times and adopted the *Gomaṭha sāmpradāya*. Attempts are made to connect the word with 'go' or cow and *gomati* is explained as having a generous mind as cow.[94]

The *Śrīvaiśyapurāṇam* contains the legendary lore of the vaiśya community.[95] Accordin to this work the vaiśyas of 74 *gotras* possessed 18 towns including Penugoṇḍa in the West Godāvari district, their headquarters. The vaiśyas formed into a corporate body and enjoyed autonomous administration of these towns each of which had an assembly called *nakaram* with a *nakarasvāmi* at its head. It further narrates the story of *kanyakā*, the daughter of the *nagarasvāmi* of Penugoṇḍa. *Kanyakā* preferred to die in order to save the honour of the community against the lust of Cālukya Viṣṇuvardhana of Rājahmunḍry. Along with her, according to the story, elders of 102 families *(gotras)* entered the sacrificial fire and perished. Vāsavīkanyakā became the diety of the *vaiśya* community and the *vaiśyas* belonging to the 102 *gotras* became pure *vaiśyas*.

The legend of Vāsavi Kanyakā is not found in any epigraph of Telangāṇa. Nor is there any reference to Penugoṇḍa as the original place of the *komaṭis*. The *komaṭis* of Telangāṇa therefore appear as a local trading community without much of an ambition for sanskritisation. It may further be assumed that this community continued to prefer Jainism which was very popular in Telangāṇa till Beta II (A.D.1076-1108) became a Śaivite.[96] The main occupation of this community was local and retail trade. Some of them were also engaged in highly prosperous trade lines. The Govindāpuram inscription (A.D. 1122)[97] refers to the grant of *taḍukambātika* (¼ of *taḍila*), a guild levy on horse traders belonging ot the *vaiśya* caste to Pārśva Jineśvara installed by one Nāgarāju, a minister of Guṇḍa, the Polavāsa ruler.

The *komaṭis* formed into a corporate body called *nakaram*[98] and elected a chief known as *nagarasvāmi* or *nagarmukhya*. He was also known as *"śreṣhṭi"* or *"seṭṭi"*. The *nakaram* looked after the affairs of the community such as the collection and payment of taxes, peaceful conduct of trade etc. The Rāchūr inscription (A.D. 1157) divides the merchant households into three classes viz., *uttama, madhyama* and *kanisṭha*.[99] This division was made on the quantum of trade carried by the merchant and his prosperity, on which depended the rate of tax levied on him.

The rich *komaṭis* exhibited social consciousness and undertook welfare activities. The Pillalamaṛṛi inscription (A.D. 1202)[100] refers to a *komaṭi ceṛuvu*, a tank built by *komaṭi* community.

2. The balāñja community

The *balāñjas* were the other major community of traders. These are generally referred to as *Vīrabalāñja Ayyāvaḷi* 500 and *Vīrabalāñja* and *Ayyāvaḷi*-500 *Vīrabalāñja*. *Balāñja* or *baliñja* apears to be a *deśi* form of the Sanskrit word, *vaṇija*, meaning a merchant. The prefix *"vīra"* suggests that this community was an armed merchant community.The guild *Ayyāvaḷi* has been discussed in the chapter on trade. These constituted an itinerent merchant community.

The *Vīrabalāñjas* had a long *praśasti*. A Tripurāntakam inscription (A.D. 1292)[101] gives a list of titles of the *Vīrabalāñja* community. The Chittāpūr inscription[102] describes the leader of the local *Vīrabalāñjya* community Bairiseṭṭi as *"Vīrabaliñjya dharmopadeśa karta"* and *"Ayyāvaḷi Pañchāśata Vīrasahasra sahasragunālankrita*". Bairiseṭṭi consecrated a *trikūṭa* temple built by this community and on the occasion, made extensive land grants to the temple complex. The *Siddheśvara Caritra*[103] mentions that 15,000 *baliñjas* lived in the city of Warangal. They were armed to protect themselves from highway robbers. During the Kākatīya period they began to settle down at political centres such as Warangal, Chiṭṭāpūr and Kūcimañci and continued their trading activity by forging alliances with the local trading communities like the *Ubhayanānādeśi Pekkaṇḍru*.

3. Teliki Community

The Telikis were a community of oil-millers and oil-mongers. They formed into a guild known as *Telikivevuru* and called themselves as Bezawāḍa *śāsanulu*. Sundaram opines that Bezawāḍa was their operational headquarters and they had met at Bejzawāḍa and given themselves a code of conduct to be followed by the members of their community.[104]

4. Sālevāru

The Sālevāru form another important aritsan merchant community. They were wholesale and ratail traders as well as manufacaturers of all types of textiles from coarse cloth to muslin and silk. The Girmājipeṭ inscription[105] refers to them as *Dharma-sālīyajanulu*. The *Sidheśvara Carita*[106] mentions that the *Padmasāli* community was residing in Warangal city. The Āvanca and Ālavā-nipalli inscriptions refer to a guild, *paṭṭasālīlu*.[107] The *paṭṭasāliulu* may be a branch of the *sāle* community who specialised in manufacturing silk cloth and supplied to the market and temples. A later record[108] mentions specialist groups in the *sāle* community. They are (1) *tantuvāya* (weaver) (2) *vastrabhedaka* (dyer) (3) *vastra-rakṣhaka* (sewre) and (4) *devānga* (spinner). The *mēre* community mentioned in *Siddheśvara Carita*[109] followed the occupations of tailoring or sewing. They are therefore identical with the *vastra-rakṣhakas* of the record.

5. Akkasālevaru and allied commuities

Several inscriptions refer to the dealers in metals. They are known by the general term *Pañchalohāla behārulu*.[110] The term means that they were merchants dealing in five metals. However, the community guild *Panchāṇamvāru* which appears in the coastal Āndhra does not figure in the epigraphs of Telangāṇa. It may be said that the *Panchalohāla behārulu* were a branch of the larger guild *Panchāṇamvāru*.

The *Panchāṇamvāru* was a significant artisan community in medieval Āndhradeśa. The mythical origin of *Panchāṇamvāru* preserved in the *Nagarakhaṇḍa* traces their lineage to Viśvakarma, whose five sons, Manu, Maya, Śilpi, Thawaṣṭra, Viśvajna-Daivajña.[111] They were considered to be the originators of the five crafts of blacksmithy, carpentary, stone-carving, metal work and jewellery respectively. The inscriptions in Telangāṇa do not use the collective term *panchāṇamvāru,* but often refer to *akkasālevāru* who figure among the *aṣṭādaśamahāpraja,* and to mūsaravāru and tagaramvāru.[112] The latter were merchants trading in metals like copper and tin. Another community is *kāsevāru*. They were workers in stone. Each of these communities acquired specialised skills in their crafts working in metals, weed and stone and treaded in the articles made of them. In an economy dominated by agriculture, the importance of the metal worker and the carpenter can never be underestimate. The stone mason also played an important role in the period which witnessed large scale building of forts, temples and tanks.

The leading members of this community added the suffix *oju* to their names.[113] *Oju* or *ojja* in Telgu means teacher. From this, we may infer that the leading member acted as teachers and trained apprentices in their own craft. The pupils, in their turn, assisted the masters in their work.

REFERENCES

1. P. H. Prabhu, *Hindu Social Organisation* (Bombay, 1961, pp. 326-328.
2. *Sacred Laws of the Āryas,* Tr.G. Bhühler, (Delhi, 1984) Part_II, *Baudhāyana dharma śāstra, Praśna* II. *Adhyāya* 6 *Khaṇḍika* II.
3. S.I.I. IV 371, S.I.I.X, 79.
4. P.I. No. 14.
5. Tel. Ins. I, pp. 55-61.
6. I.A.P. Wl. 58.

7. P. I. No. 15.
8. P.I. No. 14.
9. Ibid.
10. Ibid.
11. Tel. Ins. I, 55-61, C.I.T.D., IV, P. 142.
12. Baddena, *Sumatīśatakam* (Hyderabad, 1968) v. 7.
13. Mārana, *Mārkaṇḍeyapurāṇam*, (Hyderabad) Canto III, v. 248.
14. Tel. Ins. I. p. 118.
15. Ibid, p. 141.
16. Romila Thaper, Social Mobility in Ancient India. *Ancient Indian Social History - Some Interpretations* (Hyderabad, 1984) pp. 122-151.
17. I.AP. Kn. 28.
18. Ibid, 25.
19. Ibid.
20. Ibid, 30.
21. M. somasekhara Sarma - *A Forgotten Chapter of Āndhra History,* (Madras, 1945), p. 26.
22. Ibid, pp . 27-28.
23. P.V.P. Sastry, *The Kākatīyas* (Hyderabad, 1978) p. 128.
24. Kāse Sarvappa, *Siddheśvara Caritra,* (Hydearabad, 1960), p. 126.
25. I.A.P. Wl. 40.
26. Tel. Ins. I. 124, Ibid, 55-61, Ibid 78-79.
27. I.A.P. wl. 24.
28. Tel. Ins. I, p. 118.
29. Ibid, p. 141.
30. E.I. Vol. VIII 26.
31. E.C. Vol. VIII, Introduction, Part- IV, *śloka* 123.
32. Tel. Ins. II, pp. 45-46.
33. P.I.No.14.
34. P.V.P. Sastry. Op. cit., pp. 292-299.
35. Ibid.
36. Ibid.
37. Ibid.
38. B.S.L. Haumantha Rao, *Religion in Āndhra,* (Guntur, 1973) p. 314.
39. E.I. Vol. VIII p. 239.
40. K.C.S.C.S. pp. 156-160.
41. I.A.P. Kn. 25.
42. K.A.N Sastry—*Development of Religion in South India,* (Madras, 1962), p. 64.
43. S.I.I., VI 139.
44. M. Somasekhara Sarma—*The History of Reḍḍi Kingdoms* (Waltair, 1948), p. 314.
45. Tel. Ins. II, pp. 126-127.
46. Tel. Ins. I, p. 169.
47. Tel. Ins. II, pp. 126-127.

48. Tel. Ins. I, pp. 71-72.
49. C.I.T.D. III, Ng 2, p. 108.
50. V. Rangacharyain *Cultural Heritage*, IV, p. 176.
51. Suvira Jaiswal, Studies in Early Indian Social History. *The Indian Historical Review*, Vol. VI, Nos. 1-2, pp. 1-63.
52. S. Sankaranarayana, *The Viṣṇukuṇḍins and their times* (Delhi, 1977), pp. 24-26.
53. A.P.G.A.S. No. 6, Māruṭūru plates of Pulakeśi II, p. 1.
54. E.A. IV, pp. 55-65.
55. Suvira Jaiswal, op. cit.
56. I.A.P. Wl. p. 36.
57. I.A.P. Wl. p. 122.
58. P.V.P. Sastry, *The Kākatīyas* (Hyderabad, 1978) p. 89.
59. Ibid, p. 127.
60. I.A.P. Wl. 42.
61. I.A.P. Kn. 38.
62. K.C.S.C.S. pp. 193-195.
63. K.C.S.C.S. pp. 242-248.
64. B.S.L. Hnumantha Rao, Nāgāmba alias Nāyakurālu, Hindu College Magazine, (Guntur, 1963).
65. M. Somasekhara Sarma, op. cit., 70 ff.
66. M. Somasekhara Sarma, op. cit.
67. Suvira Jayaswal, Studies in early Indian Social history: Trends and possibilities, *Indian Historical Review*, Vol. I, 1-2, p. 40.
68. I.A.P. Wl. 89.
69. Ibid.
70. Thurston E., *Castes and Tribes of Southern India* Vol. I, p. 284-286.
71. A.A. Stuart, in *Castes and Tribes of Southern India* Vol. III, p. 13-14.
72. M. Somasekhara Sarma - *History of the Reḍḍi Kingdoms* (Waltair, 1948) p. 241.
73. I.A.P. Wl. 37.
74. E.I. II, p. 22.
75. H. Krishna Sastry, E.I. XI, p. 342-343.
76. M. Somasekhara Sarma, op. cit., chap. IV, Appendix-A, 70 ff.
77. Ibid.
78. Ibid, p. 72.
79. I.A.P. Cp. Part-I, No. 14.
80. I.A.P. Cp. Part-I No. 16.
81. H. Krishna Sastry, Op. cit.
82. S.I.I. IV, No. 1281.
83. Somasekhara Sarma, op. cit., p. 129.
84a. I.A.P. Kn. 14.
84b. Ibid, No. 15.
85. M. Somasekhara Sarma, op. cit., p. 50.
86. Ibid, p. 51.

87. Kāse Sarvappa, *Siddheśvara Caritra* (Hyderabad, 1960) p. LXXVI.
88. Tel. Ins. I, p. 89-90.
89. Kāse Sarvappa, op. cit.
90. Tel. Ins. I, pp. 83-84.
91. *Hindu Polity* (The ordinances of Manu) translated by A. C. Burnell ed. by E.W. Hoppkins, Ludhiyana, 1972, p. 316.
92. K.C.S.C.S., p. 199, Tel , Ins. I, p. 92, P.I. No. 6, etc.
93. Bharati, April-55, T. Ramachandra, *Nuḍi-Nānuḍi.*
94. E. Thurston, *Castes and Tribes of south India*, Delhi (1975), p. 306.
95. *Śrīvaiśyapurāṇam* - Published by Vavilala Ramaswamy Sastry and Sons, Madras.
96. Tribhuvanamalla Durga's Khājipeṭ inscription (I.A.P. Wl. 15, A. D. 1098) records the granting of an *agrahāra* with the name Śivapura to the Kālāmukha Śiva ascetic Rāmeśvara Paṇḍita, the ācārya of Mallikārjuna Śilāmaṭha of Śrīparvata. This is the first instance of a Kākatīya grant to a śaivite ācārya. Prola I appears to be a follower of Jainism (I.A.P. Kn. No. 15).
97. I.A.P. Wl. 26.
98. K. Sundaram, *Studies in Economic and Social Conditions of Medieval Andhra* (Machilipatnam, 1968), p. 59.
99. K.C.S.C.S., p. 199.
100. Tel. Ins. I, pp. 26-31.
101. S.I.I., X, 473.
102. I.A.P. Kn. 38.
103. Kāse Sarvappa, op. cit.
104. K. Sundaram, op. cit., p. 44.
105. I.A.P. Wl. 61.
106. Kāse Sarvappa, op. cit.
107. Tel. Ins. II, pp. 57-62.
108. A.R. 1918, P. 174.
109. Kāse Sarvappa, op. cit.
110. I.A.P. Wl. 71.
111. K. Sundaram, op. cit,. p. 25-36.
112. Tel. Ins. I, p. 89-90, I.A.P. Wl. 63.
113. Tel. Ins. I, pp. 169-172.

CHAPTER—VII

SOCIAL MOBILITY

The foregoing political events and diverse economic activities facilitated social mobility in Telangāṇa in particular and Āndhradeśa in general. Social mobility is of two types horizontal and vertical.[1] Horizontal mobility is geographical, i.e., movement from one place to another. Vertical mobility is either upwards or downwards in the social status of a family or a group of families. These movements are interrelated.

Horizontal mobility is caused mostly by the pressure of population. Political disturbances and religious conflicts also make people go about in search or patronage and security. In times of hardship or natural calamities, families move seeking better chances of livelihood. Vertical mobility may broadly be defined as rise or fall in social status of a family. Improvement in the economic status of a family generally leads to a rise in its social status and such a rise is quickly possible at a place far away from the native home.[2] However, the status of a family has two aspects ritual and actual. The ritual status is fixed by the Dharmaśāstras[3] whereas the actual status is determined by economic and political factors.

Both the aspects of mobility, horizontal as well as vertical, are present in Telangāṇa during the period of the present study. The factors that led to this in Telangāṇa region may be said as (1) stable politcal conditions (2) expansion in agriculture and trade (3) increasing bureaucratisation of administration and (4) large-scale military recruitments.

During the early phase of the period, Telangāṇa, being an integral part of the Rāṣṭrakūṭa and Cāḷukya empires, was almost free from political disturbances. There were no doubt troop movements across the region but it was free from foreign attacks and did not become the scene of any major war. With the rise of the Kākatīyas, the erstwhile *sāmantas* were also suppressed and the region was united under the effective rule of the Kākatīyas. Telangāṇa could develop a political individuality. About the same time as Vēṅgi lost her political importance and was drawn into Cāḷukya-Coḷa conflict,[4] Telangāṇa attracted different sections of people from the coastal Āndhra.

MOBILITY OF ELITE GROUPS

The elite groups in the society are generally brāhmaṇas and rulers including civil and military leaders. The radical religious movements and the widespread network of educational institutions, especially *ghaṭikas* and *maṭhas*, gave rise to a large elite section in the fourth caste also.

Mobility among brāhmaṇas

The brāhmaṇa community was one of the most mobile communities in this age. As the Rāsṭrakūṭas were patrons of Jainism, many Jain brāhmaṇas migrated from coastal Āndhra, especially from Karmarāṣṭra to Telangāṇa. The family of Pampa, the first poet in Kannaḍa is known to have left Vangipaṛṛu[5] and secured the patronage of the Vemulavāḍa Cāḷukyas. Pampa was a kamma brāhmaṇa, a brāhmaṇa from kammanāḍu. Other famous poets Ranna (C.A.D.993)[6] and Nagavarama I (C.A.D.900)[7] and Durgasimha (C.A.D.1200)[8] were also kamma *brāhmaṇas*. Some of the generals in the service of Vikramāditya VI, Sarvadeva and Chāvuṇḍa[9] were of kamma kula. It is of great interest to note that Mādirāja, the father of Basaveśvara, the founder of Vīraśaivism, is described in a Kannaḍa poem of poet Harihara as beloging to *kamma kula*.[10] One of the inscriptions from Sanigaram (A.D.1149) refers to a daṇḍanāyaka. Mandapārya of Ātreya gotra as kamma-kulābharaṇa.[11] On the other hand, the names of most of the teachers in the *Ghaṭikas* of Perūur, Alampūr suggest that they were from Karnāṭaka[12] In the inscrliptions of Telangāṇa and coastal Āndhra, we come across brāhmaṇas with the suffix of *bhaṭṭu* to their names and it is held that they were immigrants to Āndhra from Karnāṭaka.[13]

The great Kannaḍa poet Pampa was jaina brāhamaṇa and it is held that his family migrated to Vemulavāḍa for fear of persecution[14] at the hands of eastern Cāḷukyas who were śaivites. According to the *Orugallu kaifiyat*[15] many jains migrated to Anmakoṇḍa from Rājahmuṇdry because Rājarājanarendra was hostile to the Jains. Even from Tamilnāḍu during this period, jains appear to have migrated to Telangāṇa[16] and probably settled at Kollipāka,

On the other hand, it was the period when the Śaivite *acāryas* especially of the Goḷakī *maṭha* migrated from Dāhala[17] and established several branches of their maṭha in different parts of Āndhra including Telangāṇa.[18]

The head of the Golakī maṭha invited vedic scholars of different *gotras* to Āndhra from Bengāl and Tāmilnaḍ.[19]

Vedic scholars also are found migrating from place to place in search of work and livelihood. When new *agrahāras* were established, brāhmaṇas from various parts of the land were settled there. The Manthen a inscription (A.D. 1199)[20] records the establishment of an *agrahāra,* Mallikārjunapuram by *Tribhuvana-vidyā cakravarti* Manchi bhaṭṭopadhyāya, Gaṇapatideva's priest. Many brāhmaṇas from Vellankipura *agrahāra* in Vēṅgideśa migrated to Anmakoṇḍa and rose to prominence in the service of the Kākatīyas.[22] Another instance of mobility of brāhmaṇas is the case of Indulūri family.[23] These are the instances by talented brāhmaṇas who sought service at the courts.

Ruling elite

There is a strong tradition taht the Rāsṭrakūṭas appointed their own people as the rulers of the conquered regions.[24] The Rāṣṭrakūṭa subordinates, the Cāḷukyas of Vemulavāḍa and the Kākatīyas seem to have come from Karnāṭaka. But the Coḍas of Kandūru migrated to Telangāṇa from Eṛuvanāḍu[25] in Kurnool district and became prominent as the *sāmantas* under the Raṣṭrakūṭas. The Cāḷukyas who were overthrown by the Rāṣṭrakūṭas, appear to have migrated to Telangāṇa and made Anmakoṇḍa their base.[26] It is known that the predecessors of Tailapa II ruled from Anmakoṇḍa and Tailapa took the title Lord of Trilingadeśa.[27] After they rose to imperial position, the Cāḷukyas of Kalyān followed the policy of the Rāsṭrakūṭas and many of their generals and ministers are found at important places like Poṭlakere[28] Bhuvanagiri,[29] Perūr,[30] Kollipāka,[31] Gangāpuram[32] and Vemulavāḍa.[33]

During the reign of Rudradeva, after the famous battle of Palnāḍ (A.D. 1176), the *velamas* appear to have migrated to Telangāṇa from Coastal Āndhra. The *velamas*, as the name itself suggests, should have been the original inhabitants of Velanāḍu. They appear to have been an agricultural community of Velanāḍ who rose to political prominence at the court of the Durjayas of Chandol and later in Palnāḍ.[34] After their defeat at the hands of the *reḍḍis* the *velamas* might have crossed the Krishna and entered Telangāṇa. It is also not improbable that Rudradeva who was planning to invade Velanāḍu welcomed the Velamas with the hope that they could be of help to him in destroying the Durjayas. Soon, the velamas became very powerful at the Kākatīya court and justified the hopes of Rudradeva by becoming *rayasthapanācāryas*[35] in times of trouble in the Kākatīya history.

Another element that appears to have made the social texture of Telangāṇa complex was the infiltration of the Marāṭhas. Since the time of Rudradeva there had developed a conflict between the Yādavas and Kākatīyas and Rudra and his brother Mahādeva died at the hands of the *Yādavas*.[36] Rudramāmba avenged the defeats by carrying the victorious Kākatīya arms upto the gates of Devagiri.[37] with a view to create more troubles to the Yādava king, Rudrama gave one of her daughters, Rudrama, in marriage to Ellāṇadeva, a Yādava prince who was at her court.[38] In the course of these conflicts, it appears many Marāṭha soldiers and generals were left behind. They moved southward and settled in Ārebhūmi, considered to be a region around Śrīśailam inhabited by the Marāṭhas.[39] They rose to prominence at Vallūr-Gaṇḍikoṭa. Jannigadeva, the Kāyastha chief of Gaṇḍikoṭa became *bāhattaraniyogādhipati*[40] under Gaṇapati.

MOBILITY OF NON-ELITES

The mobility of non-elite groups was somewhat restricted. They were generally bound to the land and native locality. But, mobility is not completely absent among them. Expansion of agriculutre, extensive tank and temple building and development of trade gave rise to movement of people from one place to another leading to the growth of urban centres. The Warangal fort inscription of A. D. 1313[41] refers to the gift of some money to God Sahasralinga Gaṇapatīśvara by Kāmpus belonging to *Sannagarapuvāḍa* and *Pānugaṇṭiwāḍa*. Evidently, the Kāmpus of Sanigaram and Pānugal moved to the capital city, probably in search of work. Trade also made for mobility. One of the Perūr inscriptions[42] refers to *Aruvanakaram* of the place. It was a merchant guild composed of Tamil merchants. They settled down at Perūr and built a temple for Aravanakareśvaradeva.

However, the Malakāpuram inscription[43] records a grant of an *agrahāra* by Gaṇapatideva's daughter in A.D. 1261 to *Dīkṣāguru* Viśveśvara Śambhu along with the peasants and cultivators. A later inscription from Warangal district prohibited the migration of peasants from a village granted to the brāhmaṇas.[44] This might mean, as B.N.S. Yadava suggests, a restriction on the mobility on the peasants and cultivators by the ruling classes.[45]

RISE OF PEASANT-WARRIOR COMMUNITIES

The rise of the peasant-warrior communities and the absorption of aboriginal tribes into the traditional social order are two good examples of vertical social mobility during this period. This is upward movement. But earlier ruling families, supposed to have been kṣatriyas, entered tinto marriage alliances with the rising political groups. This is an instance of downward movement in social scale.

During the Kākatīya period, communities such as the velamas, reḍḍis and kammas rose to political prominence. They were originally agriculturists (*kāpus*). The constant warfare during the eastern Cāḷukyan period gave them an opportunity to join military services. War provided scope for plunder and become rich and powerful. Gradually, through royal and efficient service, they rose to high positions of status such as *mantri, pradhāni, daṇḍanāyaka, māṇḍalika* and *sāmanta*.[46] Thus, a section who took to arms was formed out of the peasant communities. This may be termed as the nāyaka community and the elite took suffixes like nāyaka, nāyaḍu and nīḍu. The *Palnāṭivīracaritra*[47] refers to *vīranāyakas* of different communities that took part in the battle of Kārempūḍi. The Mallenāyaka of Māṭeḍu *inscriptions*[48] belonged to *puḷinda* community. Rājāñāyaka and Kāṭayanāyaka of Goḍiśala inscription[49] were brāhmaṇas. Brahmanāyaḍu of Palnāḍ belonged to the velama community. Musunūri Prolayanāyaka and Kāpayanāyaka are considered to have belonged to the *Kamma* community.[50] An inscription at Yanamadala (A. D. 1251)[51] refers to a gift by the sons of Muktāsāni, Kāṭamareḍḍi and Bayya Reḍḍi. In the same epigraph, the son of her sister, Dannesāni, is referred to as Eṛṛangomminayaḍu and her brother-in-law as Sūrapanāyaḍu. Thus, the suffix *nāyaḍu* or *nāyaka* did not signify a sub-caste but only elites who achieved military authority and official position. It seems that *velamas* differentiated themselves from other *nāyaka* Communities by calling themselves *padmaṇāyakas.*

Many feudatory families ruling over Telangāṇa and coastal Āndhra under the overlordship of Kākatīyas belonged to the fourth caste and who rose in status by the strength of their arms. The Koṭas of Amarāvati, the Reḍḍis of Pillalamaṛṛi, Vardhamānapuram and Pālampeṭ are some examples. After the fall of the Kākatīyas, the Āndhra country witnessed the establishment of independent kingdoms at Rekapalli by the *kamma* chiefs of the Musunūri family, at Addanki by the *panta reḍḍis* and at Rāchakoṇḍa by the *velamas.* These examples show the upward vertical mobility of the peasant community.

Satśūdras

The peasant warrior communities who rose to political importance naturally aspired for corresponding social status. The Bekkallu inscription[52] of Malli Reḍḍi says that because they were looked down upon as they were supposed to have been born of the feet of Brahma, they accepted Jainism, practised truth, non-violence and other virtues and became *śiṣṭas* (pure). Jainism thus raised the *śūdras* in the social status. The radical śaivite sects introduced the practice of *dīkṣa*[53] initiation which gave some sort of ritual purity to the śūdras, who began to claim to be *satśūdras.* One of the *Drākṣharama* inscriptions describes the donor as *satśūdra-*

cūḍāmaṇi.[54] These śūdras began to claim even equality with brāhmaṇas. In the inscriptions of coastal Āndhra we come across statements like *Vipparla vaṁśa iti vipra kulopamānat*[55] and *Caturthavaṁśas caturānana.*[56]

The case of the Kākatīyas is itself example of upward social mobility. The early inscriptions give different origins of the family. The Bayyāram tank inscription[57] says that the Kākatīyas belong to Durjayakula. The rulers of Velanāḍu were Durjayas who clearly described themselves as śūdras.[58] The Māngallu plates[59] and the Khājipeṭ Dargah inscription[60] call the family as *sāmanta viṣṭivaṁśa* which may mean *viṣṭivaṁśa* who rose to *sāmanta* status. The term *viṣṭi* has ben discussed at length by scholars. It is held that the term meant forced labour employed also in agriculture.[61] The Telugu word *veṭṭi* which means forced labour is derivable from the sanskrit word *viṣṭi*. The early members of the family are Eṛiya Rāṣṭrakūṭa and Guṇḍaya Rāṣṭrakūṭa. The personal names give rise to the doubt that they belonged to a forest or hill tribe. It seems, therefore, that the Kākatīyas were originally an aboriginal tribe who took to agriculture and then entered the military service of the Rāṣṭrakūṭas. They soon became generals and frontier gaurds of the Rāṣṭrakūṭas. The Lingāla[62] and Vardhamānapuram[63] inscriptions attribute śūdra origin to Kākatīyas. The early members of the dynasty were Jains but from Beta II they became adherents of Kālāmukha Śaivism. As mentioned above Jainism and radical Śaivism helped the Kākatīyas in rising higher in social status. From the time of Rudradeva onwards, they switched on to brāhmānical religion and attained political supremacy. The Kākatīyas, after Gaṇapatideva's time were referred to as Kṣatriyas.[64] However, Vidyānātha, the court poet of Pratāparudra, says that the fame of the Kākatīya family excels that of solar and lunar races,[65] implying thereby that they belonged to neither.

Aboriginal tribes

From about the 7th century A. D. many of the aboriginal tribes such as the śabaras, puḷindas and boyas were absorbed into the traditional social order. Such a process of acculturation was necessitated by the expansion of agriculture through the multiplication of *agrahāras* and by increased military requirements. The Rāṣṭrakūṭas recruited śabaras into their army. Govinda IV, after conquering Vēṅgi, posted his feudatory śabara chiefs who held Vēṅgi for seven years.[66] The Eastern Cāḷukyas encouraged the boyas of *Boyavihāradeśa* to accept service under them. After the destruction of *boya koṭṭams,* the boyas had spread over entire Āndhra i ncluding Telangāṇa.[67] They seem to have been admitted into all castes of the Hindu society from brāhmaṇa to śūdra.[68] Some of them joined civil and military services under the Durjayas of Velanāḍu and rose to very high positions such as *māṇḍalika* and *mahāmaṇḍaleśvara.*[69] Jillaboya was a general in the service of Velanāṭi Rajendracoḍa. His brother Nāraboya, the ruler of Divi, was the founder of the Ayya family.[70] After the occupation of Divi, Gaṇapatideva married Nārama and Perama, the princesses of Divi and appointed their brother Jāyapa as *Gajasāhiṇi* in the Kākatīya army.[71] Jāyapa, as already noted, was a great Sanskrit scholar and wrote *Nrittaratnāvaḷi,* a treatise on dance in Sanskrit.

The puḷindas were nother tribe that were absorbed into the Hindu Social order through military service. The Māṭeḍu records dated in the A. D. 1120, states that a puḷinda chief *Mahāsamanta* Vemabola Boḍḍama Mallenāyaka of Māṭeḍu was a *baṇṭu* of *mahāmandaleśvara* Kākatīya Prolarāju, who was himself a feudatory of Tribhuvanamalla Vikramāditya VI.[72] The statement of Mallenāyaka that the puḷinda *kula* was created by Brahma to protect the four *varṇas* implies the high status he claimed. The inscriptions record the building of several temples by Mallenāyaka for gods Īśvara, Nārāyana and Āditya. He excavated a tank called Mallasamudram and granted lands to the temples of Malleśvara, Keśavadeva and Vināyaka. All these lands were irrigated by the waters of Mallasamudram.

The inscription gives a detailed account of Mallenāyaka's geneology. His forefather, Būchena, belonged to *Vemabolakula,* a clan of the puḷindas. The puḷindas as a trans-Vindhyan non-āryan tribe, have been mentioned in association with the Āndhras in the *Aitareya Brāhmaṇa.*[73] They might have lived in northern parts of

Telangāṇa and been gradually integrated into the brāhmānical social order. It is possible that Mallenāyaka remembered his ancestry at the time of the record.

Būchena was described as *koṭamalla* which means 'fighter of forts'. He might have joined the Cāḷukyan army and distingushed himself in capturing forts. Būchena's third son, Reva joined the army of Kākati Beta, perhaps Beta II, and participated in many wars and protected the Kākatīya kingdom. He received many villages and titles in recognition of their service. These two inscriptions give us to understand how the members of the hill and forest tribes rose in social and political status by the strength of arms. The present donor *mahāsāmanta* Vemabola Boḍḍama Mallenāyaka is the son of Reva. Boḍḍama might have been his mother.

Thus, the *śabaras, puḷindas* and *boyas* who were aboriginal tribes got slowly integrated into the mainstream of the society as different castes through agricultural activity and military service.

REFERENCES

1. Romila Thaper—*Ancient Indian Social History—Some Interpretations.* (Hyderabad, 1984) pp. 122-151.
2. Ibid.
3. Ibid.
4. N. Venkataramanaiah—*The Eastern Cālukyas of Vēṅgi* (Madras, 1950) 218 ff.
5. I.A.P. Kn. No. 3.
6. P.B. Desai—*Basaveśvara and his times* (Dharwar, 1968) Appendix III, Note-1.
7. Ibid.
8. Ibid.
9. Ibid.
10. Ibid.
11. I.A.P. Kn. 24.
12. The Perūr epigraph (P. I. No. 3) mentions the names of the teachers at the *ghatika*. They include Kuppana Bhaṭṭu, Kesava Bhaṭṭu, Meḍaya Bhaṭṭu, Dasena Bhaṭṭār, Atyaṇa Bhaṭṭu, Janne Bhaṭṭu and the Alampūr epigraph (T. I. II 45-46) mentions Ghaḍiaśāsi Somaya, Koṇḍu Paṭṭema Bhaṭṭu among the mahājanas at the *ghaṭika*.
13. R. Suryanarayana Murthy, A.P.H.C. 'The Bhaṭ Brāhmins of Āndhradesa' X (Guntur, 1986) p. 76.

14. N. Venkataramanayya, Bharati, 1967, B.S.L. Hanumantha Rao, *Religion in Andhra* (Guntur, 1973) p. 187.
15. L.R. Vol. XI, p. 133 ff.
16. K.A.N. Sastri, *The Colas* (Madras, 1955) p. 224.
17. S.V.Pathak, *Śaiva Cults in Northern India*, p. 28.
18. S.I.I., V, 197, Ibid, 686.
19. S.I.I. X, 395.
20. I.A.P. Kn. 28.
21. I.A.P. Wl. 58.
22. I.A.P. Kn. 25.
23. M. Somasekhara Sarma, *A Forgottern Chapter of Āndhra History*, (Madras, 1945) p. 26.
24. A. S. Altekar, in *The Early History of the Deccan*, Ed. G. Yazdani, (London, 1960), p. 302.
25. B. N. Sastri, Introduction to K.C.S.C.S. p. 1-2.
26. E.A. IV, p. 143.
27. Ibid.
28. C.I.T.D. IV., 18-22, 32-35, 36-39.
29. Tel. Ins. 2, p. 59.
30. P.I. No. 4 C.I.T.D. IV. No. 12.
31. Tel. Ins. 1. 147-152, Tel. Ins. I, 145-146.
32. Tel. Ins. p. 105, p. 118, p. 124.
33. I.A.P. Kn., No. 18.
34. P. Lakshmikantam, Introduction to Palnāṭivīra Caritra (Vijayawada, 1961), p. 7.
35. C.I.T.D. III, No. 2 Tel. Ins. I, pp. 73-79.
36. N. Venkataramanaiah and M. Somasekhara Sarma in *The Early History of Deccan* Ed, G. Yazdani (London, 1960) p. 529.
37. S.E.A.P. No. 21.
38. A.P.G.A.S. No. 6, pp. 109-116.
39. Isvaradatt, *Prācīnāndhra bhūgoḷam*, (Secunderabad, 1979) pp. 29-30, S.I.I.X, 504.
40. I.A.P. Cp. Part I. No. 142.
41. I.A.P. Wl. 89.
42. P.I. No. 6.
43. S.I.I.X 335.
44. I.A.P. Wl 110.
45. B.N.S. Yadava "Immobility and subjection of Indian peasantry in early medieval complex", Indian Historial Reiview. Vol. I, p. 827.
46. Refer Table I.
47. Srinatha, *Palnāṭvīracaritra* (Vijayawada, 1961), pp. 297-298.
48. I.A.P. Wl. 24.
49. I.A.P. Kn. 30.
50. M Somasekhara Sarma, *A Forgotten Chapter of Āndhra History* (Madras, 1945) p. 33.

51. S.I.I. IV, p. 933.
52. I.A.P. Wl 20.
53. S.C. Nandimath, *A Hankbook of Viiraśaivism* (Dharwar, 1942), p. 10.
54. A.R. No. 349, of 1893, S.I.I. IV, 1239.
55. S.I.I. X, 373, Tel. Ins, Vol. X 65.
56. S.I.I. IV, No. 1182.
57. E.A. I, p. 71 ff.
58. S.I.I. VI,123.
59. E.A. I, p. 57 ff.
60. I.A.P. Wl. 15.
61. B.N.S. Yadava, Presidential Address, Section I, Proc. of I.H.C. (Bombay, 1980) p. 31. ff.
62. C.I.T.D. III Mn. 17.
63. Ibid, Mn. 47.
64. S.I.I. X, 371, *Siddheśvara Caritra* (p. 25 ff) and *Pratāpacaritra* (p. 2 ff.) call them Kṣhartiyas of lunar race.
65. Vidyānāth, *Pratāparudrīyam, Nāṭakaprakaraṇa*, (Madras, 1865), v. 13.
66. N. Venkataramanayya, *The Cālukyas of Vēṅgi*, (Madras, 1950), p. 167.
67. B.S.L. Hanumantha Rao, J.A.H.R.S. XXXVIII, Part IV, p. 79.
68. Ibid, p. 77 ff.
69. Ibid, p. 89.
70. Ibid.
71. P.V.P. Sastry, *The Kāklatīyas*, (Hyderabad, 1978), pp. 107-108.
72. I.A.P. Wl. 24, 25.
73. *Aitareya Brāhmaṇa* VII, 318.

CHAPTER—VIII

URBANISATION

The Deccan and south India experienced urbanisation during the 11th to 14th centuries. In the region, it is the second urbanisation, the first being during the Maurya-Sātavāhana age, as evidenced by Megasthanes. The Greek ambassador mentions that the Āndhras had thirty walled towns. These towns declined with the decline of trade which the Deccan carried on with the Roman world. Again as the Cālukyas succeeded in bringing large part of Deccan under their rule, the second urbanisation may be considered to have started in the 10th and 11th C.A.D.

There are several points of view as to the factors leading to urbanisation. Scholars such as Burton Stein,[1] Kenneth Hall,[2] Champakalakshmi[3] and Amita Ray[4] have written about the factors of urbanisation in early medieval south India. Stein's ideas are summarised as 'temple urbanisation'. But it is too simplistic a description. In fact, Stein's theory consists of two important factors which have led to urbanisation in Tāmilnāḍ during the 12th and 13th centuries. They are (1) consolidation of large units of governance and economic cooperation and (2) consturction of temples.[5] The first factor appears to imply the unification of large area under a single rule and establishment of an efficient system of administration, thus putting an end to internecine warfare which was a serious hindrance to economic growth. The first factor provided congenial conditions for the second factor i.e. building of huge temple complexes which acted as the centres for urban growth. Hall expressed the view that trade centres were the nodal points for urbanisation.[6] In his opinion, the *nagaram* network and the emergence of merchant organisations to look after long distance trade were major factors of urbanisation. Champakalakshmi has taken a comprehensive view and says "that no single autononous causative factor can be identified in the nexus of social, economic and political transformations which resulted in the emergence of urban forms".[7] Still, she lays emphasis on two important factors. In the first place, in her view, that Bhakti or devotionalism which was the chief characteristic of the religious life of the Pallava-Cola age provided the ideological basis for building huge temples that became the nodal points of urbanisation.[8] Secondly, during the Vijayanagara period, militarisation of administration and the consequent establishment of feudal capitals around forts provided the nucleus for urban development.[9]

Writing about the urbanisation in ancient and medieval Bengal, Amita Ray lays emphasis on two of its important aspects. The necessary pre-condition for urban growth, according to her, is strong agricultural base producing surpluses.[10] The second one is the growth of urban culture or "urbanism" reflected in works of art.[11]

The statment of Champakalakshmi that urbanisation is a complex movement is true in the case of Telangāṇa. From the 11th century, all the factors such as political unity, administrative consolidation and strong agricultural base, Bhakti centred religions, temple building and expansion of trade progessively manifested in Telangāṇa which naturally led to the development of urban centres.

The Cālukyas of Kalyān (A.D.973-1163) united the Deccan and organised the administration of Telangāṇa. Their *mahā-sāmantas* and *sāmantas* such as the Coḍas of Kandūr, chiefs of Polavāsa and Kākatīyas of Anmakoṇḍa strove hard to develop wetland agriculture by excavating numerous tanks all over Telangāṇa. After they became sovereigns, the Kākatīyas (A.D.1158-1323) continued the policy with greater vigour. Large tracts of land were brought under irrigation, providing a strong agricultural base for all social religious movements in Telangāṇa.

Increased agricultural production led to the development of industry and growth of artisan and merchant communities. The growth of agro and non-agricultural industries has been discussed in Chapter III.

Agricultural and industrial development boosted up both inland and maritime trade. The local trade guilds known as the *nakaram* network became very active and prosperous during the 12th, 13th and 14th centuries. The itinerent trade guilds such as the *Ayyāvali*-500, carried on brisk trade. In course of time, *Ayyāvali*-500 became a federal organisation incorporating in itself a number of itinerent trade guilds. Both the local and itinerent merchants formed joint corporations like the *Ubhayanānādeśi pekkaṇḍru* which functioned at the points of intersection of local and supralocal trade. The increase in external trade gave scope for imports and exports. The Moṭupalli charter[12] by Ganapatideva issued in the year A.D. 1244 indicates the interest taken by the state in overseas trade.

In the interest of public welfare and state income, the state encouraged and regulated trade and exercised its authority on trade in several ways. The state officers with revenue and military powers supervised trade centres and collected taxes due to the state. The Jaḍcherla inscription (A.D.1162) refers to the officers of Kandūri Udayana Choḍa Mahārāja, as *Sunkādhikkārulu* and *daṇḍanāya-kulu*.[13] The title, *daṇḍanāyaka*, suggest that the officers had under their command a small force and it was necessitated by the fact that the itinerent merchant guilds had their own armed men accompanying them to trade centres, as indicated by the mummūridaṇḍas.

With the presence of the revenue and military personnel, the trade centres gained political and administrative importance. The territories surrounding the trade centres were brought under administrative control either by appointing a *māṇḍalika* or by granting it as military fief to an officer in recognition of his services. Several inscriptions even from early times furnish information on such developments. The Gūḍur epigraph records the granting of Mogaḍupalli-12 to Viriyāla Eṟṟa by Boṭṭu Beta, the Mudigoṇḍa Cālukya chief and Mūḍa-30 to Viriyāla Sūrana by Kusumāyudha.[14] In the same way Recherla Rudra Reḍḍi obtained the Palampet region from Gaṇapatideva. Rudra Reḍḍi built a town near Ātukuru as his capital which was a flourishing trade centre.[15]

In medieval times, generally centres of administration were provided with fortification and guarded by a small army unit. Many such forts came up in Telangāṇa. Munnalūr,[16] Vardhamānapuram,[17] Paṭācheru,[18] Pāngallu,[19] Ujjili,[20] Magatala,[21] Nelakoṇḍapalli[22] and Amarābād[23] are some such fortified towns. These fortified towns must have served as the headquarters of the[75] *nāyamkaras* created by Pratāpa Rudra. Where such towns were not available the *nāyamkaras* should have built new towns to serve their military requirements. As already noted these *nāyamkaras* combined in themselves civil, revenue and military powers and held sway over their respective regions as feudal lords. Even before the *nāyamkara* system fully developed in all its aspects, the Kākatīya empire collapsed in Turkish invasions.

The foregoing account outlines the political and economic developments which provided respectively peaceful atmosphere and financial wherewithal for the rise of religious institutions. It was the period when puranic theism became popular in the Deccan. This religion laid emphasis on devotion and worship of image leading to building of temples. Even sūdras supported the new religion as it admitted them into temples and gave them a place in temple ritual, thus overthrowing the monopoly of religion by the brāhmaṇa. The Western Calukyas and their subordinates built temples in Telangāṇa at Patānceruvu,[24] Perūr,[25] Gangāpuram,[26] Vemulavāḍa,[27] Kollipāka[28] and probably Pānagal.[29] The Kākatīyas followed their example and built temples at Pillalamṛṛi[30] Pālampeta,[31] Koṇḍiparti,[32] Upparapalli[33] and others. Radha Krishna Sarma, remarks that "the Telangāṇa region of Āndhra Pradesh is studded with Cālukya and Kākatīya temples, rich in variety and splendour."[34] In his work, Sarma studied nearly forty five sites, most of them containing temple complexes. The temples thus became a huge institution with a considerable population centering around it. The picturesque temple rituals and occasional festivities on auspicious days attracted pilgrims from far and near. To satisfy the requirements of service in the temple, the daily requirements of its servants and the needs of pilgrims, temple attracted trade. While describing the Cola temple, Nilakanta Sastri[35] observes that the temple was a land lord, an employer, a consumer of different articles, a patron of arts and letters, Thus the centre of the fabric of socio-economic life in the land.

The inscriptions of 11th to 14th centuries reveal that most of the temples were richly endowed. Because the religion of the age was dominated by Bhakti, not only the builders of temples but also commoners used to make gifts to temples.Generally temple-building was accompanied by tank-digging and gifts to temples included wetland, dryland and garden land. Tanks were useful for ritual ceremonial and irrigational purposes. Land was distributed among the temple servants right from the high priest to the *tomtamāli* (gardener) downward.[36]

The above study makes it clear that the following factors helped the growth of urban centres generally known as *purās* and *nagarās* :

a) an agricultural hinterland from which marketable surplus is available;

b) political or administrative headquarters of a territorial division such as a Sthala;

c) local guild of merchants;

d) artisan communities working to satisfy the requirements of the place;

e) a temple complex attracting pilgrims;

f) trade connections, which Kenneth Hall Calls vertical connections, with the neighbouring villages;

g) facility for horizontal movement of merchandise from one town to others;

h) perennial source of water;

i) fortifications and an army for purposes of protection.

IMPORTANT URBAN CENTRES

From the beginning of the rule of the Cālukyas of Kalyān, the administration of the western districts of Telangāṇa was entrusted to officers where as the eastern and South-eastern parts were kept under Mahasamantas and Samantas. They lavished patronage on both Jaina and Hindu religious centres. Hence several important and active urban centres such as Alampūr, Kollipāka, Poṭlakeṛe, Gangāpuram, Perūru, Vemulavāḍa, Pānugal, and Anmakoṇḍa developed between A.D.973-1126. The process continued till about the fall of the Kākatīyas in A.D.1323. Some of the important urban centres and factors for their rise are discussed in the following pages.(table xvii)

Alampūr

Alampūr started to develop into an urban centre under the early Cālukyas. It is situated at the confluence of the rivers Krishna and Tungabhadra. The history of this town can be traced from the times of the early Cālukyas of Bādāmi.[37] During the Cālukya period, it emerged as the headquarters of the district Yāje-300,[38] in the doab. It is adjacent to districts of Kanne-300 and Natavāḍi-500. With numerous temples, Alampūr was a major *tīrtha* during the medieval period. the *Brahmeśvara maṭha,* with a *ghaṭika*[39] was a premier temple institution which administered the endowments of land and money. The administration of the place was under a mahāsthānādhipathi, who enjoyed the powers of a *māṇḍalika* chief. Alampūr is known as the western gateway of Śrīśalim[40] and pilgrims from Karṇāṭka and coastal Āndhra, proceeding to that hill gathered here.

The regioin commanded by the town was noted for textile manufacture as seen from the epigraphical references to cotton textiles. Several merchant guilds such as *Ayyāvali*500,[41] Seṭṭikarasamaya,[42] and *nānādeśi*[43] carried on brisk trade. Alampūr became a point of interesection for the exchange of local goods including several luxury items. Thus, Alampūr was not only a temple-town and a pilgrim centre but also a politically and commercially prominent centre duirng A.D.10th-14th centuries. It continued to be a prominent town until the Vijayanagara period.[44]

Kollipāka

Kollipāka was an administrative centre[45] and a Jaina *tīrtha*[46] from the Rāṣṭrakūṭa times. In an inscription of the 9th century A.D. found at Warangal, reference is made to the large province, Kollipāka-20,000.[47] The town continued to be a prominent political and military headquarters during the period of Cālukyas of Kalyān. It occupied a position of strategic importance in the Cola-Cālukya conflicts.[48] In view of the importance of the Kollipāka province, Someśvara I recognised Kollipāka *nāḍu*-20,000 into smaller districts and Kollipāka-7000 was kept under the Eṛuva Coḍas.[49] Vikramāditya VI appointed his eldest son Someśvara as the governor of Kollipāka around A.D.1110.[50]

Kollipāka is a prominent Jaina *tīrtha* even at the present time. It may be said that the town emerged as a Jaina centre during the Rāṣṭrakūṭa period. K.A.N. Sastri recrods that the Jain temples at kollilpāka were destroyed by Rajendra Cola and again by Rājādhirāja I.[51] Apart from being a very big Jain centre, Kollipāka has several brāhmānical temples for gods Vīranārāyaṇa, Brahmeśvara, Mallikārjuna and goddess Lakṣmī and several Śaivite Maṭhas.[52]

The successive governors that ruled the Kollipāka *nāḍu* and their officers excavated numerous tanks in the region around Kollipāka which resulted in large scale wet-land irrigation. An inscription dated A.D.1077[53] records the order given by *Mahāmaṇḍaleśvara* Śankaragaṇḍarasa to the varioius merchant guilds at Kollipāka to pay one *gadyāṇa* from each shop for lthe enjoyment of *preggaḍa* Kāvaṇayya and other *karaṇams* of Kollipāka.

Thus, it may be said that Kollipāka was a major urban centre in the early medieval period. The town continued to enjoy a high political status during the Muslim period during which it was called Kulpāk.

Poṭlacheṛuvu

Poṭlacheṛuvu or Poṭlakeṛe is another city of political, religious and commericial importance during the Cālukyan phase. Before the city of Kalyān was built by Someśvara I, Poṭlacheruvu appears to be the capital of the early kings of this dynasty.[54] An inscription dated A.D. 1127[55] issued by Bhūlokamaḷla Someśvara III from this town refers to the temple of Bhogeśvaradeva, five *Śaiva maṭhas and seṭṭikara samayas.* The fact that the newly coronated emperor was in Poṭlakeṛe making extensive grants suggest that the town occupied an important position in the Cālukya administration. The inscription suggest that the emperor held his court at Poṭlakeṛe as it mentions several high officers such as *Paṭṭasāhini Mahāmaṇḍaleśvara* Mahiyanna, Mahāpradhāni, *Heggaḍe daṇḍanāyaka* Patchammayya, *Sarvādhyakṣa* Mallināthabhaṭṭa and *Śrīkaraṇa daṇḍanāyaka* and *Aḍapa* Bammanayya, the *antahpura preggade.*

Poṭlakeṛe had a rich *nakaram* organisation headed by a *nakaramukhya*. The *nakaram* had its own temple for Nakareśvara.

Gangāpuram

Vikramāditya VI followed a policy of appointing his sons as governors to supervise the *sāmantas* in Telangāṇa. Kumāra Someśvara was appointed at Kollipāka.[56] Kumāra Tailapa was appointed over southern and south-eastern regions.[57] Gangāpuram was the headquaters of Kumāra Tailapa. Gangāpuram appears to be a temple town and trade centre from the beginning of the 11th century A.D. Koḍūr, the early capital of the Eṛuva Coḍas,[58] is situated near Gangāpuram. Temples for Sāgareśvara,[59] Keśavadeva[60] and other gods are located at this town. Several itinerant merchant guilds and *samaya* organisations carried on trade activity. Several *agrahāras* including *koḍūra brahmapuri* were established here during Tailapa's rule.[61] The town therefore attracted both pilgrims and students from far and near. Ālavānipalli, a village close to Gangāpuram, had among its population an artisan community called *paṭṭasālīlu.* This comminity is supposed to have been engaged in the production of silk cloth.

It appears that Kumāra Tailapa defied the authority of his elder brother[62]Bhulokamalla Someśvara and coronated himself as a sovereign king in A.D.1137 at Gangāpuram. However, Tailapa was defeated by Prola II soon after and had to accept the overlordship of his brother.[63]

Perūr

At present a small and insignificant village situated on the banks of Ahalya, a tributory of river Krishṇa. Perūr was one of the biggest trade centres in medieval Telangāṇa.Being the headquarters of a *stalam*, the Perūrikampaṇa,[64] the town rose to prominence as a provincial capital, a market place and a temple town and an educational centre under the Coḍas of Kandūr.

A Kannaḍa inscription of Tribhuvanamalla's time[65] mentions nine itinerant trade guilds at Perūr. Another inscription (A.D. 1119)[66] records several gifts made by Perūri *nakaram*, Telugu *nakaram*, Aruva *nakaram* and *Telivāru* to a local temple. The same inscription refers to a *samayamu pēmṭa*. This might be a market place where Kannaḍa merchants carried on trade. Inscriptions refer to several agricultural and industrial products that entered the markets of Perūr. The merchant households were classified into three categories and taxes levied accordingly.

The above mentioned Kannaḍa epigraph refers to two officers, *Mudrāṇada* and *Vaḍḍerāvula daṇḍanayaka*. Somasekhara Sarma has expressed the view that *Mudrāṇada* was the master of the mint.[67] *Vaḍḍerāvula daṇḍanayaka* was, as it has already been said, a tax officer with police powers.

Temples for Svayambhu Somanātha, Mallikarjuna, Keśava-deva were built at Perūr apart from two Nakareśvara temples. Several tanks irrigated the lands in the Perūri *kampaṇam*. Tāḍimaṭṭa, a village near Perūr was converted into an *agrahāra* settlement by Mallināyaka, the governor of Perūr. Several villages were granted for the maintenance of the temples.

An important aspect about the Perūr town was the educational institution at the place. The *Ghaṭika* at perūr was a big college with thirty one teachers headed by a *Ghaḍiyaśasi*.[68] The administration of the property of the *ghaṭika* was entrusted to a *nāyaka*, apart from the *Ghaḍiyaśasi*. It appears that the college was a large residential institution. An inscription[69] at Perūr records the imposition of a levy on every child of the town *(Herjunka)* at the time of the naming ceremony. The levy was payable to an *Upādhyāya*. It may be understood that elementary education and higher learning were actively pursued at Perūr.

Vemulavāḍa

The chief town of Vennisale-70 in Sabbi-1000[70] was an ancient town. It was the seat of a subordinate dynasty, the Cālukyas of

Vemulavāḍa *(Lembula vāṭika),* who ruled a large territory as feudatories of the Rāṣṭrakūṭas.[71] Though this dynasty disappeared soon after the rise of the Cālukyas of Kalyān, Vemulavāḍa continued to be an important town. *Mahāmaṇḍaleśvara* Rājaśekhara was ruling from Vemulavāḍa as a vassal of Vikramāditya VI.[73]

Polavāsa

Polavāsa, the modern Polasa near Jagtial in Karimnagar district, was the capital of the chiefs known to historians as the chiefs of Polavāsa, a feudatory dynasty.[74] The town was the chief town of the territory known as *Ugravāḍi*.[75] A number of Jain and Śaiva temples were built at Polavāsa. A large number of tanks were excavated in the region resulting in the production of agricultural surpluses. Itinerent merchant guilds such as *Ayyāvali*-500 and *Mummūridaṇḍa*.[76] carried on trade activity at the town.

Mudigoṇḍa

Another provincial town was Mudigoṇḍa situated near the present town of Khammam. It was the capital town of the feudatory dynasty of the Cālukyas of Mudigoṇḍa.[77] Mudigoṇḍa was the chief town of the territories, Visurunāḍu and Manchikoṇḍanāḍu.[78]

Sanigaram

A number of inscriptions[79] throwing considerable light on the early history of the Kākatīyas have been discovered at Sanigaram in the present Karīmnagar district. These inscriptions mention several land grants made by Beta II and Prola I and their subordinates and refer to Sanigaram as the provincial headquarters of the territory, Pulgunūru-70.[80]

In addition to the above-mentioned cities, Anmakoṇḍa,[81] Pānugal,[82] Meḍapalli,[83] Govindāpuram,[84] Sirikoṇḍa,[85] Ujjvalakoṭa,[86] Inugurti[87] and Āvanca[88] were some other towns that were fast growing into big political and commercial centres. These towns were graduallygetting connected by roads facilicating the movement of itinerant guilds, armies and pilgrims belonging especially of the Jaina and 'Hindu' faiths. With the rise of the Kākatīyas several other places developed into urban certres.

Nagurūr

Gangādharamantri, a loyal and trusted general of Rudra was appointed as the *māṇḍalika* of Sabbi-1000.[89] He made Nagurūr (modern Karimnagar) as his headquarters and it soon developed into an important township as its hinterland was dominated by weaving industry.

Ākunūru

Ākunūru which was an important village in Warangal district from early times became a trade centre, and a military contonment with large population.

Jalālpuram

The Ceṛaku chiefs who were initially feudatories of Coḍas of Kandūr were subordinated by Rudra and a military fief was created with Jalālpuram as its chief town and was placed under Ceṛaku Bollaya.[90]

Pillalamaṛṛi

Nāmi Reḍḍi, of the Recherla family, was stationed at Pillalamaṛṛi by Rudradeva to check the forays of the Coḍas of Kandūr. Thus Pillalamaṛṛi became the headquarters of Recherla Nāmi Reḍḍy who rose as a noted general and feudatory during the regnal periods of Rudradeva and Gaṇapatideva. Between A.D. 1195 and 1208 the construction of a fort and temples of Nāmeśvara, Kāmeśvara, Eṛakeśvara and Aiteśvara and a tank called Nāma-samudram was completed.[91] Estabilshment of *maṭha* and *ghaṭika* was also referred to in the records. As a result, Pillalamaṛṛi grew into a prosperous town.

Koṇḍaparti

Koṇḍaparti, in the vicinity of Warangal, during the 13th century became the headquarters of Cauṇḍa of the Malyāla family who was the commander in - chief of Gaṇapatideva. An inscription dated A. D. 1203 records the construction of Cauṇḍa samudra tank, an agrahāra named after Cauṇḍa called Cauṇḍapura and the temple Cauṇḍeśvara.[92] In the inscriptions Koṇḍaparti is mentioned as the chief town of Sankīśa deśa.

Pālampeṭ

Recherla Rudri Reḍḍi and his son Kāṭaya Reḍḍi were appointed as māṇḍalikas in the Pālampeṭ and Māchāpuram regions. Rudra built a new town near the present Pālampeṭ called in the inscription as Ātukūru which became a trade centre.[93] The famous temple called Rudreśvara and the huge tank at Pālampeṭ are marvels of the Kākatīya age.

Among other places that came to develop into towns as a result of feudal lords, mention may be made of Vardhamānapuram, Magatalanagaram, Amarāvati (Amarabad), Munnalūr, Umāmaheśvaram, Kaṭukūr, Gārla, Kūcimanchi etc.

ANUMAKONDA/WARANGAL, THE CAPITAL OF THE KĀKATĪYAS

Early Kākatīya rulers has their capital at Anumakonda. Its antiquity can be traced to 9th century A.D. With the establishment of Kākatīya rule by Prola I, Anumakoṇḍa became the capital. The fort[94] has an area of 5 square miles protected by hillocks on the east and west. On the north and south, two big tanks Bālasamudram and Bhadrakāli Ceruvu were located. The mud fortification walls cover the entire area connecting the hillocks and the tanks. Within the fort the temples of Padmākṣi, Siddheśvara and Rudreśvara are important. Among these, the Rudreśvara temple, known popularly as the Thousand Pillar-Temple marks the imperial grandeur of the independent Kākatīya dynasty. Weaving and manuafacture of textiles formed the economic base of the town.

Warangal

Warangal, known by various names such as Orugallu, Ekaśilānagari, Āndhranagari and later named as Sultanpur by Muhammad bin Tughluq was the most prominent city in Telangāna. Rudradeva made it his capital. Gaṇpatideva and his successors reinforced the fortifications.[95] The muslim historians refer to three almost concentric fortifications of hedge, mud and stone, one inside the other, each protected by a deep moat and ramparts.[96]

Warangal was a populous city inhabited by the people emerging to the royal capital. Royal patronage to artisans and merchants encouraged these communities form various parts of the empire to settle down at the capital. The names of the various wards *(vāḍas)* of the city such as *Sanigarapuvāḍa, Pānugaṇṭivāda, Medaravāda, deśi paradeśi behārulavādalu,* Maṭṭevāḍa etc., reveal that people from towns such as Sanigaram and Pānugal, artisans and merchants from various parts of the kingdom were living in the city.[97] The *Siddheśvara Caritra* metions that there were twenty seven communities living in the city, each having a population of several thousands.[98] Mention should also be made of Turakalu (Muslim) living in the city where they had a Masjid.

Warangal was a centre for texitile menufature, wool products and metal industries. An inscription from Warangal refers to taxes called *vrittipannulu* remitted by several artisan communities.[99] The industries not only catered to the needs of the palace, the various colonies and to the resident army but also produced surplus as evidenced from the items of trade at the markets at Orugallu, Maṭṭevāḍa and Anumakoṇḍa which constituted a triple city.[100]

During the 13th and 14th centuries, Warangal emerged as the biggest trade centre. Inscriptions from Warangal fort, Girmājīpeṭ, Maṭṭevāḍa, Anumakoṇḍa and Kāzīpeṭ refer to a large number and variety of trade guilds, functioing at the capital.[101] The *Pañchalohāla nakaram, Maṭṭenakaram, baccu maṭṭe nakaram,* etc., and the apex bodies like the *aśeṣha nakaram,* and *ubhaya nānādeśi,* are mentioned in the inscriptions. Seperate markets for commodities such as *nuvvulapēmta* (oil seeds market) *maṭṭiya sthala* (silver market) busibhāṇḍālu (unhusked grains and oil seeds) and *maṇibhāṇḍālu* (Prescious stones and the like) are noted in the Warangal Fort inscription.[102]

The urban character of the city is evidenced by the provision of several clocks in the city. The maintenance of the clock *(Ghaḍiyāramu)* according to the Warangal fort inscription[103] was entrusted to the *aśeṣa nakaram* at the market centres where the bells were sounded at intervals of 24 minutes *(ghaḍiya).* Lodging and boarding houses were popular places in the city which are described at length in the literary work Krīḍābhirāmamu.[104] The urban character is also noted in the epigraphs and literature, containing descriptions of the courtesans, gambling houses, drama performances etc. Amir Khusru describes Warangal as a 'paradise of idol worshippers' which "on all sides of it for the distances of two miles, there were fountains and gardens calculalted to gratify those who are in search of pleasure".[105]

Warangal emerged as a major temple centre. The epigraphs found in the fort and suburbs refer to the temples of Rudreśvara, Sāleśvara, Somanātha, Vīrabhadra, Venkateśa, Pāñchālarāya, Kākati. Malleśvaradeva, Beteśvara, Ekavīra and Mailāradeva.[106] Reference is made to paintings depicting the stories of the heroes of Palnāḍ. In an inscription, the priests in charge of *śaivaite* temples in Sanigarapuvāḍa, Brāhmalakumṭa, uppasaravāḍa and Pānumgantivāḍa are mentioned.[107] The numerous shrines that dot each ward of the city, by and large, belong to the respective communities.

The magnificent temple, believed to be that of svayambhūdeva, the tutelary deity of the Kākatīyas stood, in the midst of the city and enclosed by four torana gateways, as a symbol of the imperial dignity of the dynasty and the splendour of the city. The entire temple, except the *toraṇas,* is in ruins.

URABANISM

The steady growth of prosperous towns as administrative and commercial centres all over Telangana led to the development of urban culture which some scholars prefer to describe as bourgeois culture and others simply as urbanism.[108] It is natural that lurbanism reflects in the day to day social life of people and in their achievements in art. However, the urbanism of the age was not limited to towns. As Amita ray says it is a "historical process in which the rural, the urban, the commerical and religious form an inseparable web..." and pervades the entire life of a people or nation giving rise to "social and cultural aflorescence" which is best revealed in perceptual vision in which art plays a dominant role.[109]

During the Kākatīya period which witnessed the culmination of the process of urbanisation, life both in rural and urban areas became sumptuous and luxuriant. People became fond of ornaments and cosmetics and the later were sold in caskets made of ivory.[110] Not only courtesans, even brāhmaṇa teachers had pet birds like parrots in their houses. The fine taste the people had cultivalted is best reflected in the visual arts of the period. People loved to witness dance and drama and invited drama troupes even from such distant places as Dwarasamudra, the capital of the Hoyasalas.[111] Jāyapa, the *Gajasāhiṇi* of Gaṇapatideva composed a classic on dance in Sanskrit called *Nrittaratnāvali* in which he discussed the two major types of dance, *deśi* and *mārga*.[112] Each important temple complex contained a *rangamaṇḍapa* where dance was performed on occasions. In palaces and even in pleasure parks dances were performed on festive days on specially arranged stages. Dance is generally accompanied by music. Sārañgadeva who is believed to have lived during the period mentions a number of *rāgas* and *tālas* where as Pālkuriki Somanātha describes different types of *Viṇa* and lists out other musical instruments that were in use.[113] In the sculptures of the temples of the age on comes across dance troupes and numerous musical instruments. No festival in temple and no domestic ceremony could be conducted without music and in aristocratic families without dance. Besides, there were street singers and street dancers who with all their histrionic talents displayed the episodes in the lives of the heroes of Palnāḍa.[114] The dancing girls who were mostly courtesans enjoyed considerable respect in society.

Painting was another art which received patronage both from rulers and commeners alike. The walls of the houses of common people were plastered and were decorated with the paintings, depicting the stories from *Rāmāyaṇa, Bhāgavata* and *Palnāṭi-vīracaritra*.[115] Mācaldevi, the courtesan of Pratāpa Rudra built a hall of paintings (Citraśāla) and it is 'truely said' that the fame of Mācaldevi, probably for her patronage of arts and letters, excelled that of the sultan of Delhi.[116]

The religion of the period with its emphasis on devotion and image-worship led to vigorous temple building activity. In the village, the temple, though a humble shrine, was the result mostly of the cooperative efforts of the *aṣṭādaśamahāpraja*. The kings, their feudatories, officers, merchants and nakarams built huge temple complexes in urban centres. The temples of this period reveal in its architectural style the northern influence which was the result of close political and cultural relations. The Kākatīya buildings reveal the influence of Yādava, and later Cālukya structures. The Bhūmija and Nāgara temple forms were current in Malwa and upper Deccan. The occurrence of those temples forms at Pillalamaṛṛi, Nandikaṇḍi, Raikal etc., and depiction of a variety of building forms on the walls of the temples amply illustrate the mutual cultural influences.[117] The presence of artists and architects and religious preceptors from Karnāṭaka, Bengal and Madhya Pradesh in the Telangāṇa region must have provide stimulus to the cosmopolitan and urban culture in all its manifestations.

The walls and pillalrs of most of the temples are decorated with sculptures. The themes of the sculpture were mostly religious-taken from the epics and purāṇas. At times, the decorative sculptures depict floral designs, beadgarlands, animals, martial arts, hunting scenes and scenes from social life. The beauty and aesthetic grandeur of Telangāṇa sculpture are best reflected in the temples of Pānagal, Anmakoṇḍa, Nāgulpāḍu and Pālampet. Especially, the *sālabhanjikas* (bracket figures) of the Pālampeṭ temple, which is the brightest jewel of Kākatīya art, reveal the fine conception of feminine grace which the artist had and his skill to delineate it in granite. Yazdani rightly observes that almost every village in Telangāṇa "possesses elegrance",[118] which are the general characteristics of urbanism in any land.

REFERENCES

1. Burton Stein, in the *Cambridge Economic History of India,* Vol.I (Hyderabad, 1982) pp. 36-42.
2. Kenneth R. Hall. *Trade and Statecraft in the Age of the Colas* (New Delhi, 1980) p. 187.
3. R. Champakalahim, *Proc. I.H.C.,* (Srinagar, 1986) pp. 45-107.
4. Amita Ray. Presidential Address. Secton I, *Indian History Congress,* (Goa, 1987).
5. Burton Stein, op. cit.
6. Kenneth Hall, op. cit.

7. R. Champakalakshmi, op. cit. p.78.
8. Ibid., p. 80.
9. Ibid., pp. 90-91.
10. Amita Ray. op. cit.
11. Ibid.
12. E.I. XII, P. 183 ff.
13. K.C.S.C.S. pp. 202-204.
14. I.A.P. Wl. 27.
15. I.A.P. Wl. 50.
16. K.C.S.C.S. p. 44.
17. C.I.T.D. III, Mn. 46.
18. Ibid. IV, pp. 36-39.
19. K.C.S.C.S. p. 44.
20. Tel.Ins. II, pp. 66-67.
21. Ibid., pp. 126-127.
22. Ibid., I. pp. 155-156.
23. K.C.S.C.S. pp. 44.
24. C.I.T.D. IV, pp. 32-39.
25. P.I. Nos. 12, 13.
26. M. Radhakrishna Sarma, *Temples of Telangāṇa*, p. 77.
27. Ibid., p. 58.
28. Ibid., p. 66.
29. Ibid., p. 84.
30. Ibid., p. 100.
31. Ibid., p. 115.
32. Ibid., p. 135.
33. Ibid., p. 141.
34. Ibid.
35. K.A.N. Sastri.
36. K.C.S.C.S., pp. 177 and 242.
37. Tel. Ins. II, p. 8.
38. Ibid., I, pp. 112-113.
39. Ibid., II, pp. 45-46.
40. M. Radhakrishna Sarma, op. cit., p. 39.
41. I.A.P. Kn. 75.
42. C.I.T.D. IV, No. 21. pp. 36-39.
43. Tel. Ins. I, p. 128.
44. M. Radhakrishna Sarma, op. cit., p. 45.
45. Tel. Ins., I, p. 123, Ibid., pp. 147-152.
46. B.S.L. Hanumantha Rao, *Religion in Āndhra*, (Guntur, 1973) p. 572; I.A.P. Wl. 3.
47. I.A.P. Wl. 3.
48. K.A.N. Sastri, *The Colas* (Madras, 1955), p. 224.
49. Tel. Ins. I, p. 123.
50. Ibid., pp. 138-141.

51. K.A.N. Sastri, op. cit.
52. M. Radhakrishna Sarma, op. cit., p. 68.
53. A.P.A.S. No. 31.
54. P.B. Desai, *Jainism in South India*, p. 102.
55. C.I.T.D. IV, pp. 36-39.
56. Tel Ins. I, pp. 138-141.
57. Ibid., pp. 133-134.
58. K.C.S.C.S., p. 118, Tel.Ins. I, p. 123.
59. Tel.Ins. I, pp. 118-119.
60. M. Radhakrishna Sarma, op. cit., p. 77.
61. Tel. Ins. I, pp. 118-128.
62. J.A.H.R.S. XXXVI-I, Appendix-II; P.V.P. Sastry, *The Kākatīyas*, p. 83.
63. I.A.P. Wl. 36.
64. C.I.T.D. IV, p. 28.
65. P. I. 4; C.I.T.D. IV, No. 12, P. 27.
66. P. I. 6; C.I.T.D. IV, No.41, p. 87.
67. P. I. 4; C.I.T.D. IV., No. 12, p. 27.
68. P.I. 3.
69. P.I. 5; C.I.T.D. IV, No. 12, p. 28.
70. I.A.P. Kn. 13.
71. N. Venkataramanayya, *The Cālukyas of V (L) emulavāḍa*, (Hyderabad, 1953). p. 15 ff.
72. I.A.P. Kn. 3. At the court of Cālukyas of Vemulavāḍa several Kannaḍa and Sanskrit Poets flourished. The first poet in Kannada, Pampa composed *Vikramārijuna Vijaya* and *Ādipurāṇa*. His brother Jinavallabha was also a poet. Somadeva Sūri, a Jain writer of great merit composed his *Nītivākyāmṛita* and *Yaśastilakacampu* and other works. The Kurkyāla inscription (I.A.P. Kn. 3) records the installation of the images of the first and last Jaina Tīrthankaras and a construction of a Basadi called *Tribhuvana Tilaka*.
73. I.A.P Kn. 13.
74. Ibid., 75.
75. I.A.P. Wl. 22.
76. I.A.P. Kn. 75.
77. P.V.P. Sastry, op. cit., pp. 50-57.
78. Ibid.
79. I.A.P. Kn. Nos. 14, 15, 19, 22, 24.
80. Ibid., 19.
81. I.A.P. Wl. 36.
82. Tel Ins. I, pp. 169- 172.
83. I.A.P. Wl. 21.
84. Ibid., 26.
85. K.C.S.C.S., pp. 193-195.
86. Tel Ins. II, pp. 66-67.
87. I.A.P. Wl. 49.
88. Tel. Ins. II, pp. 60-62.

89. I.A.P. Kn. 25.
90. Tel Ins. II, pp. 103-107.
91. Ibid., I, pp.17-19, Ibid., pp. 26-31; Ibid., pp. 40-41.
92. I.A.P. Wl. 48, I.A.P. Kn. 29.
93. Ibid., 50.
94. Proc. A.P.H.C., Hyderabad, 1982. p. 63.
95. Kase Sarvappa, *Siddheśvaracaritra*, p. 113.
96. Elliot, H.M. and Dowson, J. *The History of India as told by its own Historians*, (Allahabad, 1970) pp. 78-85.
97. I.A.P. Wl. 63; Ibid., 89.
98. Kase Sarvappa. op. cit., Introduction by K. Lakshmiranjanam, pp. XXVI-XXVII.
99. C.I.T.D. III, pp. 172-173.
100. I.A.P. Wl. 61.
101. Ibid., Nos. 15, 61, 62, 63, 68.
102 Ibid., 62, 63.
103. Ibid.
104. Vallabhāmātya, *Krīḍābhirāmam* (Hyderabad, 1960) v. 155.
105. Elliot, H. M. and Dowson, J. op. cit. Appendix p. 559.
106. M. Radhakrishna Sarma, op. cit., pp. 105-108.
107. I.A.P. Wl. 89.
108. Niharranjan Ray, *Maurya and Post Maurya Art*, New Delhi, 1974. pp. 94-95, 97. Prof. Ray descibes the medieval urban culture as bourgeois culture whereas Amita Ray (Presidential Address, Section I, Indian History Congress, Panaji, Goa, 1987) calls it urbanism.
109. Amita Ray, op. cit. pp. 47-48.
110. Vallabhamatya, op. cit., v. 77.
111. Ibid., v. 293.
112. Jāyapa, *Nṛitaratnāvali*, (ed) Ananta Krishna Sarma, R. Hyderabad, 1967. Ibtoduction.
113. Palkuriki Somanatha, *Pannḍitārādhya Caritra*, Parvataprakaraṇam.
114. Vallabhāmātya, op. cit., vv. 116-126.
115. Ibid., vv. 126 and 191.
116. Ibid., v. 185.
117. B. Rajaendra Prasad, *Art of South India, Āndhra Pradesh*, Delhi, 1980. pp. 173 ff.
118. G. Yazdani in *The Early History of Deccan* (London, 1960), p. 759.

TABLE XVII

Urban Centres in Telangana (A. D. 1000-1323)

Sl. No.	*Name (District)*	*Territorial Division*	*Tanks Mandalika*	*Samanta/ guilds*	*Temples information*	*Trade*	*other*	*References*
(1)	(2)	(3)	(4)	(5)	(6)	(7)	(8)	(9)
1.	Alampūr (Mahaboob-nagar)	Yaje 300 Kanne 300	--	Mahāsthānā-dhipatis administered the temple town	1) Navabrahma temples 2) Sūryanārā-Yaṇa 3) Nṛsimha	1) Ayyāvali-500 2) Ubhayanā-nādeśi 3) Mummuri-daṇḍa -36	A *ghaṭika* was located here	Tel. Ins. I, p. 117 A. D. 1099. Tel. Ins. I, p. 113. A. D. 1164. Tel. Ins. II, p. 45, A. D. 1089.
2.	Kollipāka (Nalgoṇḍa)	Kollipāka 1000 (Kollipāka 20,000 in early times)	--	Several Sāmantas ruled the Province	1) Several Jain temples. 2) someśvara 3) Vīranārā-yaṇa	--	--	Tel. Ins. I, p. 123, A. D. 1088. Tel. Ins. I, pp. 124-125 A. D. 1098 Tel. Ins. I, pp. 138-141. A. D. 1105

(1)	(2)	(3)	(4)	(5)	(6)	(7)	(8)	(9)
3.	Paṭānche-ṛuvu (Madak)	--	--	Early capital of the Cālukyas of Kalyān	1) Bhogīśvara 2) Nakareśvara 3) Jain temples	Nagaram	Tenginamaṭha was a residential school.	C.I.T.D. IV, pp. 18-22. Ibid., pp. 32-35. Ibid., pp. 36-39.
4.	Gangāpuram (Mahaboob-nagar)	Kandūr-1100	--	capital of Kumāra Tailapa	1) Sagareśvara 2) Keśava 3) Haleśvara 4) Somanātha	1) Samaya-samūha 2) Asakasa-maya 3) Nānādeśi	Kodūrabrāhma-puri is located here	Tel. Ins. II, p. 57, A. D. 1110 Ibid., I, pp. 105-108 (A. D. 1146-1156) Ibid., p. 118 A. D. 1079
5.	Ujjili (Mahaboob-nagar	Kallake-lagu-500	Kottakeṛe	Saudheres (governors)	1) Chenna Pārśvanātha	Aśeṣanakaram	Ujjvalakota is a major fort	Tel. Ins. II, p.66. A.D. 1097
6.	Peddaka-ḍumūr (Mahaboob-nagar)	--	Hirikeṛe Muṇḍana-Keṛe Prolakere	Saudheṛe Bollenāyaka	1) Brahmeśvara 2) Mallikār-juna 3) Keśsava	1) Ayyāvali 500 2) Mummūrin-daṇḍa 30 3) Kannaḍa-4000 4) Ubhyanāna-desi	--	Tel. Ins. II, pp. 67-73. A. D. 1116

(1)	(2)	(3)	(4)	(5)	(6)	(7)	(8)	(9)
7.	Vemulavāḍa (Karim-nagar)	Vennisale 70 (in Sabbi 1000)	Rājāditya samudram	Cpital of the Cālukyas of Vemula-vāḍa and later Sāman-tas of Cālukyas of Kalyān	1) Subhadhāma Jinālya 2) Harikeśvara 3) Rājarājeśva-ra		A *ghaṭika* is located here	I.A.P. Kn. Nos. 18,20,21
8.	Perūr (Nalgonda)	Perūr Kampanam	Seṭṭiceruvu Nalenje-ruvu Muccasa-mudram Somasamu-dram	Perūr was a māṇḍalika capital under the Coḍas of Kandur and Kakatīyaṣ	Vindhyavāsi Someśvara Keśava Nakareśvara	Nine itine-rant guilds and three nakarams are menti-oned	A large *ghaṭika* is located here	P. I. Nos. 1 to 9
9.	Śanigaram (Karim-nagar)	Pulgunūr 70 (in Sabbi 1000)	--	Śanigaram appears to be early capital of the Kākatīyas before An-makoṇḍa.	Bhīmeśvara Kommeśvara Partheśvara	--	--	I.A.P. Kn. 19, 22, 24.
10.	Polavāsa (Karim-nagar)	Polavāsa-deśa	--	Polavāsa was the capital of the family of sāmantas called pola-vāsa chiefs	Pulastyeśvara	Ayyāvali 500 Mummuridaṇḍ-36 Ubhayanānā-deśi	--	I.A.P. Kn. 75

(1)	(2)	(3)	(4)	(5)	(6)	(7)	(8)	(9)
11.	Sirikoṇḍa (Khammam)	--	Ketasamudram Sūrasamudram Somasamudram Bhīmasamudram	Capital of a māṇḍalika under the Coḍas of Kandūr	Juvveśvara Bhīmeśvara Nārāyaṇa Kedāradeva Jinadeva	Nakaram	--	K.C.S.C.S. pp. 193-195
12.	Tekumala (Medak)	Tekumbeḍḍa sthalam	--	--	Ranganātha Bhoganātha	--	--	C.I.T.D. II, pp. 166-167.
13.	Pālampet Ātukūr (Warangal)	--	Nekkoṇḍ-Smudram	Capital of Recherla Reḍḍis	Rudreśvara Gauriśvara Kāṭeśvara Kāmeśvara	--	--	I.A.P. Wl. 50
14.	Koṇdaparti (warangal)	--	Cauṇḍa samudram Bellamaceruvu	Capital of Malyāla chiefs	Cauṇḍeśvara Rudreśvara Keśava Proleśvara	--	Cauṇḍapura agrahara is located near this town.	I.A.P. Wl. 48 & 64.
15.	Inugaṇṭi (Warangal)	Natavāḍi	--	Capital of Natavāḍi chiefs in addition to Niḍigoṇḍa	Buddeśvara, Muppeśvara Rudreśvara Śiva Gopālakṛishṇa Jalandhara Bhairava	--	--	--

(1)	(2)	(3)	(4)	(5)	(6)	(7)	(8)	(9)
16.	Goḍisala (Karim-nagar)	--	Penjeruvu Kāṭnāyuni-ceruvu Rājanāya-kuniceruvu Ravvasāni ceruvu	--	Pñcaliñga Śiva	--	--	I.A.P. Kn. 30
17.	Kaṭukūr (Khammam)	--	Peddaceruvu	Chief town of the Viriyāla family	Atyeśvara Mallikārjuna Gopīnātha Keśava	--	--	C.I.T.D. III pp. 16-18.
18.	Kūcimanci (Khammam)	--	Pedda-ceruvu Tailadevuni ceruvu Tāmara ceruvu Rāviceruvu Rekapalli ceruvu Nerapu ceruvu Jeḍḍla ceruvu	Māṇḍalika capital	Gopīnātha	Vīrabalañjas	--	C.I.T.D. III pp. 19-23

(1)	(2)	(3)	(4)	(5)	(6)	(7)	(8)	(9)
19.	Nelakoṇḍa-palli (Kammam)	--	Bollasamu-dram peddaceruvu	Māṇḍlika capital	Viśveśvara	--	--	Tel. Ins. I, pp. 155-156
20.	Magtala (Mahaboob-nagar)	Magatala-sthalam	Ullisamu-dram Aśvatha taṭākam Vennasamu-dram, Kāca-samudram Naruvataḍā-kam, Sanga samudram and many other tanks	Capital of Malyāla chiefs.	Mallinātha Brahmeśvara	Nakaram	Śrīvaiṣṇava centre	Tel. Ins. II, pp. 122-127 Ibid., pp. 153-162.
21.	Vardhamāna-puram (Mahaboob-nagar)	Kandūr 1100	Sūrasamudram and many tanks	Capital of the Gona chiefs	Buddheśvara Gaṇapatīśvara Lakṣmīnṛsimha	Nakaram	--	C.I.T.D. III Mn. 46
22.	Pānugal (Nalgoṇḍa)	Pānugallu viṣaya	Udayasamu-dram Udayāditya-samudram Bhīmasamu-dram, Coḍa-samudram	Eastern capi-tal of the Coḍas of Kandūr	Abhinava Somanātha	Nibaramana-karam Pānugallu-nakaram	--	Tel. Ins. pp. 72-74. Ibid., pp. 169-172

(1)	(2)	(3)	(4)	(5)	(6)	(7)	(8)	(9)
23.	Pillalamaṛṛi (Nalgoṇḍa)	Āmanikallu 70	Nāmasamudram Lakṣmī-samudram Eṛkasamudram Sabbạsamudram Gauresamudram Viśvanātha-samudram Komaṭiceruvu and many tanks	Capital of Recherla family Reḍḍis	Kāmeśvara Kāceśvara Nāmeśvara Proleśvara Aiteśvara Bhīmanātha Eṛakeśvara Tripuradevi	--	Eṛakamaṭham was a residential school at Pillalamaṛṛi.	Tel. Ins. I, pp. 17-19. pp. 26-38
24.	Jalālpuram (Nalgoṇḍa)	--	Maṛṛikuṇṭa Baṇḍala-ceruvu Naruva-taṭākam	Capital of Ceṛaku chiefs	Bolleśvara Malleśvara Gaṇapīśvara Viṣṇu, Mallikārjuna, Keteśvara	--	--	Tel. Ins. II, pp. 115-121.
25.	Anmakoṇḍa	Anmakoṇḍa-viṣaya	Kūchikeṛe Seṭṭikeṛe Maddicaruvu Hariyakeṛe	Capital of early Kākatīyas	Kaḍalālaya-basaḍi Rudresvaram Chaturmukha-deva, Umamaheśvara	Anamkoṇḍa Puradaseṭṭi Pramukha nakaram	--	I.A.P. Wl. 15,22.

(1)	(2)	(3)	(4)	(5)	(6)	(7)	(8)	(9)
26.	Warangal	-do-	--	Capital of later Kākatīyas	Sāleśvara Gaṇapesvara Sakaleśvara Virabhadra Nakareśvara Svayambhu-nātha Somanāth Gaureśvara Rudreśvara Somanātha Bhaṭṭeśvara Rāmadeva	Cīramaṭṭi nakaram Dharmasāle-janulu Gandhya aśeṣa nakaram Nakharam Svadeśi paradeśi behārulu Nunebehārulu Santanakaram Gandhyamvāru Tangaramvāru Mūsaravāru Ubhayanāna-deśi Pañcalohāla-nakaram Pomakanakaram Baccumaṭṭe-nakaram	Warangal city consisted of Girmājipeṭ, Maṭṭevāḍa	I.A.P. Wl. 61, 63, 71 87, 89

CONCLUSION

Telangāṇa assumed for the first time politicoeconomic significance with the organisation of *sāmanta* network in the region by the Cālukyan emperors, Someśwara I and Vikramāditya VI. the *sāmanta* rulers tried to augment the economic resources of their feudal principalities by developing wetland agriculture under tanks. For the first time in her long history Telangāṇa became the seat of sovereign power. The Kākatīyas, who rose to the position of sovereigns in A.D.1163, gave further stimulus to the process of resource mobilisation, providing their state with a strong economic base in the form of industry and trade in addition to agriculture.

Neither the Cālukyan nor the Kākatīya state can be described as "despotic" or segmentary. The rulers shared the political power with a number of *mahāsāmantas* or *mahāmaṇḍaleśvaras* and *māṇḍalikas*. The *sāmanta* chiefs owed nominal allegiance to their overlords and ruled their principalities almost independently. They discharged the *sāmanta* obligations such as participating in the wars of their imperial overlords. The Kākatīyas maintained a standing army otherwise neither Rudradeva nor Gaṇapatideva would have been in a positon to make such extensive conquests. At times the *māṇḍalikas* received land for their service in lieu of salary. Instances are also found that land was granted as a reward for service without any obligations.

Rudra and Gaṇapati not only created *māṇḍalika* principalities all over Telangāṇa, but also developed an elaborate bureaucratic machinery with[72] offices *(niyogas)* headed by a high-ranking official the Bāhattara niyogādhipati. Officials like *Mahāpradhāni, Preggaḍa, Adhikāri* under them. The bureaucractic machinery reduced the evils of the semi-independent māṇḍalika system and functioned as a bridge between the central authority and local authority.

Some instances of subinfeudation are found in the Cālukyan

epoch, but no evidence of it is seen in the Kākatīya age. The king and the *māṇḍalika* were directly related without any intermediaries and under the *māṇḍalikas* only state officials and *āyagars* in the village functioned.

The existence of an official machinery leads one to the conclusion that the administration was not completely vassalised. It must also be noted that most of the civil officers were also military men holding the rank of *daṇḍanāyaka* but that was necessitated by the demands of the medieval state.

At the local and village level, people's councils like *sthalamu samastapraja, astādaśasamayāla samastapraja* were managing the local affairs. The several communities and guilds had their own codes of conduct known as *samaya*. The *āyagars* of a village that appear during the Kākatīya period were drawn from the village community itself. The *Pedakāpu* or *Gavuṇḍa*, the village headman, was not a vassal. He was a leading member of the village community, a link between the village and central bureaucracy.

As such, it may be said that conditions of political feudalism were not full-fledged by the middle of the 13th C.A.D. But, after the death of Gaṇapati, Rudrama and Pratāpa Rudra had to make changes in the *māṇḍalika* system in order to cope us with internal revolts and external aggression.Some historians have pointed out that the *nāyankara* system, started by Rudrama and strengthened by her successor, had elements of political feudalism. The kingdom was divided into more than seventy small principalities and their administration was kept under military chiefs. However, the feudal elements between the king and the *nāyankara* and the one below *nāyankara* are not known. But the Kākatīya kingdom fell before the *nāyankara* system took a definite shape. Not much information is forthcoming from epigraphs regarding the relations between a *nāyankara* and a monarch. It may be said that the *nāyankara* system was the fore-runner of the *amaranāyaka* system in the Vijayanagara period. In view of such a balanced system of administration no traces of segments-either power or territorial are found either in the Cālukyan or in the Kākatīya kingdom.

Agriculture being the mainstay of the economy, all sections

of people took interest in developing it. The kings, the *sāmantas* officials, merchant guilds and individuals showed interest in providing irrigational facilities which is very rare in medieval times. Moreover, by the Rāṣṭrakūṭa times *viṣṭi* or forced labour which was the backbone of feudal economy disappeared. The Kākatīyas were probably the last of such families engaged in *viṣṭi*. Agricultural production, both wetland and dryland, witnessed tremendous expansion. Tank irrigation led to new techniques in agriculture. A variety of food and money crops were raised. There were marketable surpluses in every commodity as evidenced by the development of inland and overseas trade.

The problem of landholding pattern is the key to the understanding of the socio-economic situation. As documented in chapter II that the cultivable and uncultivable land was distributed among many institutions such as the government, *agrahāras,* temples civil and military officials and peasant communities. In the agrahāras, the brāhmaṇas held individual proprietory and hereditary rights in land. The temple land such as the *devabhogas* and *devamānyas* were distributed among various temple servants. The temple servants held individual *vrittis,* which were generally hereditary, in the peasant villages. The uncultivable land was held in common for purposes of cattlegrazing, house-building etc. Inscriptions reveal that the cultivable land whether wet or dry, was held individually. The individual enjoyed the right to purchase, to mortgage and sell away his land. The condition of the cultivators on the government,or *devabhoga* or *agrahāra* lands was not unsatisfactory. They were called arthasīris i.e. they were allowed to retain for themselves half of the raised produce, which practice led to remarkable socio-political developments in the long run.

The agricultural surpluses were channelised into industrial activity. In addition, iron, coal and diamonds were mined and since about the middle of the the Rāṣṭrakūṭa period there was considerable development of different industries. Tank and temple construction and growth of industry became comlplimentary of one another. The Rāṣṭrakūṭas encouraged Arab merchants who became very active in the western Deccan and on the Arabian

Coast. As a result a huge *nakaram* network, both local and itinerant had spread all over Telangāṇa conducting commerical operations.

Most of the *nakarams* maintained temples of their own and the itinerant guilds had bands of armed men to protect them and their merchandise. Throughout Telangāṇa, several trade centres developed like Warangal, Polavāsa, Alampūr, Gangāpuram and Perūr. Moṭupalli on the east-coast was a great mark of foreign trade and the character of Gaṇapatideva (A.D.1244) indicates the interest taken by the rulers in the expansion of foreign trade.

The foregoing analysis shows that the concept of Asiatic Mode of production is not applicable to the age under study. Villages were not isolated. They were conncected with neighbouring villages and towns by a marketing network nursed by several merchant guilds. The peasant in the village did not produce everything only for consumption. The surpluses were channelised into industries for the production of various commodities for local consumption as well as for export through market towns. Agriculture ceased to be only occupation of the people.

However all was not rosy in the economic field. Taxation was heavy and the state took away a big share in the agricultural and industrial produce. Traders were also taxed heavily. Thus the state resorted to taxation as a method of surplus appropriate. Still, it may be said that neither the peasant nor the artisan or the trader was reduced to subject poverty. Industrial production and commerce gave scope for a variety of occupations which had its own impact on the society.

The structure of the society had undergone many changes as to fit neither into the ancient order of the Caturvarna system nor in the medieval concept of *aṣṭādaśamahāpraja*. The number of castes and communities got multiplied because of several factors such as the absorption of hill and forest tribes, new economic occupations and religious movements. As such, the society was divided into a number of occupatinal groups such as 1. priests, 2. rulers, 3. farmers and peasants, and 4. artisans and traders.

The bulk of the population belonged to the peasant community who depended mostly on land for livelihood. There were many branches in the peasant community such as *tammaḍi, reḍḍi, īdara, golla, boya, uppara* etc. who were engaged in various occupations depending on land such as wetland agriculture, dryland farming, horticulture and animal husbandry. The peasant class may generally be classified into big landowners, small farmers and landless peasants. But in the period under study, no big landlords are noticed. Most of the peasants were either small farmers or landless labourers. Tank and temple building, forming of new villages resulting in expansion of agriculture facilitated mobility of labour. Some of the peasants were engaged on the crown lands or on *brahmadeva or devabhoga* lands on *ardhasīri* basis. The ardhasīri system steadily improved the economic status of some of the members of peasant communities who joined military services as required by the frequent wars of the medieval period and rose to high social status. Such families naturally strove to rise in ritual status as well. The prevailing heterodox religions like Jainism, Vīraśaivism and Śrīvaiṣṇavism provided the means to them for gaining ritual purity as well as canonical and secular learning. Some members of this class were so highly learned as to write in sanskrit on subjects like *rājanīti* dance and music. They described themselves as *satśūdras* and claimed equality with brāhmaṇas.

The members of this new community of peasant-warriors or *nāyakas* dethroned the traditional ruling class, from positions of political power. The Kākatīyas and their successors-Prolayanāyaka, Singamanīḍu and Prolaya Vemāreḍḍi were all of that community.

The factors of social change affected the brāhmaṇa community also. The community lost its solidarity by breaking up into several endogamous branches such as vaidikas, niyogis, ārādhyas and śrīvaiṣṇavas. Through the community enjoyed ritual status, they lost their monopoly of learning and domination at the court. But most of the karaṇams in villages were brāhmaṇas. But, in the higher echelons of administration, they were out numbered by the members of the fourth *varṇa*.

The fact that the society of the period was not stagnant is borne out not only by the cases of social mobility outlined above but also by the process of urbanisation that resulted in the growth of populous towns and cities in the region. The development of strong agricultural base, large scale building of temple complexes, brisk internal and external trade and growth of *sāmanta-māṇḍalika-nāyankara* capitals resulted in the formation of a number of urban centres. Alampūr, Gangāpuram, Poṭlaceruvu, Kollipāka, Pānugal, Perūr, Polavāsa, Nagurūr, Pillalamaṟṟi, and Vardhamānapuram etc. The biggest of all such cities was of course the metropolis, Warangal which became the most prominent city in the Deccan. Warantgal grew up into a tripple city with a highly cosmopolitan population. The developed urbanism of the age reflects in a variety of art forms-literature, dance, drama, music and painting and more than all in the magnificent temple architecture and handsome sculptures which are an eloquent testimony to the high aesthetic sense of the people.

APPENDIX

COINAGE, WEIGHTS AND MEASURES

The Kākatīyas, after attaining sovereign power attempted to standardise land measures, coinage, weights and measures. They adopted earlier units but standardised them and enforced uniform usage throughout their kingdom. Pavuluri Mallana, who lived during the 11th C.A.D. described several units and measures in his *Gaṇitasāra sangraha,* a Telugu translation of sanskrit work by Mahāvīrācārya. The Kākatīya standards were generally designation by the prefix *kesari*.

Kesari prefix

The Kākatīya kings had the titles *arigajakesari, rāyagaja-kesari* and *dāyagajakesari*. Prola I built a tank called kesari-samudram, Inscriptions from Gaṇapatideva's time frequently refer to *kesarigadyāṇas*. It may thus be said, as P.V.P. sastry pointed out, that the *kesari* prefix indicates Kākatīya units.

Land Measure

Among the many types of land measure, the *Martur* was the unit widely employed in Āndhradesa and Karṇāṭaka. It was used to measure both wet and dry lands in earlier times. As more and more wet land came into use, *martur* was used for the measurement of wet land and *khaṇḍuga* became the unit of dry land. The area denoted by *martur* is not clear. In contemporary Tamil epigraphs *veli* was the land measure and it is nearly equal to 6.6 acres. It may be said that *marturu* denoted the same area. *Nivartana* was the Sanskrit word used for *martur.*

Though *khaṇḍuga* was used in measuring dry land it was also a measure of grain, equal to *puṭṭi* of grain. Other records indicates that the seed sowable in the land was one *puṭṭi*. The area denoted by *khaṇḍuga* therefore not clear.

During the Kākatīya period, a standard pole was employed

to measure both wet and dry lands. This was known as the *kesari-pāṭighaḍa*. The suffix, as noted above, indicates that it was a Kākatīya standard. The length of the kesaripāṭighaḍa is given in several inscriptions.

Coinage

The *gadyāṇa* and *dramma* were the coins in use during the Rāṣtrakūṭa period. During the time of the Cālukyas of kalyaṇ, *gadyāṇa* continued to be in currency. The sanskrit word *gadyāṇa* can be derived from the Telugu words, *Gadde+āṇe,* meaning the coin issued from the seat of royal authority. *Gadyāṇa* was a gold coin. *Māḍa and tanka* were the other words used to mean the coin (or the same amount of gold).

The Kākatīyas issued two gold coins: *kesari gadyāṇam* and kesari *cinnam*. The *kesarigadyāṇa* was nearly 3.5 gms. in weight and circular in shape with approximately 1cm. in diameter. The *cinnam* was a fraction of the *gadyāṇa* and sources are at variance as to its value ranging from 1/8 to 1/14 of a *gadyāṇa*. Other gadyanas referred to in contemporary epigraphs are *tyāgigadya* and *birudugadya*.

Other coins that were in wide use was the *rūka* and *vīsa* made of silver. Gokarṇarūka, most probably issued by the Coḍas of Kandūr, was in currency till the end of the 13th century. The Kākatīyas appear to have issued coins for fractional value of a *rūka* such as the *kesaripāṭi aḍḍugu*(½ rūka) and *kesari vīsam* (1/16 rūka). No reference is found to *kesarirūka*.

An inscription from Bollapelli and another from Bāpaṭla indicate that one *gadyāṇa* was equivalent to 10 rūkas.

Grain measures

Puṭṭi, tūmu, Kiuncamu and *mānika* were the standard measuress for grain. Same measures were used for oil and ghee. Kesaripāṭi *puṭṭi*, Kesaripāṭi *tūmu* and kesaripāṭi *mānika* are referred to in inscriptions. Evidently, these were the standard units adopted during the Kākatīya period. The following table shows the relation between these measures.

4 *mānikas*	= 1 *kuncamu*
4 *kuncamu*	= 1 *puṭṭi*

The *mānika* also had fractions as follows:

1 *mānika*	= 4 *solas*
1 *sola*	= 4 *giddas*

Weights

The *māḍa*, the equivalent of *gadyāṇ*, and *cinnam*, its fractions were also used to weigh articles such as sandal powder. Some standard weights were also referred to in inscriptions. They are *vāsa*, *tula* and *pala*. The relation between these can be given as follows:

30 *cinnams*	= 1 *tula*
3 *tulas*	= 1 *pala*
40 *palas*	= 1 *vīse*
8 *vīse*	= 1 *maṇugu* or tūmu
20 *Maṇugus* or *tūmus*	= 1 puṭṭi

The above summary on coinage, weights and measures is based on the following:

Ārudra, *Samagra Āndhra Sāhityam* Vol, Madras. 1965.

P.V.P. Sastry, *Kākatīya coins And Measures* Hyderabad, 1975.

Y. gopala Reddy, some Measures and Weights in Medieval Āndhara, JAHRS, VoL. XXXII, pp. 102-114.

BIBLIOGRAPHY

ORIGINAL SOURCES

1.Epigraphy

ARCHAEOLOGICAL SURVEY OF SOUTH INDIA

Annual Reports of (South Indian) Epigraphy.

South Indian Inscriptions:— (Pub. Archaeological Survey of India)

Vol. IV. Miscellaneous Inscriptions from the Tamil Telugu and Kannada Countries and Ceylone. ed. H. Krishna Sastri, Madras, 1923.

Vol. V. Miscellaneous Inscriptions from the Tamil, Malayalam, Telugu and Kannada Countries and ed. H.Krishna Sastri, Madras, 1925.

Vol. VI. Miscellaneous Inscriptions from the Tamil Telugu and Kannada Countries ed. K.V. Subrahmanyam Aiyer, Madras, 1928.

Vol. X. Telugu Inscriptions from the Madras Presidency ed. J. Ramayya Pantulu, Delhi, 1948.

Epigraphia India, Vol. I, V & VI.

Annual Reports on Indian Epigraphy.

Hyderabad Archaeological Series **(by the Nizam's Govern-ment)**

A corpus Inscriptions in the Telingāṇa Districts of H.E.H. The Nizams dominions, ed. P. Srinivasachar.

Part- I (Introduction) Hyderabad, 1942.

Part-II (Texts and Translations) Hyderabad, 1940.

A corpus of Inscriptions in Telangāṇa Districts of Andhra Pradesh, ed. P. Sreeivasachar.

Part-II (Texts and Introductory Notes) Hyderabad, 1956.

Telangāṇa Insctiptions, 2 Vols. 1935, 1960 anon/ Lakshmanaraya Parisodhaka Mandali, Hyderabad.

Andhra Pradesh Government Archaeological Series:

Select Epigraphs of Andhra Pradesh, by P. V. Parabrahma Sastry, Hyderabad, 1965.

Corpus Inscriptions in the Telangāṇa Districts, Part IV by M. Somasekhara Sarma ed. R., Subrahmanyam, Hyderabad, 1973.

Perūr Inscriptions (Text in Telugu and Introductions in English) by N. Venkataramanaih, Hyderabad, 1970.

Inscriptions of Āndhradeśa (Pub. Sri Venkateśwara University)

Vol. I Index ed. M. Rama Rao, Tirupati, 1967.

Vol. II Part I, Summaries of Inscriptions, ed. M. Rama Rao, Tirupati, 1968.

Śāsanasamputi (Telugu) by B. N. Sastry, Hyderabad.

Andhra Pradesh Gvernment Epigraphy Series :

Annual report on epigraphy (ed) N. Venkataramanayya, 1966, Hyderabad.

Annual report on Epigraphy (ed) P. V. Sastry, Hyderabad, 1977.

Inscriptions of Andhra Pradesh:

Warangal district (ed) N. Venkataramanayya, Hyderabad, 1974.

Karimnagar District (ed) P. V. Parabrahma Sastri, Hyderabad, 1974.

Cuḍḍapah districct Part-I (ed) P. V. P. Sastry, Hyderabad, 1977.

Cuḍḍapah District Part-II (ed) P. V. Parabrahma Sastry, Hyderabad, 1978.

2. Literature :

Sanskrit Works :

Nrittaratnāvali, Jāyapa (ed) Ananta Krishna Sarma, R. Hyderabad, 1969 (ed) Madhavaraya Sarma, J. Tanuku, 1971.

Partāparudrayaśobhūṣaṇam, Vidyanatha (ed) Narasimhacarya, Madras, 1967.

Mānasollāsa (Abhilishitārdhacintamaṇi) Gayakwad Oriental Series.

Telugu works :

Āndhra Mahābhāratam, Nannaya, Ādiparva; Tikkana, Virātparva and Śānti Parvas. Hyderabad, 1970.

Āndhrabhāṣhabhūṣhaṇam, Ketana (ed) Surayya, D. Tenali, 1953.

Āndhra Vijñānasarvasvamu III, (ed) Mallampalli Somasekhara Sarma, M. Venkatarangaiah, N. Venkataramanaiah, M. Satyanarayana, Madras, 1959.

Basavapurāṇam, Pālkuriki Somanātha, (ed) Venkata Rao N, Madras, 1958.

Daśakumāra Caritra, Ketana, Hyderabad, 1967.

Keyūrabāhucaritra, Mañcana (ed) Kodandaramayya, T. Madras, 1960 Krīḍābhirāmam, Vallabharaya, V. (ed) Tammayya, B., Madras, 1960.

Krīḍāhirāmam, V. Prabhakara Sastry, Hyderabad, 1960.

Kumārasambhavam Nannecoḍa (ed) Lakshmikantham, Vijayawada, 1916.

Ranganātha Rāmāyaṇam, Gona Buddha Reḍḍi (ed) Vavilla & Sons, Madras, 1960 (Reprint).

Sakalanīti Sammatamu, Maḍiki Singana (ed) Venkata Rao, N. and Appa Rao, P. R. Hyderabad, 1970.

Siddheśvara Caritramu—Ekamranātha, Narendra Sahitya-mandali, Tanuku, 1969.

Śrī Paṇḍitārādhyacaritra, Pālkuriki Somanātha (ed)

i) Narayana Rao, C. Madras (Reprint) 1974.

ii) Prabhakara Sastry, V, Madras, 1936.

Vijñāneśvaram, Ketana (ed) Ramacandra Rao, C. V. Nellore, 1977.

Śatakasamputamu Part I (Telugu) ed. Nidadavolu Venkatarao, Hyderabad, 1966.

SECONDARY SOURCES

Altaker, A.S., The Rāṣṭrakūṭas and their times, Poona, 1967.

Amita Ray, Life and Art of Early Āndhradeśa, Delhi, 1983.

Appadorai, A Economic Conditions in South India, Madras ,1936.

Apte,V.S. the Student's Sanskrit-English Dictionary, Delhi, 1965.

Arudra, Samagra Āndhra Sāhityam (Telugu) Vols. I and II, Madras, 1965.

Bühler (ed) The Laws of Manu, Delhi, 1984.

Bhattacharya, H. (ed) The Cultural Heritage of India, Calcutta, 1975.

Brown, C. P. (1) English-Telugu Dictionary, New Delhi, 1984.
(2) Telugu-English Dictionary, New Delhi 1984.

Dange, S.A., India from Primitive Communism to slavery (Bombay, 1947).

Desai, P. B., Basaveśvara and his times, Dharwar, 1968.

Desai, P. B. (ed) A History of Karṇāṭaka, Dharwar, 1970.

Desai, Dinkar, The Mahāmaṇḍaleśvaras of Cālukyas of Kalyāni, Bombay, 1951.

Dikshit, G. S., Local Self government in Medieval Karṇāṭaka, Dharwar, 1964.

Elliot, H. M. and Dowson, The History of India as told by its own Historians, Vol. III, Allahabad, 1970.

Gopalachari, K., Early History of the Āndhra Country, Madras, 1976.

Gopalakrishna Murty, S., The Sculpture of the Kākatīyas, Hyderabad, 1964.

Habib, I., Bhārata Caritralo Raitu (Telugu) translated by M. Ramamohan Rao, Hyderabad, 1985.

Hanumantha Rao, B. S. L., Rligion in Āndhra, Guntur, 1973.

Habib, Irfan, An Atlas of the Mughal Empire, Delhi, 1982.

Karashima, N., South Indian History and Society. Studies from Inscriptions, A. D. 850-1800, Delhi, 1984.

Kenneth, R. Hall, Trade and Statecraft in the age of Colas, New Delhi, 1980.

Kosambi, D.D., An Introduction to the study of Indian History, Bombay, 1985.

Krishna Sastry, V. V., The Proto and Early Historical Culture of Andhra Pradesh, Hyderabad, 1983.

Kuriyan, G., India—A General Survey, National Book Trust, Delhi, 1970.

Lalitamba, K., Vīraśaivism in Āndhra, Guntur, 1976.

Mackenzie, G., Manual of Krishna District, Madras, 1893.

Mahalilngam, T.V., Administration and social Life under Vijayanagar, Madras, 1970.

Max Mülier, F., The sacred Laws of the Āryas, parts I and II Delhi, 1984.

Minakshi, C., Administration and Social Life under the Pallavas, Madras, 1938.

Narasimha Rao, R., Corporate life in Medieval Āndhradesa, Hyderabad, 1967.

Nandimath, S.C., A Hand Book of Vīraśaivism, Dharwar, 1942.

Nihar Ranjan Ray, Mauryan and Post-Mauryan Art, New Delhi, 1975.

Pandarinath H. Prabhu, Hindu Social Origanisation, Bombay, 1961.

Pathak, S.V., History of Śaiva cults in North India, Varanasi, 1960.

Picchamuttu, C.S., Physical Geography of India, (Telugu translation) National Book Trust, New Delhi, 1971.

Radhakrishna Sarma, M., Temples of Telangāṇa, Hyderabad, 1972.

Rajendra Prasad B., Art of Sourth India, Andhra Pradesh, Delhi, 1980.

Rama Rao, M.1. The Kākatīyas of Warangal, Hyderabad, 1952.

2. Kākatīya Sancika, (Telugu), Rajahmundry, 1935.

3. Sātavāhana Sancika (Telugu), Guntur, 1950.

Roychaudhury, T. and Habib, I., The Cambridge Economic History of India, Vol. I, Delhi, 1982.

Sankaranarayana, S., The Vishnukuṇḍins and their times, Delhi, 1977.

Sarma, R.S. (1) Material culture and social formation in Ancient India, Delhi, 1983.

(2) Indian Feudalism, Delhi, 1980.

Sastri, K.A.N. 1) Development of Religion in South India, Orient Longmans, Madras, 1962.

2) Foreign Notices of South India, Madras, 1939.

3) The Colas, Madras, 1955.

Sastry, P.V.P. 1) The Kākatīyas, Hyderabad, 1977.

2) Kākatīya Coins and Meausres Hyderabad, 1975.

Satyanarayana, K., A Study of the History and Culture of Āndhras Vol. I and II, New Delhi, 1982.

Sherwani, H. K. and Jodhi, P. M., History of Medieval Deccan, Vol. I and II Hyderabad, 1974.

Smith, V., Early History of India, Oxford, 1904.

Somasekhara Sarma, M., The History of Reḍḍi Kingdoms, Waltair, A forgotten Chapter of Āndhra History, Madras, 1945.

Stein, B., Peasant State and Society in Medieval South India, Delhi, 1980.

Sundaram, K., Studies in Economic and Social conditions of Medieval Āndhra, Machilipatnam, 1968.

Spate, O. H. K. and Leanmonth, A. T. A., India and Pakistan—a general and Regional Geography, London, (Reprint), 1972.

Sriramachandra Murthy, S., Devalaya Sasana Samiksha (Telugu) Tirupati, 1984.

Sahitya Academy, Sūryarāyandhranighaṇṭu, (Telugu), Hyderabad, 1982.

Thapar, Romila, Ancient Indian Social History, Some Interpretations, New Delhi, 1984.

Thurston, E., (ed). Castes and Tribes of Southern India Vols. I and II.

Vaidehi, A., Social and Economic conditions of Eastern Deccan, Secunderabad, 1970.

Venkateramanaiah, N. 1) The Cāḷukyas of Vēṅgi, Madras, 1950.

2) The Cālukyas of L (V) emulavāḍa, Hyderabad, 1953.

3) Velugotivarivamśāvali, Madras, 1939.

Yazdani, G., (ed). The Early History of Deccan, London, 1960.

SELECT ARTICLES

B.S.L. Hanumantha Rao : The Boyas in Medieval Āndhra History, JAHRS., Vol. SXXXVIII, Part IV, pp. 77-91. Hyderabad, 1987.

B. Rajendra Prasad : Perūr inscriptions—A study, Proc. I.H.C., 45th Session, Annamabinagar, 1984, 911-917.

Dr. Y. Gopal Reddi : 1) Varṇa in relation to Polity and Justice under the Kākatīyas of Warangal, JAHRS, Vol. XXXVIII, part II, pp. 115-136, Hyderabad, 1986.

2) Some Measures and Weights in Medieval Andhra, JAHARS, Vol. XXXVI, I-IV Parts, pp. 102-114, Hyderabad, 1971.

T. Venkatesvara Rao : Local Self-Government in Medieval Andhra, J.A.H.R.S. XXXI, parts 1-4, pp. 113-123.

Katheleen Gough : Modes of Production in Southern India, Economic and Political Weekly, Annual Number, 1980.

Suvira Jaiswal : Studies in Early Indian Social History, The Indian Historical Review, Vol. VI, Nos. 1-2, pp. 1-63.

B.N.S. Yadava : Immobility and Subjection of Indian Peasantry in Early Medieval complex. Indian Historical Review, Volume I, No. 1, March, 1974, pp. 18-27.

Amita Ray : Urbanisation in Bengal, Proceedings of Indian History Congress, Presidential Address, Section I (Ancient India), Panaji, Goa, 1987.

Champakalakshmi : Urbanisation in South India, The Role of ideology and Polity, Proc. Idian History Congress, Presidential address, Section I (Ancient India), Srinagar, Kashmir, 1986.

✯✯✯✯

Āśaka Samayagalu 114

INDEX

B

C

L

M

N

O

P

R

S

★★★